The
LIFE
MAGNET

ALSO AVAILABLE FROM
TARCHER SUCCESS CLASSICS

The Law of Success
Napoleon Hill

Think and Grow Rich
Napoleon Hill

Your Magic Power to Be Rich!
Napoleon Hill

As a Man Thinketh
James Allen

Acres of Diamonds
Russell H. Conwell

A Message to Garcia
Elbert Hubbard

The Science of Getting Rich
Wallace D. Wattles

The Science of Being Great
Wallace D. Wattles

The Master Key System
Charles F. Haanel

The Secret of the Ages
Robert Collier

Public Speaking for Success
Dale Carnegie

In Tune with the Infinite
Ralph Waldo Trine

Prosperity
Charles Fillmore

How to Prosper in Hard Times
includes Napoleon Hill,
James Allen, Joseph Murphy

The Think and Grow Rich Workbook
Napoleon Hill

The Magic Ladder to Success
Napoleon Hill

The Master-Key to Riches
Napoleon Hill

The Game of Life and How to Play It
Florence Scovel Shinn

The Power of Your Subconscious Mind
Joseph Murphy, Ph.D., D.D.

Riches Within Your Reach!
Robert Collier

How to Be Rich
includes Napoleon Hill,
Joseph Murphy, Wallace D. Wattles,
Robert Collier

*The Think and Grow Rich Success
Journal*
Napoleon Hill
with Joel Fotinos and August Gold

Think and Grow Rich Every Day
Napoleon Hill
with Joel Fotinos and August Gold

JEREMY P. TARCHER/PENGUIN
a member of Penguin Group (USA) Inc.
New York

The
LIFE
MAGNET

ROBERT COLLIER

JEREMY P. TARCHER/PENGUIN
Published by the Penguin Group
Penguin Group (USA) Inc., 375 Hudson Street, New York, New York 10014, USA • Penguin Group
(Canada), 90 Eglinton Avenue East, Suite 700, Toronto, Ontario M4P 2Y3, Canada (a division
of Pearson Penguin Canada Inc.) • Penguin Books Ltd, 80 Strand, London WC2R 0RL, England •
Penguin Ireland, 25 St Stephen's Green, Dublin 2, Ireland (a division of Penguin Books Ltd) •
Penguin Group (Australia), 250 Camberwell Road, Camberwell, Victoria 3124, Australia (a division
of Pearson Australia Group Pty Ltd) • Penguin Books India Pvt Ltd, 11 Community Centre, Panchsheel
Park, New Delhi–110 017, India • Penguin Group (NZ), 67 Apollo Drive, Rosedale, North Shore 0632,
New Zealand (a division of Pearson New Zealand Ltd) • Penguin Books (South Africa) (Pty) Ltd,
24 Sturdee Avenue, Rosebank, Johannesburg 2196, South Africa

Penguin Books Ltd, Registered Offices: 80 Strand, London WC2R 0RL, England

First Tarcher/Penguin edition 2010

This work began as a pamphlet series called *The Secret of Gold*, under which the author published two
volumes in 1927. The following year he completed the series with an additional five volumes under the
revised title, *The Life Magnet*. The full seven volumes are collected in this edition.

Except for adjustments that bring the text in line with contemporary typographic standards, the
publisher has mostly retained the original spelling, usage, and style of the author. As this work was
written in the first part of the twentieth century, it occasionally features an antiquated reference or
word choice. For purposes of historical accuracy the publisher has left these largely intact.

Published simultaneously in Canada

Most Tarcher/Penguin books are available at special quantity discounts for bulk purchase for sales
promotions, premiums, fund-raising, and educational needs. Special books or book excerpts also can
be created to fit specific needs. For details, write Penguin Group (USA) Inc. Special Markets,
375 Hudson Street, New York, NY 10014.

Library of Congress Cataloging-in-Publication Data

Collier, Robert, 1885–1950.
The life magnet / Robert Collier. — 1st Tarcher/Penguin ed.
p.   cm.
ISBN 978-1-58542-846-5
1. New Thought.   2. Success—Psychological aspects.   3. Self-actualization (Psychology).
I. Collier Robert, 1885–1950. Secret of gold.   II. Title.
BF639.C68   2010   2010032574
158—dc22

Printed in the United States of America
1 3 5 7 9 10 8 6 4 2

Neither the publisher nor the author is engaged in rendering professional advice or services to the
individual reader. The ideas, procedures, and suggestions contained in this book are not intended as a
substitute for consulting with a physician. All matters regarding your health require medical
supervision. Neither the author nor the publisher shall be liable or responsible for any loss or damage
allegedly arising from any information or suggestion in this book.

While the author has made every effort to provide accurate telephone numbers and Internet addresses
at the time of publication, neither the publisher nor the author assumes any responsibility for errors, or
for changes that occur after publication. Further, the publisher does not have any control over and does
not assume any responsibility for author or third-party websites or their content.

CONTENTS

How then shall man so order life that when his tale of
    years is told
Like Sated guest he wend his way; how shall his even
    tenour hold?
Be true to Nature and Thy self;
Fame or Disfame court not nor fear;
Enough to thee the small still voice that thunders in thine
    inner ear.
From self approval seek applause;
Before thine inner secrets kneel;
Spurn every idol others raise;
Burn incense to thine own Ideal;
To seek the True, to glad the heart, such is of life the
    Higher Law,
Whose difference is the Man's degree, the Man of gold,
    the Man of straw.

—From *The Asidah of Haji Abdu-el-Yezdi.*

FOREWORD

THE RIDDLE OF THE SPHINX

What is it," asked the Sphinx, "that walks on four legs in the morning, on two legs at noon and on three legs in the evening?"

And all who passed her way had to answer that question—*or be devoured!*

That was the Riddle of the Sphinx of olden days. But to modern man has come a far more difficult one—

"How can I earn more money? How can I make enough to get the necessities and the comforts of life to which my family and I are entitled?"

That is the eternal question which confronts you and will haunt you every day until you solve it. That is the present-day Riddle of the Sphinx that devours all who fail to answer it.

For *lack* is the greatest evil that mankind has to contend with.

Yet every man knows that in this old earth of ours are

riches and abundance sufficient not merely for every soul now on this planet—but for all who ever will be! And in the very first chapter of the Bible, it is written that "God gave man dominion over all the earth."

Not only that, but more than half the prophecies in the Scriptures refer to the time when man shall possess the earth. When tears and sorrow shall be unknown. When riches and abundance shall be yours for the taking.

That time is here—here and now for those who understand the power and the availability of that mysterious, half recognized Spirit within which so few people know, but which, fully understood, *can do anything*.

But in no book ever written is there any complete explanation of this Spirit within, any complete directions for availing one's-self of its infinite power and understanding.

In no book, that is, but one!

And in the following pages I shall show you what that one Book is and where to find the directions which tell you how to harness this truly illimitable power, how to make it bring to you anything of good you may desire. For—

"There hath not failed one word of all His good
*   promises, which He promised by the hand of Moses,*
*   His servant."*

                       —I. KINGS, 8:56.

                    Robert Collier.

"Then opened He their understanding, that they might understand the Scriptures."

—LUKE 24:25.

I

THE GENII OF THE LAMP

"Thou gavest also Thy Good Spirit to instruct them, and withheldest not thy manna from their mouth, and gavest them water for their thirst."

—NEHEMIAH 9:20.

In an ancient town in far off Cathay, there once lived a poor young man named Aladdin. His father had been a tailor, but died before he could teach his profession to his son, and the boy and his widowed mother were frequently hard put to get enough to eat.

But despite his poverty, Aladdin was one of those cheerful souls who find life good. Many and often were the times that found him wandering joyfully in the mountains, when he should have been seeking the elusive yen in some odd job among his neighbors. And Fortune, looking down upon his cheery hopefulness, smiled—as has been the habit of Fortune since time began—for then, as now, she was a fickle jade, loving most those who worry least about her.

One day, wandering among the hills, Aladdin discovered a cave, its entrance closed by a great stone. Prying the stone away, he entered, and found therein a lamp burning upon a shelf. Thinking to use it at home, Aladdin stuck the lamp in his belt and, departing, took it with him.

Next morning, lacking the where-withal for breakfast, he bethought him of this lamp, and since it looked old and tarnished, started to polish it in the hope of thus bringing for it a better price. What was his astonishment and terror to see immediately appear before him a Genii of gigantic proportions, who, however, made humble obeisance: "I am the slave of the lamp," quoth he, "ready to do the bidding of him who holds the lamp. What would you of me?"

Terrified though he was, Aladdin could understand that. So he took heart of grace, and decided to see if this great Genii really was as good as his word. "I am hungry," he therefore told him. "Bring me something to eat." The Genii disappeared. An instant later he was back again with a sumptuous repast!

Aladdin ate and was satisfied. And when next he hungered, summoned the Genii and ate again. Thereafter, to one so used to hunger, life was one grand song—just one endless succession of eating and sleeping, sleeping and eating again.

Until one day the Sultan's daughter passed that way. Her eyes had the mischievous sparkle in their depths that has drawn hermits from their cells. Her lips were twin rubies. Her teeth pearls.

So much Aladdin saw—and was enchanted. Life took on a new meaning. There was more to it than eating and sleeping after all. Here was something to live for, work for, hope for. Even though at the moment it never occurred to him that he might ever hope to win such loveliness, such divinity, for himself.

But then he bethought him of his Genii. If the Genii could bring him food, raiment, riches—why not position and power, too? Why not the Sultan's daughter? Why not, in fact, the Sultan's place? He decided to try.

First he astonished the Sultan with the magnificence of the gifts with which his good Genii furnished him. Then he built a palace more beautiful far than that of the Sultan himself. Finally he presented himself as suitor for the hand of the beautiful princess.

The Sultan laughed at the idea. But one cannot continue to laugh at a man whose raiment is more costly, whose retinue more splendid, whose palace more magnificent than one's own. One can only vie with him in splendour, and failing that—either fight him or take him into one's own camp.

The Sultan tried to vie with him. But princely riches could not compare with those of the Genii. He tried fighting. But who could hope to cope with the powers of the invisible world?

At last he decided to share that wealth, to benefit by that power. And so it came about that Aladdin won the lovely Princess of his dreams.

Fairy tales—you will say. And of course, they are. But back of them is more than mere childish fable. There is the Wisdom and the Mysticism of the East—so frequently hidden in parable or fable.

For those Wise Men of the East had grasped, thousands of years ago, the fundamental fact—so hard for our Western minds to realize—that deep down within ourselves, far under our outer layers of consciousness, is a Power that far transcends the power of any conscious mind.

"The Holy Spirit within us," deeply religious people term it. And, truly, its power is little short of Divine.

"Our Subconscious Mind," so the Scientists call it.

Call it what you will, it is there—all unknown to most of us—a sleeping Giant who, aroused, can carry us on to fame and fortune over-night. A Genii-of-the-Brain more powerful, more the servant of our every right wish, than was ever Aladdin's fabled Genii-of-the-Lamp of old.

Health and happiness, power and riches, lie ready to its hand. You have but to wake it, to command it, to get of it what you will. It is part of you—yet its power is limitless. It is Mind—Thought—Idea. It is an all-powerful mental magnet that can draw to you anything you may desire.

Just as electricity turns the inert electric bulb into a thing of light and life—just as the gasoline vapor turns your motor into a creature of speed and action—just as steam awakens the locomotive into an engine of power and usefulness—so this mental magnet can vitalize YOU into a Being capable of accomplishing ANY TASK YOU MAY SET, capable of rising to any height, capable of winning love, honor and riches.

You have seen hypnotists put subjects to sleep. You have seen men and women, while in this hypnotic trance, do marvelous feats of mind reading or of mental arithmetic. You have seen others show wonderful endurance or physical strength.

I remember one hypnotist who, after putting his subject in a trance, would assure him that he (the subject) was a bar of iron. Then the hypnotist would stretch him out between two chairs—his head on one, his feet on another—and pile weights upon him, or have several people stand upon him. A feat of strength that the subject could never have accomplished in his ordinary mind. Yet did it without strain or difficulty under the influence of the hypnotist.

How did he do it? Simply by removing the control of the conscious mind—by putting it to sleep—and leaving the Subconscious in sole charge. The power is in your body to do anything—only your conscious mind doesn't believe that it is. Remove these conscious inhibitions— place the Subconscious in entire charge—and there is nothing beyond your capacity to perform.

The hypnotist does his tricks by putting your conscious mind to sleep and then suggesting to your Subconscious the things he wants it to do. But it is in no wise necessary to deal with the Subconscious through some third party. It is no part of the Divine plan that you must first put yourself under some outside control. On the contrary, those who learn to use their own Subconscious Minds can accomplish far greater wonders with their bodies, with their brains, with their fortunes than could any hypnotist for them.

It is to show you how to properly use this Genii-of-your-Mind, how to summon it, how to control it, that this Course is written.

"But where shall wisdom be found? And where is the place of understanding?"

—JOB 28:12.

"There is a Spirit in man; and the inspiration of the Almighty giveth him understanding."

—JOB 32:8.

II

THE SPIRIT WITHIN

"Know ye not that ye are the temple of God, and that the Spirit of God dwelleth in you?"

—I CORINTHIANS 3:16.

Y ou often hear a man spoken of as brainy. The idea being that he has more gray matter in his cranium than most of us. And for years the size of a man's head or the shape of his "bumps" was believed to indicate his mentality.

But science now shows that one man has just as good brains as another. Differences in weight or shape or size have nothing to do with it. Each of us has a perfect brain to start with. It is what we put *into* it and the way we *use* it that counts—not the size or weight!

Brains are merely the storehouse of the mind. They are not the mind itself. Each individual brain cell—and there are some nine billions of them—is like a phonograph record on which impressions are registered through the thousands of nerves from all over the body that center in the brain.

Once registered, that impression stays as long as the brain cell remains. When we have no occasion to use an impression for a long time, it is filed away in the nine-billion filing compartment—and apparently forgotten.

But it is never really forgotten. It can always be recalled by the proper suggestion to the subconscious mind. The only thing that can permanently destroy the impression is the removal of the brain cell itself. That is why injuries to the brain so frequently result in complete loss of memory as to many events in the individual's life.

But the registering of impressions is merely the first step. The animals have that. The next—and the step that puts man so far above all other creatures—is the reasoning mind. Mind uses the brain cells to recall any impression it may need. To compare them. To draw conclusions from them. In short, *to reason!*

That is the most important province of mind. But it has another—the regulating, governing and directing of the growth and functions of the body. So complicated an affair that no conscious mind in the universe could ever grope with it.

Yet the subconscious mind does it with ease—does it for the youngest infant as well as for you or me—in fact, frequently does it better.

From the earliest moment of our birth, the subconscious mind takes control. It directs the beating of the heart, the breathing of the lungs, the complicated processes of digestion and assimilation. And the less it is interfered with, the better work it does.

Your body is the most wonderful and complicated chemical factory in the world. Made up of water, coal, iron, lime, sugar, phosphorus, salt, hydrogen and iodine, no man living could figure out the changes made necessary in its composition from minute to minute by heat, by cold, by pressure from without or by food taken within. No chemist in all the world could tell you how much water you should drink to neutralize the excess salt in salt fish. How much you lose through perspiration. How much water, how much salt, how much of each different element in your food should be absorbed into your blood each day to maintain perfect health.

Yet your subconscious mind knows. Knows without effort. Knows even when you are an infant. And furthermore, acts immediately upon that knowledge.

To quote the Rev. Wm. T. Walsh—

"The subconscious mind directs all the vital processes of our body. You do not think consciously about breathing. Every time you take a breath you do not have to reason, decide, command. The SUBCONSCIOUS MIND sees to that. You have not been at all conscious that you have been breathing while you have been reading this page. So it is with the mind and the circulation of blood. The heart is a muscle like the muscle of your arm. It has no power to move itself or to direct its action. Only mind, only something that can think, can direct our muscles, including the heart. You are not conscious that you are commanding your heart to beat. The subconscious mind attends to that. And so it is with the assimilation of food, the building and repairing of the body. In fact, all the vital processes are looked after by the subconscious mind."

Whence comes all this wonderful knowledge? Whence comes the intelligence that enables day-old infants to figure out problems in chemistry that would confound the most learned professors? Whence but from the same Mind that regulates the planets in their courses, that puts into the acorn the image of the mighty oak it is to be, and then shows it how to draw from the sunlight, from the air, from the earth, from the water, the nutriment necessary to build that image into reality.

That Mind is God. And the subconscious in us is our part of Divinity. It is the Holy Spirit that Jesus so often referred to.

"But when they shall lead you and deliver you up, take no thought beforehand what ye shall speak, neither do ye premeditate; but whatsoever shall be given you in that hour, that speak ye; for it is not ye that speak, but the Holy Ghost."—Mark 13.

Christianity teaches one Universal God, Father of all things, *the life of all things animate.*

"For there are three that bear record in Heaven, the Father, the Word and the Holy Ghost; and these three are one."—I John 5:7.

And modern science shows us that *all things are animate*— even the rocks and the dirt beneath our feet. Even the supposedly dead piece of paper on which these words are printed. All are made up of tiny particles called atoms. And the atoms in turn consist of protons and electrons—bits of electrical energy, so minute as to be invisible to the naked eye, but very much alive and constantly moving, constantly changing.

In *The Secret of the Ages,* the consistency of matter is explained in detail. For those who have not read this explanation, suffice it here to quote from the New York Herald-Tribune:

"We used to believe that the universe was composed of an unknown number of different kinds of matter, one kind for each chemical element. The discovery of a new element had all the interest of the unexpected. It might turn out to be anything, to have any imaginable set of properties.

"That romantic prospect no longer exists. We know now that instead of many ultimate kinds of matter there are only two kinds. Both of these are really kinds of electricity. One is negative electricity, being, in fact, the tiny particle called the electron, familiar to radio fans as one of the particles vast swarms of which operate radio vacuum tubes. The other kind of electricity is positive electricity. Its ultimate particles are called protons. From these protons and electrons all of the chemical elements are built up. Iron and lead and oxygen and gold and all the others differ from one another merely in the number and arrangement of the electrons and protons which they contain. That is the modern idea of the nature of matter. *Matter is really nothing but electricity.*"

Everything has life in it. And life is God. Therefore, everything in this world, everything in the heavens above, in the earth beneath, or in the waters under the earth, is a manifestation of God.

God is life. He is the life in us. And the life in all created things. He is the "Father" that was in Jesus—the Father that, "before Abraham was, I am"—the Father that did such wonderful works. "Believest thou not that I am in the Father, and the Father in me? The words that I speak unto you, I speak not of myself; but the Father that dwelleth in me, He doeth the works. Believe me that I am in the Father, and the Father in me."—John 14:10-11.

That same Father is in you. He is the life-force, the God-force, that flows through every atom of your being. Make yourself one with Him, and there is nothing you cannot do. "I and the Father are one," said Jesus. And His prayer was— "That they may all be one; as Thou, Father art in me and I in Thee, that they also may be one in us."

A great religious teacher once said that there are just two things in the Universe—God and His manifestations. Really there is just one—for God is *in* all His manifestations. "If a man love me . . . my Father will love him and we will come unto him and make our abode with him."—John 14:23.

THE MESSAGE OF JESUS

What was the real message of Jesus? What was the one unforgivable thing that He taught which brought down wrath upon His head?

—What one thing did He add to the teachings of Moses, of Amos and of Hosea that changed the whole current of history?

—What has since become the basis of all Democracy?

NOT the doctrine of the One God. NOT the new idea of loving one's neighbor and forgiving one's enemies. No—that wasn't why the Pharisees and Rulers hated him and resolved to have his blood. BUT BECAUSE HE WENT UP AND DOWN THE LENGTH AND BREADTH OF THE LAND TEACHING THAT ALL MEN ARE EQUALLY THE CHILDREN OF GOD!

"As many as received Him, to them gave He power to become the sons of God, even to them that believe on His name."

Can you imagine what this meant to mankind in that

day of slavery and oppression? Just think—if God is the Father of ALL men, then ALL are His children, equally entitled to the good things of life, equally dear to Him!

"No wonder," says Bruce Barton in *The Man Nobody Knows,* "the authorities trembled. They were not fools. They recognized the logical implication of such teaching. Either Jesus' life or their power must go. No wonder that succeeding generations of authorities have embroidered His idea and corrupted it. It was too dangerous a Power to be allowed to wander the world, unleashed and uncontrolled."

That is why the idea most of us have of Jesus is so far from the reality that lived and taught and worked wonders throughout Palestine 1900 years ago.

"This was the message of Jesus," Barton explains, "that God is supremely better than anybody had ever dared to believe. Not a petulant Creator, who had lost control of His creation and, in wrath, was determined to destroy it all. Not a stern Judge dispensing impersonal justice. Not a vain King who must be flattered and bribed into concessions of mercy. Not a rigid Accountant, checking up the sins against the penances and striking a cold hard balance. Not any of these . . . nothing like these . . . but a great Companion, a wonderful Friend, a kindly, indulgent, joy-loving Father.

"Hold your heads high," He had exclaimed, "you are

lords of the universe . . . only a little lower than the angels . . . children of God."

It is the same note that rings through the Psalms of old:

"What is man that thou art mindful of him? And the son of man that thou visitest him? For thou hast made him a little lower than the angels." And Jesus echoed the refrain when he quoted from the Old Testament—"Ye are gods!"

"And it shall come to pass," cried Hosea (1:10), "that in the place where it was said unto them, Ye are not my people, there it shall be said unto them, Ye are the sons of the living God."

Jesus did not come to call attention to Himself, to get people to believe in Him as a god or demi-god; He did not come solely to reveal God to man; *he came to reveal man to himself.*"

"Beloved, now are ye the Sons of God," says John.

Not only did Jesus proclaim this in His words, but His whole life was given to teaching and showing the Divine Sonship of *man*. Thirty-seven times in the Gospel records He refers to Himself as the Son of Man! He never called Himself God. But He claimed *union* with God! And He claimed and demonstrated possession of the Father's power and all that the Father had. "All power is given unto Me in Heaven and in earth," He said.—Matthew 28:18.

But He disclaimed this as a mere personal power. "It is not Me, but the Father in Me; He doeth the works."

Furthermore, He again and again assured His followers that this same power was in them. "If ye believe in Me and My word abideth in you, the works that I do shall ye do also. And greater works than these shall ye do."

Again, speaking not of Himself but of all mankind, He said:

"Verily, verily I say unto you, the son can do nothing of himself, but what He seeth the Father do; for what things so-ever He doeth, these also doeth the son likewise. For the Father loveth the son and showeth him all things that Himself doeth. . . . For as the Father raiseth the dead, and quickeneth them, even so the son quickeneth whom he will. For the Father judgeth no man, but hath committed all judgment unto the son, that all men should honor the son even as they honor the Father."—John 5:19-23.

What, then, was the message of Jesus?

The greatest message ever brought to any planet! That *man is the son of God.* That he inherits from the Father all of life, all of wisdom, all of riches, all of power.

God is the Parent. And man's every quality is derived from Him. Not only that, *but man inherits every quality of the Father!* He has only to grow up in knowledge, to learn the Father's ways, to lean trustfully upon the Father's help, in order to be supreme "amid the war of elements, the wreck of matter and the crush of worlds."

Apart from God, man is a weakling, the sport of circumstances, the victim of any force strong enough to overpower or brush him aside.

But let him ally himself with the Father, and he becomes, instead of the creature of law, the ruler through law. Instead of the sport of circumstance, he makes circumstances. Instead of the victim of fire or water or sickness or poverty, he masters the forces of nature, demands health and prosperity as his birthright.

The God that most of us were taught to believe in was a huge patriarchal Man-God, seated upon a throne high up in the skies. A King—stern, righteous and just—chastening His children mercilessly whenever He felt it was for their good. Holding an exact scale between the good they had done and the sins they had committed. And dispensing penances or rewards to balance the two.

The King idea has gone out of fashion here on earth this many a year. And the idea of a God-King is fast disappearing from our conception of the Infinite. After 1900 years, we are at last coming around to Jesus' idea of a loving Father-God. A God that is in each one of us, whose "good pleasure it is to give us the Kingdom."

"For the works which the Father hath given me to finish, the same works that I do, bear witness of me, that the Father hath sent me."—John 5:36.

In the light of such an understanding of God, we can

readily grasp how it was possible for Jesus to heal the sick, to feed the hungry, to bring forth gold from the fish's mouth, to still the tempest—and, what is even more, to promise these same powers to us!

Man is the Son of God.

We start with that. How, then, shall we take advantage of our son-ship? How use the infinite power it puts in our hands?

The purpose of this book is to develop the divinity that is in you. What is the first thing to do? Where shall you start? What shall you do?

REACHING INTO INFINITY

The first essential is to find a point of contact with the Father.

Benjamin Franklin sent a kite up into the clouds and brought down along its string a current of electricity. Through him, man has learned to harness this electricity for his daily servant. Franklin made his contact with the source of power.

Thousands of years before Franklin—centuries even before the birth of Christ—men began to send up kites (figuratively speaking) trying to contact with the source of life itself.

A few succeeded. A few great Prophets like Elisha,

Elijah, Moses, contacted with the Source of all Power, and whenever and as long as they kept that contact, nothing could withstand them.

"For the prophesy came not in old time by the will of man; but holy men of God spake as they were moved by the Holy Ghost."—II Peter 1:21.

Franklin caught the source of electrical power, and by learning to understand and work with it, turned those terror-inspiring thunderbolts of destruction into man's greatest friend and servant. The electricity did not change. It is exactly the same now as afore time. It is merely man's conception of it that has changed.

Uncontrolled, lightning was a curse to mankind. Through understanding, man has harnessed it to serve his needs. Touch a button—and it lights your home. Touch another—and it brings to you news and instruction, entertainment and music from hundreds or thousands of miles away. The mere throwing of a switch releases the power of millions of horses. Pulling it out bridles them again. Was ever such a master servant?

Yet it is as nothing to the power latent in the Source of Life—the power of the Father of all things.

Even now, ignorant of this Power as most of us are, we occasionally contact with it, but we do it accidentally—*and we fail to maintain the contact.*

Remember "The Lost Chord," by Adelaide Procter?

Seated one day at the organ,
I was weary and ill at ease;
And my fingers wandered idly
Over the noisy keys.

I know not what I was playing,
Or what I was dreaming then,
But I struck one chord of music
Like the sound of a great Amen.

It flooded the crimson twilight,
Like the close of an angel's psalm,
And it lay on my fevered spirit,
With a touch of infinite calm.

It quieted pain and sorrow,
Like love overcoming strife,
It seemed the harmonious echo
From our discordant life.

It linked all perplexed meanings
Into one perfect peace,
And trembled away into silence,
As if it were loath to cease.

I have sought, but I seek it vainly,
That one lost chord divine,

Which came from the soul of the organ,
And entered into mine.

It may be that Death's bright angel
Will speak in that chord again,
It may be that only in Heaven
I shall hear that grand Amen!

You know how often things have come to you like that—snatches of song, or speech, or verse such as man never wrote before. Visions of wonderful achievement. Echoes of great ideas. Glimpses of riches you could almost reach—the riches of the Spirit within.

If only you could tap that boundless Reservoir at will, what success would not be yours, how puny your present accomplishments would seem by comparison!

And you *can* tap it. You can make your contact with Infinity—if not at will—at least with frequency. All that is necessary is understanding and belief.

How to do it? How to go about it? Through the Holy Spirit within you. Through your part of Divinity. Through an understanding of what is commonly known as your Subconscious Mind.

Why did the Apostles, after cowering in hiding so abjectly for ten days after the ascension of Jesus, suddenly issue forth boldly and astonish the world with their preaching and their miracles?

"It is expedient for you that I go away," Jesus had told them (John 16:7), "for if I go not away, the Comforter will not come unto you; but if I depart, I will send Him unto you."

"Howbeit when He, the Spirit of truth, is come," He promised, "He will guide you into all truth; for He shall not speak of Himself; but whatsoever He shall hear, that shall He speak."—John 16:13.

And He commanded the Apostles that they should not depart from Jerusalem, but await the consummation of His promise.

"And behold, I send the promise of my Father upon you; but tarry ye in the city of Jerusalem, until ye be endued with power from on high."—Luke 24:49.

"And when the day of Pentecost was fully come, they were all with one accord in one place.

"And suddenly there came a sound from heaven as of a rushing mighty wind, and it filled all the house where they were sitting.

"And there appeared unto them cloven tongues like as of fire, and it sat upon each of them.

"And they were all filled with the Holy Ghost, and began to speak with other tongues, as the Spirit gave them utterance.

"And there were dwelling at Jerusalem Jews, devout men, out of every nation under heaven.

"Now when this was noised abroad, the multitude came together, and were confounded, because that every man heard them speak in his own language.

"And they were all amazed and marvelled, saying one to another, Behold, are not all these which speak Galilaeans?

"And how hear we every man in our own tongue, wherein we were born?

"Parthians, and Medes, and Elamites, and the dwellers in Mesopotamia, and in Judaea, and Cappadocia, in Pontus, and Asia,

"Phrygia, and Pamphylia, in Egypt, and in the parts of Libya about Cyrene, and strangers of Rome, Jews and proselytes,

"Cretes and Arabians, we do hear them speak in our tongues the wonderful works of God.

"And they were all amazed, and were in doubt, saying one to another, What meaneth this?

"But this is that which was spoken by the prophet Joel;

"And it shall come to pass in the last days, saith God, I will pour out my spirit upon all flesh."—Acts 2:1, 12, 16, 17.

Just as the one great fact of the Gospels is the presence of the Son exalting and revealing the Father, so the one great fact of the Acts of the Apostles is the presence of the Holy Spirit inspiring all their acts.

"The Comforter, which is the Holy Ghost, whom the Father will send you in my name," Jesus had promised

them, "he shall teach you all things, and bring all things
to your remembrance, whatsoever I have said unto you."—
John 14:26.

How else do you suppose they could have remembered
all that Jesus had taught, all that he had said to them? They
took no notes. For the most part, they could not even read
or write!

And why has the power of healing so largely disappeared
since about the 3rd century of the Christian era? Why did
the Apostles at Jerusalem send Peter and John to "lay hands"
upon the Christian converts in Samaria?

"Now when the apostles which were at Jerusalem heard
that Samaria had received the word of God, they sent unto
them Peter and John:

"Who, when they were come down, prayed for them,
that they might receive the Holy Ghost:

"(For as yet he was fallen upon none of them: only they
were baptized in the name of the Lord Jesus.)

"*Then laid they their hands on them, and they received the
Holy Ghost.*"—Acts 8.

Why did Paul ask other Christian congregations, which
had as yet worked no signs or wonders, whether they had
received the Holy Ghost?

"He said unto them, Have ye received the Holy Ghost
since ye believed? And they said unto him, We have not
so much as heard whether there be any Holy Ghost.

"And when Paul had laid his hands upon them, the Holy Ghost came on them; and they spake with tongues and prophesied."—Acts 19:2, 6.

It is as Jesus said—"When the Comforter is come, whom I will send unto you from the Father, even the Spirit of truth, which proceedeth from the Father, he shall testify of me."—John 15:26.

We are most of us like the dwellers in Samaria—"we have not so much as heard whether there be any Holy Spirit," much less tried to cultivate an understanding of Him.

We stumble upon His vast power occasionally—and call our resultant deeds superhuman! We contact now and then with Infinity—and regard the result as a miracle!

There is no such thing as a miracle. The occasional wonder-works that we do—the sudden healing from sickness, the miraculous escape, the answered prayer—are all divinely natural. The miracle is that it happens so seldom. We should be able to establish and keep that contact always! We should be able to contact with and use the power of the Spirit as readily as we now can use the power of electricity.

"And it shall come to pass afterwards, that I will pour out my spirit upon all flesh; and your sons and your daughters shall prophesy, your old men shall dream dreams, your young men shall see visions."—Joel 2:28.

But just as Franklin had first to determine what the

power was that made the lightning, so have you first to learn what is this Holy Spirit within you.

To say that it is the subconscious mind is not enough. It is far more than that. The subconscious mind can be used either for good or for evil. Uncontrolled, it is as great a destructive force as the lightning. If you have read the *Secret of the Ages*, you know that you can suggest thoughts of health or of disease to your subconscious mind, of success or of failure—and whichever image you get across to the subconscious, it will proceed to work out. But the Holy Spirit can be used only for good.

The Samaritans had subconscious minds, yet they worked no wonders. It was only when Paul conferred the Holy Spirit upon them that signs and wonders followed.

What then is the Holy Spirit?

How do you acquire it? How contact with it?

Have you ever read any of the accounts you occasionally see of people who have been very sick—who have hovered for minutes or for hours right over the Valley of Death—and then come back? Remember their description of how they seemed to be looking down upon themselves, upon the whole scene, as one apart, as one having but a casual interest in what was going on? Remember how some little thing called them back and how frequently they went back with reluctance?

Stewart Edward White had a story in the *American Mag-*

azine that exactly illustrated the idea. It told of a man who, according to all scientific tests, had died—lay dead, in fact, for two hours. And here, in part, was his description of the experience:

"I was pretty ill before I died, and things about me got somewhat vague and unreal. I suppose I was half dozing, and partly delirious perhaps. I'd slip in and out of focus, as it were. Sometimes I'd see myself and the bed and the room and the people clearly enough; then again I'd sort of drop into an inner reverie inside myself. Not asleep exactly, nor yet awake. You'll get much the same thing sitting in front of a warm fire after a hearty dinner.

"Now, here's a funny one. I don't know if you'll get this: You know these pictures sent by radio? They are all made up of a lot of separate dots, you know. If you enlarged the thing enough, you'd almost lose the picture, wouldn't you? And you'd have a collection of dots with a lot of space between them. Well, that's how I seemed to myself.

"I could contract myself, bring all the dots close together, and there I'd be, solid as a brick church, lying in bed; and I could expand myself until the dots got separated so far that there were mostly spaces between them. And when I did that my body in the bed got very vague to me, because the dots were so far apart they didn't make a picture; and I—the consciousness of me—was somehow the thing in the spaces that held the dots together at all. I found it quite amusing contracting and expanding like that.

"Then I began to think about it. I began to wonder whether I held the dots together, or whether the dots held me together; and I got so interested that I thought I'd try to find out. You see, I wasn't the dots: I—the essence of me, the consciousness of me—was the spaces between the dots, holding them together. I thought to myself, 'I wonder if I can get away from these dots?' So I tried it; and I could. I must say I was a little scared. That body made of dots was a good, solid container. When I left its shelter, it occurred to me that I might evaporate into universal substance, like letting a gas out of a bottle. I didn't; but I certainly was worried for fear I'd burst out somewhere. I felt awfully thin-skinned!"

Remember how you have sometimes had similar experiences in dreams, when you seemed to be a disembodied spirit looking down on yourself from above?

That disembodied self is the soul of you—your subconscious mind. But it is something more, too. Baptize it in the waters of understanding of your oneness with the Father, confirm it with a realization of the God-life flowing so abundantly through you—and it becomes, in addition, *the Holy Spirit within you*—one with the Father, one with the Source of Life, of Power, of Abundance. In short, the Holy Spirit within you is your subconscious mind, vitalized through direct contact with the Father.

You have been told time and again how small a part of your real abilities you use when you confine your mental work to your conscious mind. Prof. Wm. James, the world-famous Psychologist, estimated that the average man used only 10 per cent of his real abilities. While Dr. Mayo compares the mind to an iceberg—one-fourth above water (the conscious mind), and three-fourths submerged (the subconscious). Think, then, if the use of your subconscious mind adds so much to your abilities, how much your value will be increased if you add to that the infinite power of the Holy Spirit!

"Now we have received, not the spirit of the world, but the Spirit which is of God; that we might know the things that are freely given to us of God."—I Corinthians 2:12.

As the ordinary man uses it, the subconscious mind is largely a bundle of habits. You practice on the piano merely to set up a certain train of actions and reactions so that, after a time, your subconscious can take over the work from your conscious mind. The skilled pianist can play from memory the most difficult pieces and at the same time carry on a spirited conversation. Why? Because two entirely different provinces of the mind are carrying on their functions—the one through the fingers, the other through speech and hearing.

The same thing applies to every physical avocation. To become really skilful at anything, you must get it into the charge of your subconscious mind. As long as your conscious mind must take active control, you are tense, doubtful, hesitant—you blunder, become excited, fail. Let the action become automatic, however—in other words, let your subconscious have charge of it—and you relax naturally and do whatever is required of you without effort and will.

A man's responsiveness to subconscious reactions is usually the measure of his luck or ill luck in avoiding accidents. In the New York Herald-Tribune there was an editorial recently along this very line entitled—"Whom Ill Luck Pursues":

"The Industrial Fatigue Research Board has made an interesting report on the reasons for industrial accidents. It is already well known to thoughtful managers of factories that some men are persistently unlucky. If any one is to suffer a broken leg, it will be one of these individuals. When minor accidents are being dealt out by Fate these unfortunates never fail to receive more than their reasonable shares. No definite fault can be found with them. They are not noticeably careless or foolhardy. The poor things seem simply to possess an incurable propensity for being at hand when anything happens. Like the conventional innocent bystander, they are, almost by definition, the persons who get hurt.

"Armed with the modern magician's wand of careful record and exact statistical inquiry, two investigators for the research board have traced these instances of persistent ill luck to their cause. No demon of bad luck is concerned, although the uninstructed may well think so when they read that the cause's name is aesthetakinetic co-ordination. Translated into English, this means a lack of that instinct and exact correspondence between warning and action which some people possess and some do not. If a board in the floor is loose and happens to fly up when stepped on, some people will jump instantly and in the right direction. Others will move the wrong way or not at all. If a chair breaks some sitters will land on their feet, others on the floor. Under the conditions of modern civilization it is usually the latter who are being taken to the hospital."

The functions of your body—your heart, lungs, stomach, liver, the continual breaking down and rebuilding of all the cells—these, too, are the province of your subconscious mind. And as long as they are left to it in the full assurance that it knows its work and is tending faithfully to it, all will be well with them.

But let the conscious mind interfere, and as in playing the piano or doing any other difficult stunt, trouble will ensue.

Have you ever seen a football team whose classmates did nothing but "knock" it, tell it how rotten it was individually and collectively, how little chance it had of ever winning a game? You know how little chance that team would have of getting even a single goal.

But take that same team, put a real class spirit behind it, surround it with boosters and urge it on with a stirring college yell—and then watch it go!

So it is with your subconscious mind and your body. It knows perfectly how to rebuild your body—how to keep it well. But if you tell it, in effect, that you have no confidence in its ability to do this—if you are continually trying to take over the control through your doubts and fears and worries—you will soon have a mutinous or discouraged crew on your hands, that no longer believes in you or itself. And the result will be nervousness, apathy, failure.

As the Rev. W. John Murray put it—

"Whatever order we issue to the subconscious mind, it promptly undertakes to carry out. Whatever state of existence you declare to be in being, the subconscious mind assumes exists and works within you accordingly. If a friend asks you: How do you feel today? and you reply: I am not well; I have a headache; I am all in; I don't feel up to the mark at all, you are unconsciously setting the subconscious mind to work to realize the state you declare yourself to be in. On the other hand if you say: I am well, happy and strong, the subconscious mind undertakes to realize this state for you.

"Hence you can see what a wonderful power is within your control for your happiness or unhappiness, your condition of body and mind, and how necessary it is for you to use this power always in a positive direction. *You are, in*

a word, what you think you are. This is not a theory, a fancy
or a fad. It is a law. And the reason why the world is filled
with sin, disease, misery and misfortune is because it requires effort to think positive thoughts while negative
thinking is the result of inertia."

But it is not only in running the body-machine that the
subconscious shows the power of the Spirit that is behind
it. It has all knowledge of outside things as well. Contact
with it, and you can learn what you will.

Some time ago there was an article in the "American"
telling of the experiences of a convict, formerly the editor
of a large newspaper.

Morphine had brought this man to prison. He had
started taking it when, as a newspaper man, his body would
be so worn out that he could no longer write. By "doping"
the conscious mind into unconsciousness, he would bring
the subconscious to the fore, with the result that the most
wonderful articles flowed from his pen. In one case, without a clue to guide him, he traced a gang of criminals who
were in hiding!

But his was not merely an impossible way to contact
with the Holy Spirit—it was the wrong way to contact with
the subconscious as well—and he paid a fearful price for it.

Take Theodore Roosevelt, on the other hand. When he
entered Harvard in 1876, he was thin of chest, be-spectacled,
nervous, weighing only 90 pounds. He was afraid to get on
his feet and try to make a speech. Compare that with the

man he became—the wonder of the world for efficiency, endurance, working power, and joyousness in life. He was a cowboy, a soldier, a lawyer, a statesman, a writer. And he did each of these things phenomenally well.

That is one example of what the right attitude towards the subconscious will do. Then there are those frequent cases you hear about like the one described in Psychology Magazine. Henry A. Wight never studied art—never knew he had any talent for painting. He went into the matter-of-fact-business of steel and coal, and was successful in it. Then when he was getting along in the thirties, he found himself with the desire to paint. So, to use his own laconic explanation, "he did it—that's all." And his monotypes have won the praise of the best critics.

I know a famous song writer who never studied a note. Her music "just comes to her." I know a man—a successful business man of nearly fifty—who suddenly started writing poems. Wonderful poems—that have been eagerly accepted by the best magazines. And he doesn't know a rule of prosody! I know an eminent geologist who never consciously examines a stone. He just walks over his ground abstractedly and then tells—for a very high fee—what is underneath it.

Contacting with the Subconscious—contacting haphazardly, accidentally—yet getting marvelous results while the contact holds!

Whatever you want to know, whatever you wish to

do—the knowledge and the power are there. "When He, the Spirit of Truth is come," promised Jesus, "He will guide you into all the truth."

Ordinary contact with the subconscious is comparatively easy. The first essential is relaxation. To find a really comfortable easy chair or lounge or bed, where one can be quiet, undisturbed, unconscious of oneself and one's surroundings. To stretch luxuriously and then let every muscle relax. To review before your mind's eye every phase of the problem or the subject—not worriedly, not striving for the answer—but merely laying them before the spirit within in the way you would put them before some all-wise Solomon. To *know* that he *has* the answer— and will presently give it to you. To relax thankfully in this knowledge into slumber, with the contented feeling that you have got what you wanted. Do that—and your answer will come.

Dr. W. Hanna Thomson, in "Brain and Personality," gives some instances of how this sometimes works out even when the person doing it has no knowledge of how to put his problem up to his subconscious mind. The first was told him by a fellow student at college. One night his roommate sat up late working at a difficult problem in mathematics. Failing to solve it, he rubbed his slate clean, put out the light and went to bed.

Later on that night the first student was awakened by the light shining in his eyes. Looking up, he saw his friend working away at his slate. The next morning he commented on it, only to have his roommate indignantly deny that he had been up at all during the night.

To prove his assertion, the first student got the slate, and there on it was the problem that had puzzled his friend—*all worked out to the correct conclusion!*

The other case Thomson tells of was that of a British Consul in Syria. He had been studying Arabic diligently in an effort to better fit himself for his position, and one night tried to compose a letter to the Emir at Lebanon. After a couple of hours of fruitless effort, he finally lost all patience with the language and the job, and went to bed.

What was his astonishment to find on his desk in the morning a freshly written letter, in his own handwriting, couched in the purest Arabic, that the Slave-of-the-Lamp himself could not have improved upon!

Then there is the classic case of Herman V. Hilprecht, Professor of Assyrian at the University of Pennsylvania: He had worn himself out trying to decipher certain mysterious inscriptions on some old Assyrian rings. Finally he had given up the problem in despair—no living man could solve it. One night, still thinking and studying over it, he had gone to bed exhausted. He fell asleep and dreamed.

In his dream, a tall thin priest of the old Pre-Christian Nippur temple appeared to him and led him to the treasure chamber of the temple. In a low-ceiled room without windows he saw a great wooden chest with scraps of agate and lapislazuli lying on the floor.

"The fragments over which you have been working," spoke the priest, "are not finger rings. King Kurigalzu once sent to the Temple of Bel an inscribed votive cylinder of agate. Later we priests suddenly received a hasty and imperative summons to make a pair of agate earrings for the great God Ninib.

"We had no new agate at hand, and were in great dismay. At last we decided to cut the votive cylinder into three parts, thus making three rings. The two fragments which have given you so much trouble are portions of them. If you will put them together you will find this to be true. The third ring you will never find."

Professor Hilprecht awoke, roused his wife and told her the dream. Then ran to his study. Before long she heard him cry: "It is so! It is so!" Next winter he went to Cairo to study the objects from the Temple Nippur which were in the Imperial Museum. He found there complete evidence of the truthfulness of his dream in every detail.

The subconscious mind is your Slave of the Lamp. Use him, in the ways outlined above—and there is no problem he cannot work out for you.

But recognize your Sonship with God, your oneness with the Source of all life and Power—in short, contact with the Source of Power—and that subconscious mind becomes the Holy Spirit within you, *to whom nothing is impossible!*

"The natural man receiveth not the things of the Spirit of God," says Paul (I Corinthians 2:14), "for they are foolishness unto him; neither can he know them, because they are *spiritually* discerned."

III

THE LODE STAR

*"And I will pray the Father, and He shall give you
another Comforter, that He may abide with you forever.
Even the Spirit of Truth; whom the world cannot receive,
because it seeth Him not. But ye know Him. For He
dwelleth with you and shall be in you."*

—JOHN 14:16-17.

There once lived in a town of Persia two brothers,
one named Cassim, the other Ali Baba. Cassim
had married a very rich wife, and become a
wealthy but miserly and greedy money-lender. Ali Baba
had married a woman as poor as himself, and lived by
cutting wood, and bringing it upon his donkeys into the
town to sell. But he had married for love and he worked
cheerily, asking only of Allah that He watch over his little family and help him to teach his son to tread in the
right path.

One day, when Ali Baba was in the forest cutting wood,

he saw a great cloud of dust coming towards him from the distance. Observing it attentively, he soon distinguished a body of horsemen, and as honest people had little business that far from the haunts of men he suspected they might be robbers. Greatly frightened, he determined to leave his donkeys and save himself. Yet he was not so frightened as to lose all curiosity, so he climbed up a tree that grew on a high rock, whose branches, while thick enough to conceal him, yet enabled him to see all that passed beneath.

The troop, which numbered about forty, all well mounted and armed, came to the foot of the rock and dismounted. Each man unbridled his horse, tied him to some shrub, and hung about the animal's neck a bag of corn. Then each took off his saddle-bag, which from its weight seemed to Ali Baba to be full of gold and silver. One, whom he took to be their captain, came under the tree in which Ali Baba was concealed; and, making his way through some shrubs, pronounced these words—"Open, Sesame!" The moment the captain of the robbers had thus spoken, a door opened in the rock; and after he had made all his troop enter before him, he followed them, when the door shut again of itself.

The robbers stayed some time within the rock, during which Ali Baba, fearful of being caught, remained in the tree.

At last the door opened again, and as the captain went in last, so he came out first, and stood to see them all pass by him. Then Ali Baba heard him make the door close by pronouncing these words, "Shut, Sesame!" The robbers forthwith bridled their horses, and mounted, and when the captain saw them all ready, he put himself at their head, and they returned the way they had come.

Ali Baba followed them with his eyes as far as he could see, and afterward stayed a considerable time before he descended. Remembering the words the captain of the robbers had used to cause the door to open he was curious to see if his pronouncing them would have the same effect. Accordingly, he went among the shrubs, stood before it, and said, "Open, Sesame!" Instantly the door flew wide open.

Ali Baba, who expected a dark, dismal cavern, was surprised to see a well-lighted and spacious chamber, receiving its light from an opening at the top of the rock. Scattered around in profusion were all sorts of rich bales of silk stuff, brocade, and valuable carpeting, gold and silver ingots in great heaps, and money in bags The cave must have been occupied for ages by robbers, one succeeding another.

Ali Baba fell on his knees and thanked Allah, the Most High. "Here," thought he, "is the provision I have prayed for to keep us in our old age and to provide our son with a start in life."

So he went boldly into the cave, and collected as much of the gold coin, which was in bags, as he thought his three donkeys could carry. When he had loaded them with the bags, he laid wood over them in such a manner that they could not be seen. After he had passed in and out as often as he wished, he stood before the door, and pronounced the words, "Shut, Sesame!" and the door closed of itself.

When Ali Baba got home, he drove his asses into a little yard, shut the gates very carefully, threw off the wood that covered the panniers, carried the bags into the house, and ranged them in order before his wife. He emptied the bags before his astonished wife, raising such a great heap of gold as to dazzle her eyes. Then he told her the whole adventure from beginning to end, and, above all, recommended her to keep it secret.

The wife rejoiced greatly at their good-fortune, but woman-like, wanted to count the gold piece by piece. "Wife," replied Ali Baba, "never try to number the gifts of Allah. Take them—and be thankful. To number them is to limit them. As for this treasure, I will dig a hole and bury it. There is no time to be lost." "You are in the right, husband," replied she.

"But," she thought, as he departed into the garden with his spade, it will do no harm to know, as nigh as possible, how much we have. I will borrow a small measure, and measure it."

Away she ran to her brother-in-law Cassim, who lived

hard by, and begged his wife for the loan of a measure for a little while. Her sister-in-law asked her whether she would have a great or a small one. The other asked for a small one. She bade her stay a little, and she would readily fetch one.

The sister-in-law did so, but as she knew Ali Baba's poverty, she was curious to know what sort of grain his wife wanted to measure, and, artfully putting some suet at the bottom of the measure, brought it to her, with the excuse that she was sorry that she had made her stay so long, but that she could not find it sooner.

Ali Baba's wife went home, filled the measure with gold and emptied it in the corner. Again and again she repeated that, and when she had done, she was very well satisfied to find the number of measures amounted to so many as they did, and went to tell her husband, who had almost finished digging the hole. While Ali Baba was burying the gold, his wife, to show her exactness and diligence to her sister-in-law, carried the measure back again, but without taking notice that a piece of gold had stuck to the bottom. "Sister," said she, giving it to her again, "you see that I have not kept your measure long. I am obliged to you for it, and return it with thanks."

As soon as Ali Baba's wife was gone, Cassim's wife looked at the bottom of the measure, and was in inexpressible surprise to find a piece of gold sticking to it. Envy immediately possessed her breast. "What!" said she, "has Ali Baba gold so plentiful as to measure it? Whence has he all this wealth?"

Cassim, her husband, was at his counting-house. When he came home his wife said to him, "Cassim, I know you think yourself rich, but Ali Baba is infinitely richer than you. He does not count his money, but measures it." Cassim desired her to explain the riddle, which she did by telling him the stratagem she had used to make the discovery, and showed him the piece of money, which was so old that they could not tell in what prince's reign it was coined.

Cassim, after he had married the rich widow, had never treated Ali Baba as a brother, but scorned and neglected him; and now, instead of being pleased, he conceived a base envy at his brother's prosperity. He could not sleep all that night, and went to him in the morning before sunrise. "Ali Baba," said he, "I am surprised at you! You pretend to be miserably poor, and yet you measure gold. My wife found this at the bottom of the measure you borrowed yesterday."

By this discourse, Ali Baba perceived that Cassim and his wife, through his own wife's folly, knew what they had so much reason to conceal; but what was done could not be undone. Therefore, without showing the least surprise or chagrin, he told all, and offered his brother part of his treasure to keep the secret.

"I expect as much," replied the greedy Cassim haughtily; "but I must know exactly where this treasure is, and how I may visit it myself when I choose; otherwise, I will go and inform against you, and then you will not only get no more, but will lose all you have, and I shall have a share for my information."

Ali Baba told him all he asked, even to the very words he was to use to gain admission into the cave.

Cassim rose the next morning long before the sun, and set out for the forest with ten mules bearing great chests, which he designed to fill, and followed the road which Ali Baba had pointed out to him. It was not long before he reached the rock, and found out the place, by the tree and other marks which his brother had given him. Walking up to the entrance of the cavern, he pronounced the words, "Open, Sesame!" Immediately the door opened, and when he was in, closed upon him.

On examining the cave, his avaricious soul was in transports of delight to find much more riches than he had expected from Ali Baba's relation. Quickly he laid as many bags of gold as he could carry at the door of the cavern; but his thoughts were so full of the great riches he should possess, and how with them he should become the richest money-lender and usurer in the city, that he could not think of the necessary words to make the door open. Instead of "Sesame" he said, "Open, Barley!" and was much amazed to find that the door remained fast shut. He named several sorts of grain, but still the door would not open.

Cassim had never anticipated such a contingency as this, and was so frightened at the danger he was in, that the more he endeavored to remember the word "Sesame," the more his memory was confounded. He threw down the bags he had loaded himself with, and walked distractedly up and down the cave, for the first time in his greedy life appreciating that to put your trust in money alone is to pin your faith to the most elusive thing in the world. Yet he had looked to it alone for so long a time that he knew now no other way to turn.

About noon the robbers visited their cave. At some distance they saw Cassim's mules straggling about the rock, with great chests on their backs. Alarmed at this, they galloped full speed to the cave, drove away the mules, which strayed through the forest so far that they were soon out of sight, and went directly, with their naked sabres in their hands, to the door, which on their captain pronouncing the proper words, immediately opened.

Cassim, who heard the noise of the horses' feet, at once guessed the arrival of the robbers, and resolved to make one effort for his life. He rushed to the door, and no sooner saw it open, than he ran out and threw the leader down, but could not escape the other robbers, who with their scimeters soon deprived him of life.

There is more to this old Eastern legend, but the meat of it lies here—that if you learn the Magic Secret, the

"Open Sesame" of life, wealth and honor are yours for the taking.

But if you become like the greedy Cassim, and get so taken up with the riches that you can think of nothing else—you not only lose the Magic Secret, but you bring down speedy retribution on your head as well.

THE "OPEN, SESAME!"

What is this "Open, Sesame" of life? What is the Philosopher's Stone which turns everything it touches into gold?

It is any controlling idea or desire so intense, so alive and real, that it carries utter faith with it and thus involuntarily establishes a contact with the Holy Spirit within, which attracts to itself everything it needs for its fulfillment.

It is, in short, the Lode Star—the Polar Magnet by means of which we may draw from the heavens above, from the earth beneath or from the waters under the earth anything that is necessary to our controlling idea or desire.

Ridiculous? Stop and think for just a moment.

Have you ever concentrated for days or weeks on the writing of an article or story, on the making of some device, on the discovery of some new formula—on anything that required the deepest thought and faith and concentration?

Remember how there seemed to pour in upon you all sorts of facts and information and material pertinent to the idea you had in mind? Remember how things came to you from the most unlikely and unexpected sources—from the chance words of associates or even strangers; from newspaper and magazine articles, picked up in the most casual way imaginable; from books you happened to see in the windows or in the hands of some friend; from *out of the air,* as it were, unsought, unbidden—except as they were sought out and brought to you by that Mental Magnet within.

"If any of you lack wisdom," said James, "let him ask of God, that giveth to all men liberally, and upbraideth not; and it shall be given him. But let him ask in faith, nothing wavering. For he that wavereth is like a wave of the sea driven with the wind and tossed. For let not that man think that he shall receive anything from the Lord."—James 1:5-6.

The earnest desire for some definite thing, coupled with the sincere belief in your power to get it through the Spirit within, is the most powerful force in the world. As Marie Corelli says in "Life Everlasting":

"Nothing in the universe can resist the force of a steadfastly fixed resolve. What the spirit truly seeks must, by eternal law, be given to it, and what the body needs for the fulfillment of the spirit's demands will be bestowed. From the sunlight and the air and the hidden things of space strength shall be daily and hourly renewed. Everything in nature shall aid in bringing to the resolved soul that which it demands. There is nothing within the circle of creation that can resist its influence. Success, wealth, triumph upon triumph come to every human being who daily 'sets his house in order'—whom no derision can drive from his determined goal, whom no temptation can drag from his appointed course."

I know that when I first conceived the idea for this book and began to look for different works of reference to bear out the thought I had in mind, I was almost flooded with material—wonderful material that I had never even heard about, much less knew where to look for. Three of the best works on the subject I have ever seen, literally walked into my office—unsought, unbidden and without cost—and have been of more help to me than anything else I have found. And I am far from being alone in this experience.

In a recent issue of *Advertising and Selling,* Floyd W. Parsons tells how a piece of cheese tossed by one workman at another during the lunch hour missed its mark and dropped into the plating bath used in the production of copper disks from which wax phonograph records were stamped. Later the disks from that bath were found to be far superior to the others, and an investigation revealed that the casein in the cheese had done the trick. This disclosed a possible improvement worth several thousand dollars.

The top of a salt cellar fell off, and the outcome was a new flux for welding permalloy, making possible a six-fold increase in the speed with which we can send messages by cable.

By inadvertently opening the wrong valve, a French scientist found the answer to the long search for liquid oxygen. Again an accident created an industry and gave us an explosive safer and mightier than dynamite.

A great corporation ordered its industrial chemists to produce a paint that could be applied quickly, would dry rapidly, and be tough, hard and resistant to the elements. It had to have some of the properties of glass and yet not crack, and it had to be proof against the action of oil, grease, and acid.

Everything went well up to the point of finding a way to keep the solution in a liquid condition so that it could be applied with a brush. All efforts to solve this problem failed until one day the machinery broke down and the material had to stand for days in the tank until the repairs were completed. When work started again, the chemists were amazed to find that the paint now retained its liquid form. The long-sought secret had finally been discovered, and an accident had again shaped the destiny of a business.

In short, when you have put all of your reasoning, all of your information into the cauldron of thought, there frequently flashes out an idea that is not the logical development of anything you have had before—but a direct inspiration from the Holy Spirit within.

"And thine ears shall hear a word behind thee, saying, This is the way, walk ye in it, when ye turn to
the right hand, and when ye turn to the left."

—ISAIAH 30–21.

"The key to successful methods," says Thos. A. Edison,
"comes right out of the air. A real new thing like a general
idea, a beautiful melody, is pulled out of space—a fact
which is inexplicable."

Inexplicable? Not at all! It is simply that all knowledge
already exists in Divine Mind—in the Father who fills all
space and animates all things. There is nothing for us to
discover—merely to *seek,* to *unfold.* Columbus did not discover America. It was here all the time. As the Englishman
said after three days of traveling on a California-bound
train—"How could he have missed it?" Columbus—and
all of Europe—merely learned something that Divine
Mind had known all the time.

Galileo did not discover that the earth was round; Copernicus did not discover the movement of the planets;
Newton did not discover the law of gravitation; any more
than your young son discovers the law of mathematics by
which $2+2=4$. He learns it—yes. He makes the information his own. And to him it partakes of discovery. But the
law was known to Divine Mind since time began.

We are God's children, grasping a little at a time of the

infinite knowledge He is constantly writing on the black-board before us—and hailing each bit as a grand discovery of our own. Sir Isaac Newton, one of the greatest geniuses of all time, compared himself to a boy, gathering pebbles on the shore of the vast, unknown ocean of truth.

"God looked down from heaven," said David, "upon the children of men to see if there were any that did understand."—Psalms 14:2.

The great essential is to realize that the Father HAS all information—that the "vast ocean of truth" IS there—and that if we will do our best in the trustful knowledge that the Father *can* and very gladly *will* supply anything beyond our own powers to grasp, our faith and trust will be justified. "There is nothing hidden," saith the Scripture, "which shall not be revealed; neither hid which shall not be known." "When God is with us," quoth Josephus, "the impossible becomes possible."

When any problem confronts you that seems beyond your ability to solve, just say to yourself—"I am one with the Infinite Intelligence of the Universe. And Infinite Intelligence HAS the correct answer to this problem. Therefore, I too have the answer, and at the right time and in the right way will manifest it."

There are no new gold deposits. No new diamond fields. All of them have been known to the Father for millions of years.

You don't need to discover anything. You don't need to

create something new. All you need to do is to seek the riches and the methods that have been known to the Father for all time. And the place to seek them is not far afield—but in Mind. "Seek and ye shall find," said Jesus. "Knock and it shall be opened to you."

A RADIO WITH A THOUSAND AERIALS

Our bodies are, in effect, radio stations powerful or otherwise as our controlling ideas are strong or weak. The nerves that come to the surface all over our body act as thousands of aerials gathering in impressions from every source. And just as any station properly attuned and powerful enough to "get" it, can pick what it wants out of the air any minute of the day or night, so can you "get" anything you may want—be it riches or success, happiness or health—if your thought be properly keyed and powerful enough to receive it.

For our minds are vast magnets that can attract to us anything we may desire. The only requisite is—they have got to be *charged*. A demagnetized magnet won't draw to it or hold even the weight of a pin. Nor will a demagnetized man attract to himself a single idea or a single penny.

There are two ways of charging your mental magnet:

1. By occasional but heartfelt prayer—like the radio fan who lets his batteries run down until,

when something special comes along that he particularly wants, he finds them so weak he can scarcely raise a sound, and forthwith hies himself to the battery man to have them recharged.

2. By heeding Jesus' admonition to pray without ceasing—to go back to the simile of the radio fan again, to attach your batteries to the electric light socket and keep them constantly charged to capacity, ready and able at all times to bring you anything you may wish.

Which method is yours? Old Mother Nature adopts the second. The flowers turn their faces to the sun not just once a day or once a week—but always. The waving grain, the shrubs, the trees, drink in the light and life of the sun every day and all day. They recharge themselves with life and fragrance whenever and as long as opportunity offers.

That is what you too must do. You must first charge the magnet of your mind with a compelling desire. Then keep it recharged with faith in the power and the willingness of the Father to give to you anything of good that may be necessary to the fruition of your prayer. Not only that, but you must realize your ability (through the Father) to draw to yourself anything of good. In short, you must realize your Sonship with God, and the consequent fact that all of good is already yours—that God has done his part—that it is up to you merely to manifest, to unfold, to SEE the good things that the Father has provided for you in such profusion.

When Hagar and Ishmael were wandering in the desert, and could find no water and seemed about to perish, then Hagar cried aloud to the Lord.

"And God heard the voice of the lad; and the angel of God called to Hagar out of heaven, and said unto her, What aileth thee, Hagar? Fear not; for God hath heard the voice of the lad where he is.

"And God opened her eyes, and she saw a well of water; and she went, and filled the bottle with water, and gave the lad drink."—Genesis 21:17, 19.

Again, when the three kings in the desert sought water for their men and horses, the Prophet Elisha told them: "Thus saith the Lord—Ye shall not see wind, neither shall ye see rain, yet make this valley full of ditches."—II Kings 3:16-17.

And though it looked a hopeless task, the three kings set their men to work as directed, and after they had prepared the ditches, the rains came and filled them.

Wherever you are and whatever you need, supply is always there—for supply is in the Father, and the Father is everywhere. It is like the air we breathe—it is all around us, always available, always plentiful—unless we lock ourselves into the air-tight houses of limitation.

The trouble is that we have for so long been taught that everything of good must be fought for, struggled for, taken away from some one else, that we can't believe when we are told that all we need do is to open up the windows of our souls and let in the Holy Spirit—open up the channels of supply and let riches flow freely to us. To quote Trench's beautiful poem—

"Make channels for the streams of love,
Where they may broadly run,
For Love has overflowing streams
To fill them every one;

"But if at any time we cease
Such channels to provide,
The very founts of Love for us,
Will soon be parched and dried;

"For we must share if we would keep
Such blessings from above,
Ceasing to give, we cease to have,
Such is the law of Love."

We see others breathing deeply of the air about us, and we don't begrudge them it because we know there is plenty for all. We see others enjoying the sunlight; the clear water from the spring; and we rejoice with them in it. But let another make a lot of money, and immediately we become envious, for we think he has made it that much harder for us to get any.

The best things in life, the greatest essentials to life, are free. Air, sunshine, water—all are free, because the supply of them is inexhaustible.

What we fail to realize is that there is just as inexhaustible supply of the things that money will buy as there is of sunlight or water or air. And they can be drawn just as freely from the Father through the magic of faith and a compelling idea.

But you can't do it if you dam up the source of supply with doubts and fears. You must not limit supply as did the widow in the Scriptural story. Left destitute, her creditors were pressing her hard; and her sons, as was the law in that day, were to become bondsmen for the debt she owed. In her distress she came to the prophet Elisha, and he asked—"What have you in your house?" She replied—"I have nothing but a vessel of oil." He said—"Send out to your neighbors and borrow all the vessels you can; take them empty into a room, and pour into them the oil which you have." She did not question him but did as she was told; she poured the oil from the vessel which contained all that she possessed and filled all those which she had borrowed. Then she told her sons to get others, but they said—"We have no more." And as soon as they made that announcement, the oil stopped flowing—not one drop came after all the vessels were full—II Kings 4:2-6. Do you see who determined the quantity that should come to the widow? Was it God? I know your answer—"It was the woman herself." She received just the amount for which she had made preparation.

IT'S NOT THE SUPPLY
THAT IS LIMITED—IT IS OURSELVES!

Too many of us are like the little colored boy and the watermelon. An old gentleman, seeing the difficulty the boy was having in storing away so large a melon, stopped and asked, "Too much melon, isn't it, son?" "No, suh!" replied the youngster with conviction, "just not enough niggah."

Why does so large a part of humanity suffer hunger and want?

Certainly not from lack on the part of old Mother Earth. Ask the farmers and they will tell you their trouble is over-production—not scarcity. Ask the scientists, and they will tell you that there is food in plenty in the very air. And not only food—but power and riches. Ask the miners—whether of gold, or silver, or diamonds, or coal, or iron—and they will tell you that the supply exceeds the demand. Go to the manufacturer and ask him—and again your answer will be the same.

Evidently there is plenty to go around. Evidently the Father has not failed us, any more than he fails the birds of the air or the beasts of the field, in providing the supply. The problem is merely one of our ability to receive—to receive and digest and distribute and exchange.

There is plenty for all—of everything of good. The poor are hungry, the needy are in lack, not because there is not enough supply, but because their mental magnets have become so weak through discouragement, their channels so stopped up with fear and worry, that the stream of supply no longer reaches them.

If you cut your finger, what happens? You call upon your heart for an extra supply of blood to rebuild the damaged part. And the heart immediately responds.

If you have urgent need of money or other worldly goods, what should you do? Call upon the Heart of all things to send you an extra supply for your emergency— and He will just as promptly and cheerfully respond.

There's a little comedy on one of the Broadway stages that illustrates this idea clearly. A couple of young darkies are boxing—the first, an active, alert little fellow, on the go every minute—the second a tall, shambling, lazy sort, slow-moving, slow-thinking.

The big one is too lazy to really fight his active opponent. He contents himself with trying to guard himself. But every time he moves a hand, the little one gets in a punch.

Finally the big one catches hold of the little fellow by the shoulders, holds him off at arm's length and studies him for a minute. Then he puts one hand in the other's face and lets the little one jab at him, the while he holds him off at arm's length.

The little one swings and punches, but his arms are too short. He can't quite reach the big fellow. The lazy one throws back his head and laughs as he prepares to swing his good right arm at leisure. *"That's all I wanted to know,"* he says.

And all you need to know when that little devil of fear or worry or lack assails you and you want to hold him off for a while until you can swing your good right arm to put him out for the count is that the answer to any trouble, the remedy for any lack, the antidote for any ill is just around the corner. Charge your mental magnet with earnest desire and faith—and the need does not exist which you cannot satisfy.

"The Lord's hand is not shortened, that it cannot save," promised the Prophet Isaiah 59:1. "Neither His ear heavy, that it cannot hear."

The principal reason there is so much truth in the Scriptural quotation—"To him that hath shall be given," is that the man who has a tidy sum safely put away loses all worry about supply. Like the darkey in the play, he feels that his money gives him that bit of extra reach with which he can easily fend off the attacks of want and fear and worry, while he is getting in his good licks elsewhere. True, he places his dependence upon money rather than upon the Spirit, but the belief that he has money enough not to have to worry emboldens him to demand more. He loses all sense of fear. He expects and demands only the *good* things of life—and consequently the good things of life come to him. To put it in the words of Solomon—"He that hath a bountiful eye shall be blessed"—Proverbs 22:9.

"He who dares assert the I,
May calmly wait, while hurrying fate
Meets his demand with sure supply."

Remember the story of the merchant who saw ruin staring him in the face unless he could raise money immediately? He went to a wise friend, who gave him a great nugget of gold—on condition, however, that he was not to use it except as a last resource.

Knowing that he had the gold to use at need, the merchant went boldly about his business with a mind at ease—faced his creditors so confidently that they gladly trusted him further—with the result that he never needed to use the gold.

But you don't need to go to the pages of fiction for such examples. Most of us have seen similar instances ourselves. There is the classic case of George Muller, of Bristol, England, who maintained orphanages which spent millions, through which hundreds of children were rescued from the slums and fitted for places of trust in the world—*all without any visible means of support!*

Like the oil from the widow's cruse, the money came through his perfect faith in the Giver of all good. Many and many a time utter penury stared him in the face, so that any man of less Job-like faith would have been discouraged. Once hundreds of hungry children sat waiting for their breakfasts—and there was not a mouthful to give them.

But always in time—though sometimes at the very last moment—his faith was justified and some generous donation would supply all their wants. Like Job, he might well have said—"I know that my Redeemer liveth."—Job 19:25. "Though He slay me, yet will I trust in Him."—Job 13:15.

Or with David—"Yea, though I walk through the valley of the shadow of Death I shall fear no evil, for Thou art with me."—Psalms 23:4.

For nothing stands between you and the dearest wish of your heart but doubt and fear. When you can pray without doubting, when you can believe as the Master bade us believe—"Whatsoever ye ask for when ye pray, believe that ye RECEIVE it and ye SHALL HAVE IT"—every desire of your heart will be instantly filled.

What, then, is the "Open, Sesame," of life? What is the Magic Secret that will bring to you everything of good you may wish?

It is simply a "Message to Garcia." There is within you

a Holy Spirit who is your part of Divinity—who knows all, sees all and can do all things. Give him a definite task, magnetize Him with your absolute belief in His ability and His readiness to accomplish it—charge Him with such absolute faith that you can actually SEE HIM DOING IT—and "as thy faith is, so it will be unto you." The Spirit within you can draw from the heavens or the earth or the waters under the earth whatever you may need for the consummation of your desires.

How do men talk 3,000 miles across the Atlantic—without wires, without cables? In the Marconi beam system, they do it by focusing the electric waves into one great beam, just as a searchlight focuses all the light waves into one powerful ray. Ordinary broadcasting stations let their waves radiate in all directions like the ripples a pebble makes in a pool of water. The Marconi beam system focuses them all into one powerful beam and then directs it straight across the Atlantic, with the result that they will carry your message wherever you wish it to go.

Focus your desires in the same way. Instead of frittering away your energy in a thousand directions, bring them all to bear in one powerful beam on one single desire at a time. Do that, and you can attract to yourself anything of good you may wish.

"All that the Father hath is yours." And—"there is no lack in Him in whom all fullness lies."

So what do you want?

Is it money? Then know that the Father is the source of all wealth. Go to Him—tell Him your need—ask Him for money in abundance to meet your needs. Bless the money you now have—know that the Father is in it even as he is in all good things—then see it, in your mind's eye, *multiplied* as Jesus multiplied the loaves and fishes.

Send forth the Holy Spirit within you to the source of supply for as much as you need or can use to good advantage. Then SEE HIM DRAWING THAT SUPPLY! See a golden stream flowing to you in the sunlight, in the moonbeams!

Actually speak the word that sends your Spirit forth. Tell Him—"Holy Spirit, you know that the one Law of Supply is abundance—plenty for every right purpose, plenty for every right desire. You know that the Father has all of abundance, that there is unlimited money available for me right now, that as His son I am heir to it. Go you, therefore, bring to me of the infinite abundance that is mine, all that I may need for this purpose. If there is anything you wish *me* to do, give me a definite lead."

Speak the word, then cast your burden upon the Holy Spirit—and forget it! "My word shall not return unto me void, but shall accomplish that where unto it is sent."—Isaiah 55:11. Every doubt, every fear, every worry that you entertain is a shackle holding Him back. If you can release Him from all dominion of the conscious mind, if you can have the faith in Him that you have when you give a task to a trusted servant and thereafter look upon it as done—depend upon it, He will bring you what you ask for.

But it is so hard for us to let go. We are like a man on a desert isle, daily releasing our one carrier pigeon with a message for help, yet as often bringing him back to earth again by the string on his foot that we are too distrustful to untie.

Yet when at last in desperation we do cut off the shackles, our faithful messenger flies straight home with his message of need and brings succour to us immediately.

That is why so often our prayers are not answered until the eleventh hour. We won't turn loose the string. We won't trust entirely in the Spirit. We think He needs our help, too. When all that we need is a little trust.

"If we have faith as a grain of mustard seed, ye shall say unto this mountain—remove hence to yonder place, and it shall remove. And nothing shall be impossible unto you."—Matthew 17:20.

It is the same no matter what you may want. Are you seeking a position? Know that in the Mind of the Father there is one right position for you—one position that in the present stage of your development, is best fitted for you even as you are best fitted for it. You have a definite place in the great scheme of things. And there is one right position that marks the next step in your forward progress.

That position IS yours. You have only to *know* this and to realize it. Then send forth the Spirit within you to bring that position to you or you to it. *Speak the word.* Throw the burden upon Him, asking Him only, if there is anything you can do to forward the work, to give you a definite lead. Then rest content in the knowledge that the Spirit *is* doing the work.

"Prove me now herewith, saith the Lord of Hosts, if I will not open you the windows of heaven, and pour you out a blessing that there shall not be room enough to receive it."—Malachi 3:10.

What, then, is the answer? Is this a lazy-man's world, where all that one needs to do is to fast and pray?

By no means! It is a worker's world—and the only ones who ever get anything out of it that is worth while are the workers. Mere wishing never magnetized the Spirit within to bring anything of good.

Look at all of Nature—busy every moment, never idle—*but never worrying.* Model after her. Whatever it is you may want, remember that you must get it first in Mind. See yourself with it there—see yourself receiving it. Make it as real as you can. Be thankful for it!

Then set about manifesting that dream in the material world. Do anything you can think of that will help to bring it about. Concentrate your thought upon it in every conceivable way. But never worry as to the outcome. Know that after you have done all that is possible for you to do— if you are still lacking in some essential, you can sit back in the utter confidence that the Holy Spirit within will supply that lack. Give of your best—and you need never fear for the outcome. Your best will come back to you—amplified an hundredfold.

"Ye know in all your hearts and in all your souls, that not one thing hath failed of all the good things which the Lord your God spake concerning you; all are come to pass unto you, and not one thing hath failed thereof."—Joshua 23:14.

IV

THE MAN OF BRASS

"Behold, now is the accepted time. Behold, now is the day of salvation."

—II CORINTHIANS.

Away back in the 13th century, there lived a scientist so far ahead of his times that he had to record most of his discoveries in cypher—to keep from being burned at the stake.

Even as it was, he was thought by the ignorant to be a sorcerer, a magician, an apostate who had sold his soul to the devil. Only among the initiate was he known as "The Wonderful Doctor."

His name was Roger Bacon.

And wonderful he truly was. Many of the chemical formulas he discovered are in use today. He made gunpowder.

He discovered the possibilities of the magnifying glass. He was a forerunner of Galileo and Copernicus.

Innumerable legends grew up about him, some of which

will be touched upon in the later volumes of this Course—notably his "Elixir of Life." But the most persistent of these legends deals with "The Man of Brass."

Bacon, you must know, had mastered seven different languages in his efforts to wrest from every possible source the secrets of science that had been known to previous ages. Among these languages was the Arabic. And one day there was brought to him an old Arabic manuscript which some wandering knight had picked up in far-away Palestine.

Bacon read the work and marvelled. It told first how to fashion a man of brass. Then, by means of clock-work and wires leading to certain jars of chemicals (the first crude storage batteries), how the eye-balls could be made to glow, the tongue to move, smoke to issue from the nostrils, and noise from the mouth. But most important of all—how, by adhering to certain directions, the Man of Brass could be made to speak *and reveal a secret of the utmost importance to every Englishman.*

For seven years, Roger Bacon toiled over his Man of Brass. He is reputed to have spent a fortune in scientific experiments, and no small part of it must have gone into this brazen image. At last it was finished. Everything had been done with the greatest care, strictly in accordance with the directions given in the manuscript.

Then he sat down and waited. For more than a month, there was never a minute when Roger Bacon or his friend and confidante Friar Bungay was not sitting before the brazen image, listening for any sound it might utter. But neither friars nor philosophers can keep on without sleep.

One night, when Friar Bungay had gone home, Bacon was nodding in his chair before the image. "If I can keep awake but a few hours longer," he muttered, "the wonderful voice will speak and the great secret will be known." But he could not keep awake. His eyes would close in spite of himself. Finally he called his servant, admonished him to wake him immediately if the image should speak and went off to snatch a bit of rest.

The servant sat near the door, his eyes fastened in frightened fascination upon those of the image, his fingers gripped about the stout oaken cudel in his hands.

Suddenly the eyes of the image glowed, its lips moved and in a sybilant whisper there issued from its mouth the words—

"TIME IS!"

The servant jumped to his feet and started to run, but as the brazen image seemed to remain rooted to the one spot, he paused on the threshold to see what more it might have to say.

Presently again the eyes lighted up, the lips moved, and a voice like the rattling of a kettle-drum shrilled out—

"TIME WAS!"

This time the servant all but fled. But before he could get the door open, the eyes glowed once more and in a voice of thunder there issued the words—

"TIME IS PAST!"

And with that the image fell and smashed into a thousand pieces.

Bacon is said to have been so bitterly disappointed at what he considered the wasting of all his seven years of labor that he burned his books, closed his study and spent the rest of his life in a monastery.

But had his work been wasted? Is there any secret of greater importance than the knowledge that—*"Time is NOW"?* Most of us are so busy regretting the past or planning what we are going to be and do in some far distant day or state that we overlook the chances for happiness and success that are all around us now.

The past is gone and done with. No amount of regrets will bring it back. So let us forget it—except in so far as we may draw lessons from it. Let our motto be "Yesterday ended last night."

As for the future—it is still ahead of us, and no man may tell what it holds.

But the present is ours to do with as we will. So let us live it to the utmost. *"Time IS"*—not has been or will be. "Time *passes*"—you will never have one bit more of time than you have this minute.

So what do you want to do with it? What have you to ask of the Father of Life—not next year, or ten years from now, or in some indefinite future state—but NOW?

There's an old Eastern legend that the gates of Paradise

are opened only once in each thousand years. And judging by most people's attitude toward life, that belief seems to have obtained credence among us, for most of us look forward to happiness and success as something in the far distant future. We pray—but look for the result of our prayers in some vague future state.

"Behold, *now* is the accepted time," declared Paul.

All of supply is already in existence. Why put off drawing upon it six months—or a year—or ten years? Why not charge the magnet of your mind to draw from Infinite Supply what you may want NOW?

"I cause those that love me to inherit substance, and I will fill their treasures."—Proverbs 8:21.

If you were to take a vote of the Christian peoples of the world, you would find them practically unanimous in believing that God intended to save their souls in the next world—but that in so far as their present existence is concerned, you've got to leave Him out of the reckoning!

Yet if you took from the Scriptures all those parts that tell of His succoring those in trouble—not in some far-off future state, but in this life; if you left out all His promises of protection and reward here on earth to those that loved Him and kept His commandments—how much of the Bible would there be left?

"And the Lord shall guide thee continually, and satisfy thy soul in drought, and make fat thy bones; and thou shalt be like a watered garden, and like a spring of water whose waters fail not."—Isaiah 58:11.

If only all could realize that even in the heart of the humblest laborer, of the poorest scrub-woman, lies the key to riches inexhaustible, what a world of poverty and misery we might avoid.

"God shall supply all your need, according to His riches."—Philippians 4:19.

Most of us find it easy enough to believe this when our pockets are full and all is going well with us. But let the wolf start scratching at the door and then watch us. Yet that is the very time when we most need faith! The fact is that we have more confidence in the weekly pay-envelope, uncertain as it is, than we have in the Almighty! Well might the Prophet of old say to us, as he sarcastically said to the idolaters of his day—"Ye have gods that ye carry, but *we have a God that carries us.*"

"God is able to make all grace abound toward you, that ye always having all sufficiency in all things, may abound in every good work."—II Corinthians 9:8.

Consider the lilies of the field. Consider the birds; the denizens of the field; of the forest; of the air and the water; they don't lack for what they need. The big difference between them and you is that you have been given free will. You don't need to go to the Father unless you wish. You can struggle and toil on your own account. You can look upon this as a vale of tears—and find it so. Or you can do your best—and then rest in the arms of the Father while "He doeth the works."

"Yea, the Almighty shall be thy defence, and thou shalt have plenty of silver."—Job 22:25.

All that you need, all of good that you want, is right at your hand. Remember, when the disciples had been fishing all night and caught nothing, how Jesus told them to cast their nets on the *right* side—and they caught so many fish that their nets were full to overflowing?

If He could fill the nets of these discouraged fishermen with fish, don't you suppose He can just as easily fill your nets with whatever it is you may be fishing for?

"The soul answers never by words," says Emerson, "but by the thing itself sought after."

Have you ever seen the Hopi Indians' Snake Dance—their prayer for rain? It is probably the oldest religious ceremony on this continent, and it is said that it never yet has failed to bring the rains.

> "Speak to Him thou, for He heareth
> When Spirit with Spirit doth meet;
> Closer is He than breathing,
> And nearer than hands and feet."

Scientists may talk learnedly of atmospheric conditions and natural laws, but the fact remains—the Indians send up their heartfelt prayers to the Holy Spirit in simple faith—and so far as is known, the rains have never failed to promptly come!

"Whither shall I go from thy Spirit?" cried the Psalmist of old, "Or whither shall I flee from Thy presence? If I ascend up into heaven Thou are there; if I make my bed in hell, behold Thou are there. If I take the wings of the morning and dwell in the uttermost parts of the sea; even there shall Thy hand lead me and Thy right hand shall hold me. If I say, Surely the darkness shall cover me; even the night shall be light about me."—Psalms 139:7-11.

There is in this universe a Power that hears the cry of the human heart. There is behind us a Father "whose good pleasure it is to give us the Kingdom." You don't have to beg Him for the good things of life any more than you have to beg the sun for its heat. You have only to draw near and take of the bountiful supply He is constantly holding out to you.

"Before ye call, I shall answer."

So what is it you want of the Father of Life? A house? A toy? A car? Success in this or that undertaking? Health? Love? Happiness?

Whatever it is, you can have it. Whatever of good you ask for with earnest desire and simple faith, the Father will gladly give.

Does this sound too simple, too direct? Do you feel that it is a bit sacriligious to be asking the Father for worldly things? Just listen:

"And I say unto you, Ask, and it shall be given you; seek, and ye shall find; knock, and it shall be opened unto you.

"For every one that asketh receiveth; and he that seeketh findeth; and to him that knocketh it shall be opened.

"If a son shall ask bread of any of you that is a Father, will he give him a stone? Or if he ask a fish, will he for a fish give him a serpent?

"Or if he shall ask an egg, will he offer him a scorpion?

"If ye then, being evil, know how to give good gifts unto your children: how much more shall your heavenly Father give the Holy Spirit to them that ask him?"—Luke 11:9-13.

And those words came—not from any Prophet or Disciple, but from the lips of the Master Himself!

So have no hesitancy in going to Him about little things. Don't you suppose He is as glad to see you clothed in a new suit or new dress as He is to see the birds preening their new feathers, the wild things of the forest in their shining new coat, the snake and his like in their new skins? Don't you suppose it gives Him as much pleasure to give you something you have been longing for as it gladdens the heart of an earthly father to give a much-desired toy to his little boy?

"Thou openest thy hand and satisfieth the desire of every living thing."

I have had people write me that prayer has brought to them such simple little things as flowers, as toys for the children, as an automobile. Last Christmas one reader wrote me that he had needed $500. That he had put his problem before the Father confidently, believingly. Then left it with Him. To use his own words, "the $500 came from so unexpected a source that if the President himself had sent it to him, he would not have been more surprised."

"No good things will He withhold from them that walketh uprightly."

The very fact that you have some earnest desire is the best evidence that the answer to that desire is in the great heart of God.

"Time is NOW!"

That earnest desire of yours is in the present. And the supply is just as much so. The Father is just as much present here and now as He will ever be. So why put off the realization of your desires to some vague and distant future? Why not realize them in the now?

What is it that you want?

Whatever it is, it already exists somewhere, in some form. And if your desire be strong enough, your faith great enough you can attract it to you.

There are riches in abundance for you. They already exist. They are labeled YOURS in the mind of the Father. And until you get them, they will remain idle. You don't have to take them from someone else. You don't have to envy anyone else what he has. All you have to KNOW is that somewhere all of riches that you can ever desire are lying waiting for you.

Don't try to get them all at once.

If you had a million dollars on deposit in some bank, you wouldn't rush there and draw it out, to carry around with you or to hide about the house. No—as long as you had confidence in the integrity of the bank, you would leave your money on deposit there, drawing upon it merely as you needed it.

Have you less confidence in the Bank of the Father than in those of man? Must you ask It for all your heritage at once for fear the Bank will fail? Or can you do as Jesus did, as He told us all to do, ask each day for that day's needs—"Give us this day our daily bread"—in the simple faith that our every draft will be met promptly, fully, no matter what the size?

The man who has that simple faith will not try to pinch pennies. He won't "pass by on the other side" when a worthy need approaches him. Neither will he throw away money foolishly—"casting pearls before swine."

He will spend cheerfully—for any right purpose. He will bless the money he sends out—as Jesus blessed the loaves and the fishes—putting it to work in the confident knowledge that when used gainfully, it will come back increased and multiplied.

The same thing applies to your home, to your surroundings. There is a perfect home for you already built in the Father's mind. Know this—realize it—then, like Hagar in the wilderness, pray that your eyes may be opened that you may SEE this perfect home that is yours.

There is a perfect position for you. A perfect mate. A perfect work. A perfect idea of each cell and organism in your body. In later volumes of this set, I shall try to show you how through the promises of the Scriptures these may all be realized. Suffice it now to say that they all exist in the Father's mind. It is up to you merely to *seek* that you may find them.

You have the most powerful magnet on earth right within your own mind. Uncover it! Charge it with desire and faith. Speak the word that sends the Holy Spirit that is within you in quest of what you wish. Then cast the burden upon Him and thereafter look upon your desire as an accomplished fact.

"Whatsoever ye ask for when ye pray, believe that ye *receive* it and ye shall have it."

Prepare for the thing you have asked for, even though there be not the slightest sign of its coming. Act the part! Like the three Kings in the desert, dig your ditches to receive the water, even though there be not a cloud in the sky. And your ditches will be filled—even as were theirs.

"Be still—and know that I am God!" Wait calmly, confidently, in the full assurance that the Father has what you want and will gladly give it to you.

One's ships come in over a calm sea.

THE LAW OF KARMA

You have probably heard of the Law of Karma. It is Sanskrit, you know, for "Comeback." It is one of the oldest laws known to man—yet perhaps the least regarded.

It is the law of the boomerang. Jesus quoted it: "Whatsoever a man soweth, that shall he also reap."

In the parlance of today, it is—"Chickens come home to roost." Even in science we find it, as Newton's Third Law of Motion—"Action and reaction are always equal to each other."

Wherein does this law affect us now? Only in that, if you wish riches, if you long for happiness, health, success, you must *think* abundance, you must charge your mind with happy thoughts, healthy thoughts, optimistic thoughts.

If you are seeking riches, you will never get them by stopping up all the avenues of outgo, and waiting for your vessel to fill up from the top. I remember one man who wrote me from down in West Virginia that when he received *The Secret of the Ages* he was a farmhand, working for $1 a day. Through the confidence and knowledge acquired through the books, he had landed a job at $6.20 a day of eight hours, where before he had labored for twelve hours on the farm. But, he wrote, "I've returned the books. You gave me time to get out of them what I wanted and return at your expense without buying them. I think now I can make a million. So I don't want to spend any money now. I want to make my million." That man was like a funnel—big at the receiving end, but little at the outgoing part. The Law of Karma will get him before he has gone far. You have got to cast your bread upon the waters, in the secure confidence that it will come back to you multiplied an hundredfold.

If you are longing for a beautiful home, you will never get it by thinking thoughts of poverty and lack. Forget the state of your pocketbook. Your supply is not there. All supply is in the Father, "with Whom is no variableness nor shadow of turning." So go to the Father with your desire. Try to picture in your mind's eye the perfect home that already is yours in Divine Mind. Make it complete in every detail. Realize that this perfect home *is yours*—that it already exists—in the mind of the Father. Then send forth the Holy Spirit to bring it to you or you to it.

Don't ask for some particular house. Ask, if you wish, for one like it. Don't try to take that which is another's. Know that the one perfect home for you already exists in Divine Mind, even though you may never have seen it. Then leave it to the Holy Spirit to manifest it.

"All that the Kingdom affords is yours."

Speak the word—then cast the burden upon the Holy Spirit within. The Father sends His gifts in His own way, even as earthly fathers frequently do. Make all preparations for them—dig your ditches—open up the windows of your soul. Be ready to receive.

Remember, in Genesis I:1-2—"In the beginning, God created the heaven and the earth. And the earth was without form and void; and darkness was upon the face of the deep. *And the Spirit of God moved upon the face of the waters.*"

That Spirit of God still moves upon the face of the waters. And upon the face of the land. That Spirit of God is the Holy Spirit within you. And just as He helped to form the earth from the void, so will He bring form to your dreams, your desires. If only you do your part. If only you have the faith. If only you can cast the burden upon Him—confidently, believingly!

"Oh Judah; fear not; but tomorrow go out against them, for the Lord will be with you. You shall not need to fight this battle; set yourselves, stand you still, *and see the salvation of the Lord with you.*"

And the time to do it is NOW.

V

START SOMETHING!

"And I have filled him with the Spirit of God, in wisdom, and in understanding, and in knowledge, and in all manner of workmanship,

"To devise cunning works, to work in gold, and in silver, and in brass,

"And in cutting of stones, to set them, and in carving timber, to work in all manner of workmanship.

"And I, behold, I have given with him Aholiah, the son of Ahisamach, of the tribe of Dan: and in the hearts of all that are wise hearted I have put wisdom, that they may make all that I have commanded thee."

—EXODUS 31:3-6.

A Spanish adventurer gets together a following of a couple of thousand out-at-elbows soldiers of fortune like himself—and with them conquers a nation! A disciplined, well-led warlike nation numbering millions! Defeats armies ten times the size of his little force, time after time! Captures a walled city garrisoned by a great army and protected by dykes and canals, and makes its emperor prisoner!

I refer to Hernando Cortez, conqueror of Mexico.

Another Spaniard, with a handful of followers, enslaves the whole of Peru, carries away the vast treasures of the Incas, makes Spain the richest nation on the globe!

That was 400 years ago, but it is easy enough to find their counterparts today. A few years ago Persia had been almost dismembered by Russia and England. And Reza Khan was but a poor trooper in the Persian army. Today Persia has been restored to an independent state—and Reza Khan is its Ruler.

Ebert, a saddle-maker before the war—becomes President of the new German Republic. Trotsky, a waiter in a cheap New York restaurant—is made War Minister of Soviet Russia. Mustapha Kemal, a good soldier—but until the war unknown—makes himself Ruler of Turkey. Every day brings its grist of new stars in the world firmament—new and comet-like rises to fame.

How do they do it? What is the secret behind such phenomenal successes?

Not education—many of these men had no education to speak of. Not training—none of them was ever trained for real leadership. Then what is it?

Just one thing these men all had in common—the daring to *start something!*

If Cortez had been content to sit around in Cuba and wait for something to turn up, do you suppose we should ever have heard of him?

If Reza Khan had been content to do his mere duty as a Persian trooper; if Ebert had been satisfied to keep on making saddles; if Mustapha Kemal had merely obeyed whatever orders he received; do you suppose their countrymen would have started out on a still hunt for them, routed them out of their obscurity and put them at the head of their governments?

Not in a thousand years!

You may—and do—possess latent ability equal to any man on earth; you have ready to your call, through the Holy Spirit within you, not merely the wisdom of a Solomon but the Wisdom of God! Yet all of this will not get you anywhere—all of this will never result in the world calling upon you to lead it—unless you *use it to start something!*

"BUBBLES"

You know the air castles a young fellow builds when he is planning his future with his Best Girl. You know what pictures of wonderful achievement he can paint for her. The wealth of the Indies is but a trifle compared with the fortune he is going to lay at her feet.

"Day dreams," we call them—and laugh good-naturedly at the fondness of youth and love for believing in such bubbles, such figments of the imagination. But these dreams are very real and very dear to every boy—and girl. They embody all those things they hope some day soon to see materialize.

The only trouble with them is, that with most of us these bubbles are so soon pricked. We meet with discouragement. The fine point of our enthusiasm and ambition is blunted. Soon we lapse into a regular grind, and the man we hoped to be, the man we painted in such glowing terms to our Sweetheart—the man she really married—quietly passes out, leaving nothing but the husk of what might have been.

Is it any wonder there are so many unhappy marriages, when you compare the realities a man actually gives to the girl who marries him, with the "Bubbles" he promised her before?

The wonder is that so many girls shed only a few tears

over their shattered dreams, forget their disillusionment, and knuckle down to the tiresome, dispiriting daily round of cooking and housework—of tending babies and being good wives to their plodding husbands.

The greatest waste in business today is the waste of the enthusiasm of all the fine young fellows that go into it. True—their enthusiasm is frequently misdirected—but that is *your* opportunity. Go look at Niagara Falls!

For uncounted years the Niagara River dashed over its rocky cliff, the power of millions of horses behind it—a beautiful sight for the occasional tourist—but nothing more!

Today that same Niagara turns the wheels of a hundred great industries—gives light and power to all of Western New York—is soon to become the basis of a giant super-power system for the entire Northeast.

What made the difference? The Niagara has not changed—it had exactly the same power afore-time. 'Tis simply that man has learned how to *direct* that power, to *use* that energy for useful purposes.

"Give instruction to a wise man, and he will be yet wiser," says the Proverbs (9); "teach a just man, and he will increase in learning."

Remember the story of the young King of the Black Isles? He started out full of high ambitions. But the wicked enchantress (Lack of Initiative) turned him into black marble from the waist down. So he was condemned to sit in his palace and bemoan his fate until there came a new King to lift the spell, to inspire him for high emprise, to keep him from ever again lapsing into the state of half man and half statue.

"And Moses said unto the Lord, O my Lord, I am not eloquent, neither heretofore, nor since thou hast spoken unto thy servant: but I am slow of speech, and of a slow tongue.

"And the Lord said unto him, Who hath made man's mouth? Or who maketh the dumb, or deaf, or the seeing, or the blind? Have not I the Lord?

"Now therefore go, and I will be with thy mouth, and teach thee what thou shalt say."

The world's most tragic figure is the man who never starts anything. He is dead from the waist down. He sits and wishes and dreams; he goes through motions, doing routine things that a machine could do just as well, but he never gets anywhere.

How did Carnegie make his millions? By finding a new way to make steel—and then starting to *do* it! How did Woolworth, how did Penney, make their successes? By trying out new methods of merchandising—by starting something. How did Ford become the richest man in the world? By visioning the new transportation within the reach of every one—and then starting to put it there!

You want to get out of the rut—to grow—to develop into something better. And there are unnumbered new methods in industry, new inventions, new ideas—waiting merely to be uncovered.

To whom will these prizes go? Nine times out of ten to the man who starts something—to the man who dreams great dreams, and then has the courage, the belief in himself, in his Spirit, in his Destiny, to make the start, to take the plunge, *to go!*

"And the Spirit of the Lord shall rest upon him, the spirit of wisdom and understanding, the spirit of counsel and might, the spirit of knowledge and of the fear of the Lord.—Isaiah II.

THE THINGS THAT CAN'T BE DONE

When John MacDonald first proposed to build the great New York subways, people laughed at him. He went to one "big" financier after another, and the answer of all was the same. "Dig a tunnel under all these streets and houses, with their maze of pipe lines and electric cables and gas mains and sewers? Impossible!"

But through it all he held to the one main idea. "You have a cellar under your house, haven't you?" he asked them. "And you dug it without much trouble, didn't you? Well, I'm not thinking of building a tunnel the length of this island. I'm planning to dig a string of cellars—*and then connect them together!*"

And he finally found a man big enough to see the idea—and to back it.

"Thou shalt make thy prayer unto Him, and He shall hear thee, and thou shalt pay thy vows.

"Thou shalt also decree a thing, and it shall be established unto thee: and the light shall shine upon thy ways."—Job 22:27-28.

In this day of miracles, it would be a hardy spirit that would say that anything is impossible. The time is not far distant when men will harness the tides, get motive power and much of their food from the air and from the tropic seas, talk to anyone anywhere and see them while they talk. These and a thousand other inventions even more wonderful are in the very air. Why shouldn't you be the one to start some of them?

You don't need to be an engineer. You don't need to be an inventor. Pasteur was not a doctor, yet he did more for medical science than any doctor. Whitney was not a cotton planter. Not even a Southerner. He was a Connecticut school teacher. Yet he invented the cotton gin! Bell was a professor of elocution, and he once said that he invented the telephone because he knew nothing of electricity. He didn't know it couldn't be done! Morse, of telegraphic fame, was a portrait painter—not an electrician. Dunlop (maker of tires) was a veterinary surgeon. Gillette was a traveling salesman. Eastman a bank clerk. Ingersoll a mechanic. Harriman a broker. Gary a lawyer.

In fact, most of the great inventors and pioneers have been outsiders. Why? They don't know the things that can't be done—*so they go ahead and do them!*

"Opportunity," says Doc Lane, "is as scarce as oxygen; men fairly breathe it and do not know it."

"But as it is written, Eye hath not seen, nor ear heard, neither have entered into the heart of man, the things which God hath prepared for them that love him.

"But God hath revealed them unto us by His Spirit: for the Spirit searcheth all things, yea, the deep things of God.

"For what man knoweth the things of a man, save the spirit of man which is in him? Even so the things of God knoweth no man, but the Spirit of God."—I Corinthians 2:9-11.

It is not necessary to have a "pull" to succeed. In fact, a "pull" is more often than not just that—a pull *backward*. What we need is the "push" of necessity. For most of us are so constituted that, unless we have to put into the fight all our strength and energy, we just jog along in a slothful, ambitionless sort of way, getting nowhere.

The saving event in many a man's life has been the blow that knocked the props out from under him and left him to look out for himself. As Emerson put it: "It is only as a man puts off all foreign support and stands alone that

I see him firm and to prevail. He is weaker by every re-
cruit to his banner."

So never envy the man with a "pull." Pity him. He has
lost the greatest thing there is in business—the need for
individual initiative.

You say you have to start at the bottom, while Bill Smith's
father left him enough money to begin at the head of a real
business? Never mind. Start something—even if it be only
a peanut stand—and ten years from now you will have not
only some very valuable experience, but a business that will
be paying you dividends and give you an insurance for the
future. Whereas the chances are that though Bill Smith may
have the experience, that is all he will have. Most of the big
businesses of today, you know, started on a shoestring.

"Thus saith the Lord; Refrain thy voice from weeping,
and thine eyes from tears: for thy work shall be rewarded,
saith the Lord."—Jeremiah 31.

Democracy is equality, not of place, but of opportunity.
Just because you were born on Fifth Avenue doesn't mean
that you are going to stay there. And just because you were
born on the East Side doesn't mean that you have got to stay
there. Al Smith is but one of thousands who have come up
from humble surroundings to the topmost rung of the ladder of success.

"Always the real leaders of men," says Dr. Frank Crane,
"the real kings, have come up from the common people.
The finest flowers in the human flora grow in the woods

pasture and not in the hot-house; no privileged class, no Royal house, no carefully selected stock produced a Leonardo or a Michelangelo in art, a Shakespeare or Burns in letters, a Galli Curci or Paderewski in music, a Socrates or Kant in philosophy, an Edison or Pasteur in science, a Wesley or a Knox in religion."

The Law of Compensation is constantly at work. When men grow to put too much dependence upon the fortune or the institution or the position that has been given them, these props are suddenly removed. When through grim necessity they have learned not to rely upon anything short of the Infinite, the channels of supply are reopened to them.

"Put not your trust in Princes," advised the Psalmist. Not because Princes are so much more unreliable than ordinary men, but because they are mere tributaries—even as you are—to the King of Kings.

Put not your trust in some other man or institution. Go direct to the Fount! Don't tap some other man's channel. Go direct to the main Source of Supply!

"By me kings reign, and princes decree justice.

"By me princes rule, and nobles, even all the judges of the earth.

"I love them that love me; and those that seek me early shall find me.

"Riches and honour are with me; yea, durable riches and righteousness."—Proverbs 8:15-19.

BE KING IN YOUR OWN THOUGHTS

"Every man," says a medieval writer, "has within him the making of a great saint."

And every one of us has in him the making of a great success.

"Less than a year ago," reads a letter to me from W. Bruce Haughton, "I started in the automotive business in Jacksonville with $23.00 in my pocket. I bought $14.40 worth of tools and rented a two-car garage in the back yard of the house where I rented a room. I then went to several of the city professional men and told them what I could do for their cars. In thirty days I had a net return of $476.80 with an overhead of about $50.00.

"In June, 1926, I had to find bigger quarters to handle my business, for I then had 591 regular customers coming to my 'Back Yard' for service they could not buy elsewhere. Today I am negotiating with a concern for another corner in the best part of this city to handle my patrons who live in that section."

In the newspaper the other day, I read how Palmer C. Hayden, a negro, 33 years old, was quitting his scrub bucket to study art in Europe. He had just won the $400 prize in art awarded by the Harmon Foundation. He had the courage to start something.

I know a young fellow who, while still in College, got the idea through a chance occurrence that there was an entirely virgin field among the undertakers for raincoats—black raincoats. He reasoned that there were so few undertakers in each city that no store could afford to carry a complete range of sizes for them, whereas one central store, selling to the whole country, could do so.

So he borrowed a few dollars and tried out his idea by mail. Today he is a millionaire—and it has all been the logical outcome of that one idea.

He started something.

If you could only realize that you have a definite place in a scheme so big that God has been working millions of years to bring it about; if you would only remember that every forward step you take has His approval and help; if you would look upon Him as a loving Father watching you, His little son, taking a few faltering steps, ready to catch you when you stumble, ready to help you over the difficult places, ready to strengthen and support you—how much of fear and worry you would avoid, how much more surely you would progress.

"If ye walk in my statutes, and keep my commandments, and do them;

"Then I will give you rain in due season, and the land shall yield her increase, and the trees of the field shall yield their fruit.

"And your threshing shall reach unto the vintage, and the vintage shall reach unto the sowing time: and ye shall eat your bread to the full, and dwell in your land safely.

"And I will give peace in the land, and ye shall lie down, and none shall make you afraid."—Leviticus 26:3-6.

But to progress, it is necessary that you learn to take a few steps for yourself. You can't remain tied to the Father's apron-strings if you are to become a man or woman worthy of the name.

You know how much these "Mother's darlings" are good for when they get out among other boys. You know how long these pampered children of the rich usually last, when they are thrown upon their own resources.

The Father above has the wisdom and the courage to do what very few earthly fathers can. He gives his children free will. He turns them loose, in a world full of pitfalls and dangers, to learn self-reliance, to become real men and women, worthy Sons of God.

Yet He is always just behind us. His arms ready to support us. His hand to guide us. His wisdom to counsel us— if only we will realize His presence, His solicitude, His Fatherly love and care.

"He giveth power to the faint; and to them that have no might, he increaseth strength."—Isaiah 40:29.

He has given us free will, so He will not force Himself upon us. He has untied our apron-strings, so He won't *make* us take the great place He plans for us in the Divine scheme of things. But if we will learn to work with Him, if we will treat Him as a Father, run to Him with our joys as with our sorrows, have Him at the back of all our plans, know that we can rely upon His help in all our undertakings, what a difference it will make!

You need never hesitate then to start anything of good, because you will know that with Him behind you, it can not fail. You will never lack the faith, the enthusiasm, the power to carry through even the most difficult undertaking. Most of all, you will never lack the will to begin, for you will know that even the Father can not help you to accomplish, until you yourself have taken the first step by STARTING SOMETHING!

"Since receiving your first books," writes M. D. C. of Capitola, California, "I have made from insurance premuims in a new company which I was instrumental in forming, more than $100,000.00 in a little over six months' time. My previous income over a period of years has been approximately $7,500.00 per year."

He started something!

"And we know that all things work together for good to them that love God."—Luke 11:28.

THE STARTING POINT

Now, how about you—have *you* started anything? Do you want to? Then let's take stock of you for a moment:

1. The first thing to do is to list all of your successes, no matter how unimportant they may seem. Go

back to your boyhood days. What was your favorite game? Was it one that required initiative, quick thinking, prompt action? Were you a
better "individual-player" or "team-player"? In
other words, were you a brilliant "star," or one
of those who could sink his own individuality for
the good of the team? Did you ever captain any
team successfully? Did your teammates like you,
work with you enthusiastically? Could you inspire loyalty, co-operation, weld your team into
a single unit with a common purpose?

Qualities such as these can be acquired, of course, but
if you had them naturally as a boy, then you have them
now, so by all means develop them to their fullest extent.
They can be made your most valuable assets in business.

2. What sort of game do you prefer now? One that
depends primarily upon yourself—or one that
demands mostly team-work? Games are wonderful indicators, you know, of your innate characteristics. I used to know a very shrewd old fellow
who never formed a business friendship until after
he had played poker with his prospective friend.
How do you play bridge—*with* your partner or
regardless of him? How do you play tennis—as
two individual players, or as a team?

Don't misunderstand me—I am not decrying brilliant individual play. I am just trying to get you to analyze your innate characteristics. If you play best alone, by all means concentrate on the kind of work or the kind of business that is built up around one single figure. On the other hand, if your forte is team-work, cooperation—go in for organized effort where your leadership and fairness and good-fellowship will have the greatest play.

3. List your characteristics frankly. Ability in particular lines, quickness in picking up new ideas, open-mindedness, versatility, honesty, sociability, interest in others, power to convince others, courage, aggressiveness, stick-to-it-iveness.

In short, analyze yourself frankly—then from that analysis, from your past failures and successes, pick the work you have the greatest aptitude for—and go into it!

Don't go into it blindly. First study it. There are good books on every phase of business today. There are correspondence courses as good as any taught in colleges. Get them. Read them. Set your goal. Make your plans carefully. Start them in a small way first. Test each step before you put your weight upon it. But once sure of it, put your *whole* weight into it—your money and your ability and all your thought—*particularly all your thought.*

Don't scatter your energies. You can do it with the

work of your hands but you can't do it with your thought. To make a great success, your thought has to be concentrated on your goal in the same way that the Marconi beam system concentrates all the power of its rays in the one direction. "No man can serve two masters"—with justice to either.

Choose your goal; then, like the search-light, concentrate all your efforts, all your energies, all your thoughts in the one direction. Don't go running off after false gods. Don't fritter away your energies on inconsequential side-issues. Focus them—focus them as you focus the rays of the sun through a magnifying glass. Do that—and you will speedily start something!

There is a definite place for you in the Divine plan. There is a work which you are to do, which no one else can do quite as well. Pray, therefore, to the Father that He may open your eyes to your right work, that He may open your ears to the promptings of His voice, that He may open your understanding of the right way.

"I will instruct thee and teach thee in the way which thou shalt go: I will guide thee with mine eye."—Psalms 32:8.

VI

ROUGH DIAMONDS

"And he hath filled him with the Spirit of God, in wisdom, in understanding, and in knowledge, and in all manner of workmanship.

"And to devise curious works, to work in gold, and in silver, and in brass.

"And in the cutting of stones, to set them, and in carving of wood, to make any manner of cunning work."

—EXODUS 35:31-33.

Over in the northwestern corner of Pennsylvania a few years ago, there lived a farmer who was interested in oil. His brother was in the oil business in Canada and had told him that fortunes were being made in it every day. So he sent for all kinds of books that told how and where to locate oil, took a course in geology, spent two years getting ready—and then sold his farm and went to Canada to work in the oil fields.

The man who bought the farm, walking over the place next morning, came to a little brook that ran through the middle of it. There was a heavy board across the brook to hold back the surface drift, and back of it for some yards the water was coated with a thick scum.

It seems that this scum had troubled the previous owner for a long time. The cattle wouldn't drink the water with it on it. So he had conceived the idea of the board to clear the scum from the surface and let the cattle drink from the water below.

To the new buyer, that "scum" looked and smelled and tasted suspiciously like oil! He sent for experts. They bored. And opened up one of the richest oil fields in Pennsylvania!

It is natural to think that the first step towards success is to go somewhere else or into some new business. The distant pastures always look greenest. But more often than not, our best opportunities lie right under our own nose.

When the original Pennsylvania oil wells seemed to be worked out, most of the oil men set off for fields and pastures new. But a few stayed. And those few found that the surface had merely been scratched! Instead of being worked out, scarcely 15 per cent. of the oil had been taken out of the ground. By the pressure system, or by boring deeper and striking new deposits, they found the other 85 per cent.!

And that is only one industry out of hundreds where fortunes have been made out of what other men had thrown away as worthless. No one has yet exhausted any line of thought. The inventions that mankind has already made are merely the introduction to bigger and greater things—the open door to opportunity. The most brilliant scientists are the first to tell you that their discoveries are but as a drop of water to the great ocean of achievement that lies beyond.

"For the earth shall be filled with the knowledge of the glory of the Lord, as the waters cover the sea."—Habakkuk 2:14.

Nearly a century and a half ago, Malthus propounded his famous theory that population, when unchecked, tends to increase in geometrical proportion, whereas subsistence increases only in arithmetical proportion. In other words, that population increases many times as rapidly as the means of subsistence. And he visioned a time in the very near future when artificial checks would have to be put on population, or the world would starve.

Population has increased very near to the point he feared, but what has happened? We are farther away from the saturation point than in his day! The age of machinery came along; the age of scientific experiment; and not only opened up new fields through better transportation, but greatly increased the yields in present fields. Now Prof. Albrecht Penck advances the belief that by the year 2227 there will be 8,000,000,000 people here on earth—and famine will be continuous, because the earth cannot support that many!

What little faith some of these economists have! They get so wrapped up in their own calculations that they can see nothing else. "By that time (2227 A. D.)," says the New York Herald Tribune, "man may be taking foodstuffs from the sunlight, from the air or from the power of the revolving earth! The only safe prediction about the future of man is that no limit dare be set to what he and Nature may cooperate to do."

"For I know the thoughts that I think towards you, saith the Lord, thoughts of peace and not of evil, to give you an expected end. Then, shall ye call upon me, and ye shall go and pray unto me and I will hearken unto you. And ye shall seek me, and find me, when ye shall search for me with all your heart."—Jeremiah 29:11-13.

For 5,000 years men have built houses of brick, and in all of that time there had been no change made, either in the tools used, or in the manner in which the work was done.

Along came Frank Gilbreth, studied the motions involved in laying brick, reduced them from eighteen to five, and increased the hourly output from 120 to 350 bricks!

Simple enough—but it took 5,000 years for someone to think up this simple solution.

For 5,000 years mankind has been taught that some

men are born with ability—some without—and that those
without must serve those who have it.

No greater mistake was ever made. Every man is born
with ability sufficient to carry him upward to the highest
rung of success. "Ordinary ability, properly applied," said
Theodore N. Vail, "is all that is necessary to reach the highest rung in the ladder of success."

Life's biggest blunder is to underestimate your own
power to develop and accomplish. What if you are handicapped by lack of education, by poverty, by self-consciousness,
by sickness, by some physical disability?

Thank God for it! A handicap is the greatest urge you
can have towards success. Like the eagle which uses ad-
verse winds to rise higher, you can mount to success on
your handicap.

In an editorial some time ago, the New York Globe observed: "Nature is not democratic. She gives some women
beauty and leaves others, of equal or greater merit, plain.
She makes some persons intelligent and some stupid. In
brief, we are not born free and equal nor do we become
so. To some the Gods bring gifts and others they pass by.
There are aristocracies of voices, of beauty and of intelligence. The best that democracy can ever do is to give every
Caruso a chance to sing."

That is the general belief. That is the idea that prevails
among most casual thinkers. But the man who thinks thus
is overlooking the greatest force in life—the reserve force

that lies so dormant in most of us—the power of the Spirit within to rise superior to any inequality, to overcome any seeming handicap or difficulty.

The greatest thing that can happen to any man is the discovery of this all-powerful Spirit within him. If it is necessary for him to undergo hunger, if it is necessary for him to suffer sickness or injury in order to make the discovery, let him suffer it cheerfully, gladly! No price is too high to pay to bring into your affairs the power of the Holy Spirit. For everything you have suffered, everything you have paid, will be made good to you an hundredfold. There is no maybe about this. I have seen it work out hundreds of times. I have learned it from very bitter experience. As in the case of Job of olden times:

"The Lord gave Job twice as much as he had before.

"So the Lord blessed the latter end of Job more than his beginning; for he had fourteen thousand sheep, and six thousand camels, and a thousand yoke of oxen and a thousand she asses.

"He had also seven sons and three daughters."—Job 42:10, 12, 13.

THE LAW OF COMPENSATION

What was it made Demosthenes the greatest orator of all time. NOT his natural gifts—but his natural *handicaps!* He was self-conscious. And he stuttered. Had he not been thus handicapped, he would probably have become a mediocre orator—and lived and died unknown to the world. But he had to study so hard to overcome his natural handicaps, he had to practice and work so long and so wholeheartedly, that when at last he was ready to appear before the public, his conscious efforts were backed by all the powers of the subconscious. He had so often called upon the Spirit within to help him in his practice that it came to his aid of Itself when the real need arose. It stood at his back to give him confidence, to lend him inspiration, to supply the power that moved his hearers as they had never been moved before.

In "Organ Inferiority and Its Psychic Compensation," Dr. Adler brings out the well-known scientific fact that any physical weakness or inferiority brings with it an extra urge to strive for superiority in some compensating way.

Napoleon, Caesar, Prince Eugene were little men, but the urge within them made them the biggest men of their day.

Whistler, the greater painter, had poor eyes. He was said to be color blind. So he became a master in nuances. Edison was deaf—so he perfected the talking machine.

Beethoven, Mozart, Franz—all had defects in hearing. And worked so hard at their music that they became masters of technique, and musical geniuses.

The same principle applies to nations. Take Alaska and

Switzerland as an instance. Alaska has enormous resources of gold and silver and copper and coal, vast virgin forests, 1,000,000 square miles suitable for agriculture, and the greatest fisheries in the world. Yet if Alaska were as densely populated as Switzerland it would be supporting 120,000,000 inhabitants!

The Swiss have few natural resources, so they are constrained to use their ingenuity instead. They take a ton of metal and put it together in such form as to make it worth a million dollars. They take cotton thread at 20 cents a pound, and convert it into lace worth $2,000 a pound. They take a block of wood worth 10 cents and convert it into a carving worth $100. And because as a nation they have learned the art of utilizing their talents, they have prospered abundantly.

Where is the moral? Simply this:

There is no lack, no handicap, *nothing,* that can defeat you. Obstacles are the greatest blessings God can give you. They bring out the soul of you. They bring the Holy Spirit to your help. And anything which acquaints you with the Spirit within you, anything that gives you an understanding of the infinite power within you, anything that brings the Holy Spirit into your daily affairs, is worth while no matter what its cost.

"And Jacob was left alone; and there wrestled a man with him until the breaking of the day.

"And when he saw that he prevailed not against him, he touched the hollow of his thigh; and the hollow of Jacob's thigh was out of joint, as he wrestled with him.

"And he said, Let me go, for the day breaketh. And he said, I will not let thee go, *except thou bless me.*

"And he said unto him, What is thy name? And he said, Jacob.

"And he said, Thy name shall be called no more Jacob, but Israel: for as a prince hast thou power with God and with men, and hast prevailed.

"And Jacob asked him, and said, Tell me, I pray thee, thy name. And he said, Wherefore is it that thou dost ask after my name? *And he blessed him there.*"

That is what you, too, must do. Wrestle with every difficulty until you have learned something from it. Don't let go of any trouble until you have made it bless you.

Remember that back of you always is the power of the Holy Spirit and if the need arises, it can give you the strength—not merely of one man, but of ten! Like David going out to meet Goliath, realize that it is not you who is fighting the battle, but God. "Be not afraid, nor dismayed by reason of this great multitude; for the battle is not yours but God's."—II Chronicles 20:15. Knowing that, no obstacle need deter you, no experience terrify you. With God on your side, you are always in the majority. Struggles and trials are mere growing pains of your soul, to teach you that, though terrifying to you alone, they are as nothing to you when allied to the Father through the Holy Spirit.

"When thou liest down thou shalt not be afraid; yea thou shalt lie down, and thy sleep shall be sweet. Be not afraid of sudden fear, neither of the desolation of the wicked when it cometh. For the Lord shall be thy confidence, and shall keep thy foot from being taken. My confidence is in Him in whom I live and move and have my being."

Before you give up where you are and move to distant fields, before you seek your fortune afar, look around you! See if some of the riches in your own back yard won't bear cultivating.

There is a story told of an old Boer farmer living on a rocky bit of ground on the road between Kimberley and Pretoria. Scattered here and there over the ground, they often found dull looking pieces of crystal. The boys used them to throw at the sheep. Until one day a Cecil Rhodes engineer happened that way—*and discovered them to be diamonds!*

Many of us are just as literally walking on diamonds in the rough as were that farmer's boys. Only most of us never know it until someone comes along and points them out to us.

Let us resolve to do some of this discovering for our own selves. Let us look at every job with the question— how can this be done easier, quicker, better? Let us devote part of our thoughts to finding new outlets, new methods, new needs. Let us get a fixed objective—and then work towards it. Some great thinker once said that we should be a world of successes if the idea of a fixed objective and a set goal possessed us.

A fixed objective—it serves much the same as the controlling idea outlined in Chapter 3, magnetizing your thoughts and your work and yourself with the one intense desire. Add to that a sublime faith that shall bring the Holy Spirit within into cooperation with you—and your objective is assured.

"First have something good," said Horace Greeley, "then advertise!" First have your fixed objective, then call upon the Holy Spirit to help you, and there is no goal you cannot win.

"For the vision is yet for an appointed time, but at the end it shall speak, and not lie; though it tarry, wait for it; because it will surely come; it will not tarry."—Habakkuk 2:3.

I know a man who had a $2,500 job. He had just been offered another paying $500 more. And he went to a friend of mine to ask his advice about changing. The first question my friend asked was what he had to offer these new people. He told him, the usual round of routine knowledge.

"That isn't worth much," my friend informed him. "These people are in the same line of business that you have been working at for years. If in all those years you haven't thought out ways in which that work could be vastly improved, if you haven't been perfecting in your own mind short cuts, money-saving ways, practical ideas— then hold on to your $2,500 job until you do. You're not worth a cent more.

"My advice to you is to go home and write down on paper what you have to offer this new firm. What new methods you can show them that any other $2,500 man can't. What new ideas you have that will make money for them.

"When you get them all down, center your attention on the best of them, and work it out. Then go to these people and tell them you will give them your idea and your services—NOT for $3,000, but for $6,000!"

That talk woke this man up. He did some really serious thinking for the first time in his business life. With the result that he refused the $3,000 offer then, but kept the position open for a few weeks until he could get his big idea ready.

Then he not only landed his $6,000, but made good on his idea so completely that within six months that $6,000 was increased to $7,200.

"There is guidance for each one of us," says Emerson, "and by lowly listening we shall hear the right word." Give of your best—not merely in manual labor but in ideas— and you can safely leave the rest to the guidance of the Holy Spirit within.

As pointed out in *The Secret of the Ages,* the basic principles of all business are the same, be they as big as the Steel Trust or as small as the corner newsstand. The whole practice of commerce is founded upon them. Summed up, and boiled down to the fewest possible words, they are two:

1—Give to get.

2—This one thing I do.

1—You can get away with dishonest values, with poor service, for a little while. You can take two dollars worth of value for every one you give. But the Law of Karma will get you soon or late. If you intend to stay in business, it pays to make it a rule to try to give a little more of value or of service than you are paid for.

2—Remember that each task, no matter how great, is but a group of little tasks, any one of which you can easily do. Like the great New York subways, it is but a succession of cellars connected together. Find a place to start. Take the first step. The rest will follow easily.

So many are afraid of giving too much for the amount that is paid them. And so many wives get inflated ideas of their husband's value to or work in a business, and urge them not to give so much unless the business pays them more for it.

Poor things—they mean well. But no man ever has to be urged not to work too hard at his business. He can work too hard at worrying about it—yes. But every bit of honest work he puts into his business will pay him an honest return. He is not working merely for some man or some institution. He is doing God's work. And God is the most generous Paymaster there is. He doesn't label His paychecks. He doesn't say—"This is in payment of such-and-such invoices." But the pay comes—just as surely as the day follows night.

"I cause those that love me to inherit substance; and I will fill their treasures."—Proverbs 8:21.

There is a place for you in the Divine plan—a place that no one but you can fill. There is a work for you in the great scheme of things—a work that no one can do as well as you.

So, if you have been drifting, if your work has been joyless, your business profitless, look around you for the right niche that was made for you to fill. Don't mind how humble it may seem. To do even the most humble thing supremely well is artistry—and will bring its reward. "Who sweeps a room as for God's law, makes that and the action fine."

"Now he that planteth and he that watereth are one; and every man shall receive his own reward according to his own labour. For we are labourers together with God."—I Corinthians 3:8-9.

Let your daily prayer to the Spirit within you be that He manifest the Divine design in your life—that He bring you to your proper work, your right place.

Say to Him each day, as F. S. Shinn suggests in *The Game of Life and How to Play It*—"Infinite Spirit, open the way for the Divine design in my life to manifest. Let the genius within me now be released. Let me see clearly the perfect plan."

And then, if you like, ask Him to give you a lead, an indication of the next step for you to take.

"Call upon the Almighty," says the old Eastern Sage. "He will help thee. Thou needst not perplex thyself about anything else. Shut thy eyes and while thou art asleep, God will change thy bad fortune into good."

"Blessed *is* the man that trusteth in the Lord, and whose hope the Lord is.

"For he shall be as a tree planted by the waters, and *that* spreadeth out her roots by the river, and shall not see when heat cometh, but her leaf shall be green; and shall not be careful in the year of drought, neither shall cease from yielding fruit."

—JEREMIAH 17:7–8.

VII

I SERVE

"For the kingdom of heaven is as a man traveling into a far country, who called his own servants, and delivered unto them his goods.

"And unto one he gave five talents, to another two, and to another one; to every man according to his several ability; and straightway took his journey.

"Then he that had received the five talents went and traded with the same, and made them other five talents.

"And likewise he that had received two, he also gained other two.

"But he that had received one went and digged in the earth, and hid his lord's money.

"After a long time the lord of those servants cometh, and reckoneth with them.

"And so he that had received five talents came and brought other five talents, saying, Lord, thou deliveredst unto me five talents: behold, I have gained beside them five talents more.

"His lord said unto him, Well done, thou good and faithful servant: thou hast been faithful over a few things, I will make thee ruler over many things: enter thou into the joy of thy lord.

"He also that had received two talents came and said, lord, thou deliveredst unto me two talents: behold, I have gained two other talents beside them.

"His lord said unto him, Well done, good and faithful servant; thou hast been faithful over a few things, I will make thee ruler over many things: enter thou into the joy of thy lord.

"Then he which had received the one talent came and said, Lord, I knew thee that thou art an hard man, reaping where thou hast not sown, and gathering where thou hast not strawed:

"And I was afraid, and went and hid thy talent in the earth; lo, there thou hast that is thine.

"His lord answered and said unto him, Thou wicked and slothful servant, thou knewest that I reap where I sowed not, and gather where I have not strawed:

"Thou oughtest therefore to have put my money to the exchangers, and then at my coming I should have received mine own with usury.

"Take therefore the talent from him, and give it unto him which hath ten talents.

"For unto every one that hath shall be given, and he shall have abundance: but from him that hath not shall be taken away even that which he hath.

"And cast ye the unprofitable servant into outer darkness: there shall be weeping and gnashing of teeth."

—MATTHEW 25:14:30.

Y ou want riches. You want five talents, ten talents, a thousand—a million. But what have you to offer in return? Has it never occurred to you that you must make an accounting of them?

If some one were to offer you a million right now, what

would you do with it? Buy a yacht—an automobile—have a good time! But what sort of an accounting would that make for the Master? And why should He put Himself out to place riches in hands no better prepared to use them to good purpose than that?

Suppose you went to a banker for money—a banker who knew you well—and asked him to lend you $100,000. What is the first question he would ask of you? "What are you going to do with it?"

If you could give him no better answer than—"Buy a yacht, an automobile, have a good time"—how much do you suppose he would lend you? Not a red cent! No more will the Father which is in Heaven.

You have got to have an idea first before you can borrow money from a bank. And if the banker is wise, he will make you prove your idea in a small way before he will advance you any great sum to spend upon it.

And when you approach the Father for ten talents or a thousand, you must first have an idea that will be of some benefit to mankind.

Henry Ford is worth a billion dollars. He is probably the richest man in the world. How did he get it?

He started out with an idea—an idea that the automobile should be put within reach of everyone. That idea was of definite benefit to mankind. It opened up remote districts. It brought light and life into the lives of millions of farm dwellers. He was entitled to a generous reward.

Woolworth accumulated a fortune of millions. He performed a definite service. So did Penney. So has many another merchant on a smaller scale. And the supply flows to him in proportion. But before reward, must come the idea. You must give to get.

The United States has become the richest of all peoples. Half the world's gold is in our possession. In 75 years the wealth of the country has increased fifty times over. All the world has become richer, but in no other country has the wealth increased to anything like that extent.

Why?

Some will say because of our great natural resources. But Mexico has great natural resources. So has Russia. And China. Yet all these countries are backward.

What then is the answer?

The fact that in America manufacturers have learned to share with the workers the fruits of industry. America began to forge ahead of the rest of the world the moment its manufacturers learned that every worker was entitled to a share of the good things of life.

Automobile manufacturers saw every workman as a potential automobile owner. And then proceeded to make that ideal feasible. Telephone companies, gas companies, electric light and equipment companies, radio manufacturers, saw every home as a user of their products—and proceeded to put them within the reach of all.

Never since life first appeared upon this planet has there

been so much of comfort, happiness and contentment among *all* the people as there is in these United States. And the reason? Free education. Equal opportunity. And the realization on the part of manufacturers that their best market and their biggest one is right among the workers— that the more they share with the workers, the more will come back to them.

You must give to get.

Russia has enormous resources of land and minerals and oil. So has China. And Mexico. Why then are they so poor?

Because the ruling classes have tried to keep all these riches for themselves. They wanted to take all—and give nothing. That may work for a little while, but always there is an accounting.

"For they have sown the wind, and they shall reap the whirlwind: it hath no stalk: the bud shall yield no meal: if so be it yield, the strangers shall swallow it up."— Hosea 8:7.

You must give to get.

There is a story by Samuel Butler that describes the idea exactly:

"In Erehwon," he says, "he who makes a colossal fortune in the hosiery trade and by his energy has succeeded in reducing the price of woolen goods by the thousandeth part of a penny in a pound, this man is worth ten professional philanthropists. So strongly are the Erehwonians impressed with this that if a man has made a fortune of over £20,000 a year they exempt him from all taxation, considering him as a work of art and too precious to be meddled with. They say, 'How much he must have done for society before society could be prevailed upon to give him so much money!'"

Unfortunately, we have not yet reached the ideal state visioned by Butler, where every millionaire earned his money through unusual service to the community. Too many are still robber captains or greedy money-lenders like Cassim.

The Law of Karma is steadily at work. Give it time. There is always an accounting. Meantime, thank God for the Fords and the Edisons and the Burbanks and the thousands of others of their kind who are not only making this the richest country on earth, but are helping to spread those riches around and make it also the happiest.

THE BANK OF GOD

The true purpose of every worthy business is to help in the distribution of God's gifts among men.

Judge your work, your ideas, by that standard. If you want money, if you seek riches, ask yourself—"Could I go to God and tell Him as my banker that the purpose for which I want this money is anything but a selfish one? Could I honestly assure Him that my primary idea is service—giving to people a little better value, a little more of service, a little greater comfort or convenience or happiness than they are now getting?"

Don't misunderstand me. You are entitled to money to meet your daily needs. You have a right to ask for all those things necessary to your happiness, as long as they do not infringe upon the happiness of others. You even have a right to demand just as much more than that as you can use to advantage. *But you have got to account for it!*

Given a right idea, given a controlling thought, dollars will seek you, even as iron filings seek the magnet. You can claim all that you can use to good advantage.

So get your thought right first. Make sure that you have something the world needs. Then draw on the Great Banker for all the money you need, never fearing, never doubting that He will honor your draft.

"For the Lord God is a sun and shield. The Lord will give grace and glory. No good thing will he withhold from them that walk uprightly."—Psalms 84:11.

After all the proofs of God's power to supply them with food and water. After He had brought them safely through every conceivable danger. When another crucial time came, the children of Israel fearfully called out—"Can God furnish us a table in the wilderness?"—Psalms 78:19.

Of course He can!

"Hast thou not known? Hast thou not heard? That the everlasting God, the Lord, the Creator of the ends of the earth, fainteth not, neither is weary?"—Isaiah 40:28.

Draw on Him as you need. Don't wait to start until you have all the money in hand. How many businesses—big and successful today—do you suppose would have been started if their founders had waited until they had all the money in hand they were going to need? Use the talent you have. Your credit is good for just as much more as you can use to advantage. More than that is a weight around your neck.

If you had a business proposition, and knew that your banker would extend you credit to the extent of a million dollars to develop it, you wouldn't think of drawing that million all at once. No—you would ask for credit as you needed it. You would draw upon it only as your business required it. You wouldn't burden yourself with one cent more of interest than was necessary.

Do likewise with the Lord. If your banker promised you the money as you needed it, you would go ahead with your plans, secure in the knowledge that his word was just as good as the actual money in the bank. Do you rate the promises of the Father any lower than those of man?

"Be glad then, ye children of Zion, and rejoice in the Lord your God: for he hath given you the former rain moderately, and he will cause to come down for you the rain, the former rain, and the latter rain in the first month.

"And the floors shall be full of wheat, and the vats shall overflow with wine and oil.

"And ye shall eat in plenty, and be satisfied, and praise the name of the Lord your God, that hath dealt wondrously with you: and my people shall never be ashamed.

"And ye shall know that I am in the midst of Israel, and that I am the Lord your God, and none else: and my people shall never be ashamed.

—JOEL 2:21, 23, 24, 26, 27.

What is it you want money for? Get your idea clearly in mind. Satisfy yourself that it is for a worthy purpose. And when you are thoroughly satisfied of that, then go right ahead with your plans.

How much do you need for this stage of them? How much would you draw on the bank for, this moment, if you had unlimited credit there? $100? $1,000? $10,000? Explain your need to the Father just as you would to a very wise and sympathetic banker. Then tell Him you are drawing upon Him for that amount. Actually write out a draft and mail it—anywhere—to me if you like. Then go about your plans as confidently, as believingly, as though the Father's Bank were just around the corner.

But don't try to fool yourself. Above all, don't try to

deceive the Father. Don't camouflage merely selfish desires in some high and mighty guise as benefits to mankind.

Remember the old Spanish Conquistadores? Freebooters they were—neither more nor less—searching for booty, and caring not how they came by it. They robbed the Indians, they massacred thousands, they enslaved whole nations—all for lust of gold.

But that wasn't their tale about it. They put it all upon the high and mighty plane of spreading Christianity, of saving the souls of the heathen.

It worked for the Spaniards for a little while. But they became so puffed up that they thought to use the same ideas upon the heretics of England, of the Netherlands, upon the entire world. Then came the disastrous Armada, followed by swift and certain decline.

It was only 300 years ago that Spain was the richest nation in the world, her power pre-eminent in Europe, her sovereignty extending over most of America. Now look at her—even the Riffians laughed at her until France came to her aid.

We reap what we sow. A grain of corn planted reproduces only corn. A grain of wheat brings forth wheat. And the seed of the deadly night-shade brings forth poisonous flowers.

God cannot be mocked. We reap in kind exactly as we sow. "Be not deceived. God is not mocked; for whatsoever a man soweth, that shall he also reap."—Galatians 6:7.

What then shall you do to succeed? What is the modern law of business? The same two commandments that Jesus gave to us 2,000 years ago.

"Thou shalt love the Lord thy God with all thy heart and with all thy soul and with all thy mind. This is the first and great commandment. And the second is like unto it. Thou shalt love thy neighbor as thyself. On these two commandments hang all the law and the prophets."—Matthew 23:37-40.

"Thou shalt love the Lord thy God." Thou shalt use the talents He has given thee. Thou shalt use them to benefit thy neighbor, to benefit all of mankind, and in so doing thou shalt benefit thyself. Do that, and thy Lord will say unto thee: "Well done, thou good and faithful servant; thou hast been faithful over a few things, I will make thee ruler over many things: enter thou into the joy of thy Lord."

But to those who fail to use, or who *abuse* their talent, the Lord says even as he did of the unprofitable servant: "Take therefore the talent from him and cast him into outer darkness: there shall be weeping and gnashing of teeth."

VIII

THE COMING
OF THE SPIRIT

"Now about the midst of the feast Jesus went up into the temple, and taught.

"And the Jews marvelled, saying, How knoweth this man letters, having never learned?

"Jesus answered them, and said, My doctrine is not mine, but His that sent me."

—JOHN 7:14–16.

There was a certain Sultan of the Indies that had three sons, the eldest called Houssain, the second Ali, the third Ahmed.

He had also a niece, remarkable for her wit and beauty, named Nouronnihar, whom all three Princes loved and desired to wed.

Their father remonstrated with them, pointed out the

troubles that would ensue if they persisted in their attach-
ment, and did all he could to persuade them to abide by
his choice of which of them should wed her.

Failing that, he sent for them one day and suggested
that the three Princes should depart on a three-months'
journey, each to a different country. Upon their return,
whichever one should bring to him the most extraordinary
rarity as a gift, should receive the Princess in marriage.

The three Princes cheerfully consented to this, each flat-
tering himself that fortune would prove favorable to him.
The Sultan gave them money, and early next morning they
all went out at the same gate of the city, each dressed like a
merchant, attended by a trusty officer habited as a slave, and
all well mounted and equipped. The first day's journey they
proceeded together; and at night, when they were at supper,
they agreed to meet again in three months at the khan
where they were stopping; and that the first who came should
wait for the rest; so that as they had all three taken leave
together of the Sultan, they might return in company. The
next morning, after they had embraced and wished each
other success, they mounted their horses, and took each a
different road.

Prince Houssain, the eldest brother, had heard of the
riches and splendor of the kingdom of Bisnagar and bent
his course toward it.

Arriving there, he betook himself to the quarters of the
traders, where a merchant, seeing him go by much fatigued,

invited him to sit down in front of his shop. He had not been seated long before a crier appeared, with a small piece of carpeting on his arm, for which he asked forty purses. The Prince told him that he could not understand how so small a piece of carpeting could be set at so high a price, unless it had something very extraordinary about it which failed to show in its appearance. "You have guessed right, sir," replied the crier; "whoever sits on this piece of carpeting may be carried in an instant wherever he desires." "If that is so," said the Prince, "I shall not think forty purses too much." "Sir," replied the crier, "I have told you the truth. Let us go into the back warehouse, where I will spread the carpet. When we have both sat down, form the wish to be transported into your apartment at the khan, and if we are not conveyed there at once, it shall be no bargain."

On the Prince agreeing to this, they went into the merchant's back shop, where they both sat down on the carpet; and as soon as the Prince had expressed his wish to be carried to his apartment at the khan, he in an instant found himself and the crier there. After this convincing proof of the virtue of the carpet, he paid over to the crier forty purses of gold, together with an extra purse for himself.

Prince Houssain was overjoyed at his good fortune, never doubting that this rare carpet would gain him the possession of the beautiful Nouronnihar.

After seeing all the wonders of Bisnagar, Prince Houssain wished to be nearer his dear Princess, so he took and spread the carpet, and with the officer whom he had brought with him, commanded the carpet to transport them to the caravansery at which he and his brothers were to meet, where he passed for a merchant till their arrival.

Prince Ali, the second brother, designed to travel into Persia, so, after parting with his brothers, joined a caravan, and soon arrived at Shiraz, the capital of that empire.

Walking through the quarters of the jewelers, he was not a little surprised to see one who held in his hand an ivory tube, about a foot in length, and about an inch thick, which he priced at fifty purses. At first he thought the man mad, and asked him what he meant by asking fifty purses for a tube which seemed scarcely worth one. The jeweler replied, "Sir, you shall judge yourself whether I am mad or not, when I have told you the property of this tube. By looking through it, you can see whatever object you wish to behold."

The jeweler presented the tube to the Prince, and he looked through it, wishing at the same time to see the Sultan his father. Immediately he saw before him the image of his father, sitting on his throne, in the midst of his council. Next, he wished to see the Princess Nouronnihar; and instantly beheld her laughing and talking with the women about her.

Prince Ali needed no other proof to persuade him that

this tube was the most valuable of gifts in all the world, and taking the crier to the khan where he lodged, paid him his fifty purses and received the tube.

Prince Ali was overjoyed at his purchase, for he felt fully assured that his brothers would not be able to meet with anything so rare and admirable, and the Princess Nouron-nihar would be his. His only thought now was to get back to the rendezvous as speedily as might be, so without wait-ing to visit any of the wonders of Shiraz, he joined a party of merchants and arrived without accident at the place ap-pointed, where he found Prince Houssain, and both waited for Prince Ahmed.

Prince Ahmed had taken the road to Samarcand, and the day after his arrival went, as his brothers had done, into the merchants quarters, where he had not walked long be-fore he heard a crier, with an artificial apple in his hand, offer it at five-and-forty purses. "Let me see your apple," he said to the man, "and tell me what extraordinary property it possesses, to be valued at so high a rate." "Sir," replied the crier, giving the apple into his hand, "if you look at the mere outside of this apple it is not very remarkable; but if you consider its miraculous properties, you will say it is invalu-able. It cures sick people of every manner of disease. Even if a person is dying, it will cure him instantly, and this merely by his smelling of the apple."

"If that be true," replied Prince Ahmed, "this apple is

indeed invaluable; but how am I to know that it is true?"
"Sir," replied the crier, "the truth is attested by the whole
city of Samarcand; ask any of these merchants here. Several of them will tell you they had not been alive today
had it not been for this excellent remedy."

Many people had gathered round while they talked,
and now confirmed what the crier had declared. One
among them said he had a friend dangerously ill, whose
life was despaired of; so they could now see for themselves
the truth of all that was said. Upon this Prince Ahmed told
the crier he would give him forty-five purses for the apple
if it cured the sick person by smelling it.

"Come, sir," said the crier to Prince Ahmed, "let us go
and do it, and the apple shall be yours."

The sick man smelled of the apple, and was cured; and
the prince, after he had paid the forty-five purses, received
the apple. He then joined himself to the first caravan that
set out for the Indies, and arrived in perfect health at the
caravansery, where the Princes Houssain and Ali waited
for him.

The brothers embraced with tenderness, and felicitated
each other on their safe journeys.

They then fell to comparing gifts. Houssain showed the
carpet and told how it had brought him thither. Ali brought
out the ivory tube, and nothing would do but they must
at once look through it at their beloved. But—alas and

alack! for the sight that met their eyes. The Princess Nouronnihar lay stretched on her bed, seemingly at the point
of death.

When Prince Ahmed had seen this, he turned to his two
brothers. "Make haste," he adjured them, "lose no time; we
may save her life. This apple which I hold here has this
wonderful property—its smell will restore to life a sick person. I have tried it and will show you its wonderful effect
on the Princess, if you will but hasten to her."

"If haste be all," answered Houssain, "we cannot do
better than transport ourselves instantly into her chamber on my magic carpet. Come, lose no time, sit down, it
is large enough to hold us all."

The order was no sooner given than they found themselves carried into the Princess Nouronnihar's chamber.

Prince Ahmed rose off the carpet, and went to her bed-
side, where he put the apple to her nostrils. Immediately the
Princess opened her eyes, expressed her joy at seeing them,
and thanked them all for their efforts in her behalf.

While she was dressing, the Princes went to present
themselves to the Sultan, their father. The Sultan received
them with joy. The Princes presented each the rarity which
he had brought, and begged of him to pronounce their fate.

The Sultan of the Indies considered what answer he
should make. At last he said, "I would that I could declare
for one of you, my sons, but I cannot do it with justice. It
is true, Ahmed, that the Princess owes her cure to your

artificial apple; but let me ask you, could you have cured her if you had not known of the danger she was in through Ali's tube, and if Houssain's carpet had not brought you to her so quickly? Your tube, Ali, discovered to you and your brothers the illness of your cousin; but the knowledge of her illness would have been of no service without the artificial apple and the carpet. And as for you, Houssain, your carpet was an essential instrument in effecting her cure. But it would have been of little use, if you had not known of her illness through Ali's tube, or if Ahmed had not been there with his artificial apple. Therefore, as I see it, the carpet, the ivory tube, and the artificial apple have no preference over each other, on the contrary, each had an equal share in her cure."

The story goes on to tell how the Sultan, after repeated trials, finally did choose a husband for the Princess. How Prince Ali wed her. How Prince Ahmed wandered away, disconsolate. How he met the Fairy Princess Banou. And how through her he finally won the greatest prize of all—contact with the Spirit within that knows all, sees all and can do all things.

In *The Secret of the Ages*, I endeavored to show how your subconscious mind can be made to serve as the Ivory Tube, giving you the answer to any problem you may put up to it in the right way.

In later volumes of this set, I shall try to prove to you how the Spirit within can and gladly *will* serve you better than Magic Carpet or Curative Apple. Length of days is in His right hand, freedom from fear, protection from harm, health, happiness and prosperity.

Do I promise too much? Just listen:

"But be ye glad and rejoice for ever in that which I create: for, behold, I create Jerusalem a rejoicing, and her people a joy.

"And I will rejoice in Jerusalem, and joy in my people: and the voice of weeping shall be no more heard in her, nor the voice of crying.

"There shall be no more thence an infant of days, nor an old man that hath not filled his days:

"And they shall build houses, and inhabit them; and they shall plant vineyards, and eat the fruit of them.

"They shall not build, and another inhabit; they shall not plant, and another eat: for as the days of a tree are the days of my people, and mine elect shall long enjoy the work of their hands.

"They shall not labour in vain, nor bring forth for trouble; for they are the seed of the blessed of the Lord, and their offspring with them.

"And it shall come to pass, that before they call, I will answer; and while they are yet speaking, I will hear."

—ISAIAH 65:18-24.

But how to find this Kingdom? Let us see what Jesus says—"Except a man be born again, he shall in no wise enter into the kingdom."

How shall man be born again? "Master," asked His disciples, "do you mean that a person must go back into his mother's body, must have a birth again on this earth, before he can enter into the kingdom of which you tell us?"

"Ye must be born again of water and of the Spirit," Jesus told them.

"Of water and of the Spirit." Let us see how this Spirit came to Jesus Himself.

> "Now when all the people were baptized, it came to pass, that Jesus also being baptized, and praying, the heaven was opened.
>
> "And the Holy Ghost descended in a bodily shape like a dove upon him, and a voice came from heaven, which said, Thou art my beloved Son; in thee I am well pleased."
>
> —LUKE 3:21–22.

"IT IS THE SPIRIT THAT QUICKENETH"

"And Jesus being full of the Holy Ghost returned from Jordan, and was led by the Spirit into the wilderness.

"And Jesus returned in the power of the Spirit

into Galilee: and there went out a fame of him
through all the region round about."

—LUKE 4:1,14.

Then Jesus went up into the Temple to preach. "And
there was delivered unto him the book of the prophet
Esaias. And when he had opened the book, he found
the place where it was written."—

"The Spirit of the Lord is upon me, because he
hath anointed me to preach the gospel to the poor;
he hath sent me to heal the broken-hearted, to preach
deliverance to the captives, and recovering of sight to
the blind, to set at liberty them that are bruised.

"To proclaim the acceptable year of the Lord."

—MATTHEW 61.

What, then, shall we do to be saved? How shall we
bring the Holy Spirit into our lives? How find the Kingdom here on earth?

Step by step, Jesus showed us the way. He "was led by
the Spirit into the wilderness"—into rest, into quiet, into
thought. He retired to where he could be alone for a while,
where he could concentrate his thoughts without outside
distractions, where he could commune with the Father.

"Praying, the heaven was opened, and the Holy Ghost
descended upon Him." And if we will pray rightly, the

heaven will open to us and the Holy Ghost will come upon us.

But He will never do it for the mere repetition of lip prayers that we have learned by rote.

THE SOUL'S SINCERE DESIRE*

Do you know what prayer is? Just an earnest desire that we take to God—to Universal Mind—for fulfillment. As Montgomery puts it—"Prayer is the soul's sincere desire, uttered or unexpressed." It is our Heart's Desire. At least, the only prayer that is worth anything is the prayer that asks for our real desires. That kind of prayer is heard. That kind of prayer is answered.

Mere lip prayers get you nowhere. It doesn't matter what your lips may say. The thing that counts is what your heart desires, what your mind images on your subconscious thought, and through it on Divine Mind. "And when thou prayest, be not as the hypocrites are; for they love to pray standing in the synagogue and at the corners of the streets, that they may be seen of men. Verily I say unto you, they have their reward."—Matthew 6:5.

What was it these hypocrites that Jesus speaks of really wanted? "To be seen of men." And their prayers were

———

*From The Secret of the Ages.

answered. Their sincere desire was granted. They were seen of men. "They have their reward." But as for what their lips were saying, neither God nor they paid any attention to it.

"But thou, when thou prayest, enter into thy closet, and when thou hast shut the door, pray to thy Father which is in secret, and thy Father which seeth in secret, shall reward thee openly. But when ye pray, use not vain repetitions, as the heathen do. For they think that they shall be heard for their much speaking. Be not ye therefore like unto them. For your Father knoweth what things ye have need of, before ye ask Him."—Matthew 6:6-8.

Go where you can be alone, where you can concentrate your thoughts on your one innermost sincere desire, where you can impress that desire upon the Spirit within, and so reach the Father.

But even sincere desire is not enough by itself. There must be BELIEF, too. "What things soever ye desire, when ye pray, believe that ye *receive* them and ye shall *have* them." You must realize God's ability to give you every good thing. You must believe in his readiness to do it. Model your thoughts after the Psalmists of old. They first asked for that which they wanted, then killed all doubts and fears by affirming God's power and His willingness to grant their prayers.

What is it you want most right now? Ask yourself frankly—Is it good that I should receive this? Is it right? Will it work no injustice to anyone else? Then have no hesitancy in asking it of the Father—secure in the knowledge that anything of good He will gladly give to you. Here is His promise. Read it, and see if you can still doubt:

"I will say of the Lord, He is my refuge and my fortress: my God; in Him will I trust.

"Surely He shall deliver thee from the snare of the fowler, and from the noisome pestilence.

"He shall cover thee with His feathers, and under His wings shalt thou trust: His truth shall be thy shield and buckler.

"Thou shalt not be afraid for the terror by night; nor for the arrow that flieth by day.

"Nor for the pestilence that walketh in darkness; nor for the destruction that wasteth at noonday.

"A thousand shall fall at thy side, and ten thousand at thy right hand; but it shall not come nigh thee.

"Because thou hast made the Lord, which is my refuge, even the most High, thy habitation.

"There shall no evil befall thee, neither shall any plague come nigh thy dwelling.

"For He shall give His angels charge over thee, to keep thee in all thy ways.

"They shall bear thee up in their hands, lest thou dash thy foot against a stone.

"Thou shalt tread upon the lion and adder:

the young lion and the dragon shalt thou trample under foot.

"Because he hath set his love upon me, therefore will I deliver him: I will set him on high, beceause he hath known my name.

"He shall call upon me, and I will answer him: I will be with him in trouble; I will deliver him, and honour him.

"With long life will I satisfy him, and shew him my salvation."

—PSALMS 91:6.

"Surely goodness and mercy shall follow me all the days of my life. And I will dwell in the house of the Lord forever."

—PSALMS 23:6.

So far we can follow in the footsteps of Jesus. So far we can contact with the Holy Spirit. But how about His miracles? How about His miraculous cures of the sick, the lame, the halt and the blind? Can we follow Him there, too?

Let us see what He says. "The works that I do shall ye do also, and greater works than these shall ye do."

That was a promise. A promise that was made—not merely to His immediate followers—but to ALL who believed! And that promise held good throughout the first three centuries of the Christian era, while it remained fresh in men's minds. It was only when Christianity became the State religion, and Constantine broidered it with too many forms, that the healing power was forgotten and lost.

Again, when Jesus sent His disciples forth, He told them to—"Go, preach, saying, The kingdom of heaven is at hand. Heal the sick, cleanse the lepers, raise the dead, cast out devils; freely ye have received, freely give."

Nothing indirect or obscure about that, is there? The command to preach the Gospel is no more positive than the command to heal the sick. If one was to be kept up by succeeding generations, surely the other was, too.

And in the way Jesus prepared His disciples for their work, in the directions He gave to them, and in the detailed accounts they have left for us of how Jesus performed his miraculous cures and of how the power came to the Apostles we find, step by step, methods that we too can use.

They were simple folk—these Apostles—unlearned, inexperienced, and until the coming of the Holy Spirit, most amazing timid. Jesus' instructions had need to be plain to be grasped by their unpracticed minds.

Don't you suppose that you, with all the advantages of a modern education, can follow them quite as easily, can practice them just as successfully?

Let's try! In the volumes to come, I am going to do my humble best to show the way.

"All Scripture is given by inspiration of God, and is profitable for doctrine, for reproof, for correction, for instruction in righteousness.

"That the man of God may be perfect, thoroughly furnished unto all good works."

—II TIMOTHY 3:16-17.

THE PROMISE

"The promise is that we may do all things through the mind that was in Christ Jesus."

IX

THE PROMISE

*"For the earth shall be full of the knowledge of the Lord,
as the waters cover the sea."*

—ISAIAH 11:9.

What was the greatest terror of primitive man? What, even in the golden days of Greece and Rome, was thought to be the wrath of God? What, right down to the beginning of the last century, seemed the most wholly destructive force in creation?

The Lightning.

Primitive man crouched in his cave in abject fear when the thunder rolled and lightning darted out of the sky, taking its toll of devastation and death. He might flee from his enemies of the jungle. He might overcome his savage adversaries. But when the lightning sought him out—that, indeed, to him was the wrath of God.

When Benjamin Franklin with his kite drew lightning

quietly from the clouds, he drew out of them a lot more than a mere current of electricity. He drew one great dread from the soul of man.

For thousands of years this greatest force in the material universe had roamed the world unleased—the terror of mankind—a powerful Genii uncontrolled, loose in a land of pigmies. And all the while it stood there ready and waiting to be harnessed, lashing out impatiently at times at man's failure to grasp the availability of this wonderful servant standing at his very elbow.

Just so it is with the greatest Genii of them all—the subconscious mind within you.

Through this spirit within, you can do anything right you may wish. If there is an unpardonable sin, it is to ignore or neglect it. For there is nothing right you can ask of it that it cannot give you.

Since publishing the first two volumes of this set, many people have written me that the ideas outlined in them seem wonderfully hopeful, wonderfully promising—*but how can they know them to be true?*

The promises in them were made through Prophets, through Apostles, through Christ Himself—they are taken word for word from the Bible—but what proof have I that the Bible is to be believed? What proof, indeed, have I that there is a God at all—much less a Divine Plan that takes cognizance of such unimportant creatures as ourselves?

Well, let us see. Science is generally supposed to be at

odds with the Bible, so let us see what science has to say about the question of a God.

Dr. Michael Pupin, Professor of Electro-mechanics at Columbia University, is an acknowledged authority on things electrical and scientific. Let us get his opinion:

The only mystery in connection with electrical science, he tells us, is the question of the origin of the proton and the electron. And that baffling question of when, where and how the tiny electron and its partner the proton came into existence can only be answered, he continues, by saying—"God created them."

Dr. Pupin asserted that when man discovered the electrons he discovered the oldest and most efficient workers and the most law-abiding servants in the cosmic universe. When man learned how to employ their services, he caught the first glimpse of the divine method of creative operations.

God created the electrons to be His assistants in the creation of the universe.

The electron is the most law abiding creature in the universe; the most ordinary intelligence can manage it. It loves, honors and obeys the law and its eternal mission is to serve. It is the service of the electron which carries the human voice around the terrestrial globe; it carries the power from coal mines and mountain streams to our homes and makes us comfortable; it pulls our subway trains.

To teach electrical science as it ought to be taught, Dr. Pupin said, is to teach theology in its most concrete and

intelligible form. It is the electrons, constituting an infinitely numerous host of law-abiding celestial workers,
which the Milton of today can glorify just as the Milton of
300 years ago glorified his heavenly hosts of angels.

God employed the heavenly host of electronic workers
to build the atoms, the molecules and the galaxies of burning stars. These celestial furnaces, throbbing with the blaz-
ing energy of the electronic host, are molding all kinds of
planetary castings and tempering them so as to be just
right for organic life.

Thus Dr. Pupin. Nothing at odds with religion in it, is
there? It all goes back to the one great Source. Everything
is made of protons and electrons. Everything consists of
electrical energy. BUT—

WHO MADE THE ELECTRICAL ENERGY?

There can be but one answer—GOD. What matters
whether you call Him God or Nature or Mind or merely
the Creator? So long as you ascribe to Him His attributes
of all-power, all-presence, all-life and all-love—what does
the name you give Him matter?

So much for the science of electricity. Let us see what
the doctors say. They have taken apart everything that is
in man's body. They have analyzed all its elements. They
know exactly of what we are made. But though they have
explored every nook and cranny of the brain—living and

dead—they have never found a thought, they have never discovered what makes it work. Just listen to what Dr. Charles Mayo, one of the foremost surgeons of the day, has to say:

"Like the small boy with the watch," he says, "we have taken man's form apart and put it together again. But we are still hazy about the force that makes it run."

Any great surgeon could put together the mechanical organs of a man. He might even, with the right electrical contrivances, force the heart to do its work; send the blood coursing through the arteries, the veins, through the brain itself. As a matter of fact, it was recently announced that a Russian scientist has invented an electrical device which can take the place of the heart. But the greatest surgeon in the world cannot make the creature of his hands *live*, cannot make it *think*, cannot make it work for one minute longer than his outside agencies propel it.

In short, man can put together all the component parts of any machine, even the machine of the body. But he cannot supply the soul that runs it. He cannot breathe into it the spark of life. *Only God can do that!*

So much for the doctors. Now let us hear from the chemists, the men who have analyzed all elements:

"There are about a hundred elements," says John Gunther in *The Red Pavilion*. "When you finish listing the first eight or so, then you find that the second group forms a new series analogous to the first series. That is, you start over again with number nine, which is neon, and you find neon almost identical in properties with number one, which is helium. Both are inert gases. And number ten (sodium) is almost precisely similar to number two (lithium). And number eleven, which is magnesium, corresponds exactly with number three, which is beryllium. Do you see? Each group runs its gamut, shades from the one end to the other, and then repeats itself in an ascending order.

"I speak, of course, very loosely. But you must see what I am getting at. Anyway, when you get all the elements lined up you find them arranged in families both ways— up and down the pattern. Each element has a particular place in the scheme of things. Each element has its fore-ordained nook and cranny. You can't move it. It fits. It fits there mathematically.

"Isn't that superb? Don't you see, it shows that all matter—everything in the world—belongs somewhere, *fits in its place in the scheme of things*. No one knows why it happens that way. No one can know. It just is. In a perfectly mystical way each element, and thus all matter, finds its position and stands there like a good soldier—for eternity.

"And that isn't all. When Mendeleef announced the law some elements were undiscovered. The pattern was not complete. There are still some elements not discovered for that matter. But before the elements came to light Mendeleef was able to predict what they would be. He filled the gaps in his chart with hypothetical elements, and

after his death these same elements, just as he predicted
them, were discovered.

"I think that's the most stupendous thing in the world.
I think it is somewhat frightening. To think of elements
of matter, unborn, so to speak, waiting for the day of their
emergence, waiting patiently, and all the time, though we
can't find them, can't isolate them, we know their names,
their weights, their properties, even their colours.

"It is like a vast and thrilling battle. We on our side wait
because we know some time that element must come out of
hiding and take his place with the rest and fit in the super-
nal pattern which is ready—and on the other side the elements also wait, they hide deep in ore and crust and earth
and defy us to prove that we are right, that we know better
than they. They are unborn, but we know they must be
born and finally they come.

"And all the time the pattern is complete and every
unit—including the undiscovered ones—is at work.

"Well, now that's why I suppose I must be honest and
say I do believe in some kind of directed force which, if
you want to, you can call God."

Sounds like taking a long way around, of course, but the
Science of Chemistry brings you home to the same goal at
the last, doesn't it? For—"Who knoweth not in all these
that the hand of the Lord hath wrought this?"—Job 12:9.

Then there is the astronomer, the student of the
heavens—of "the older Scripture, writ by God's own hand."

To quote Young—"An undevout astronomer is mad." And truly, the astronomer who did not believe in God would be an anomaly, for the Hand that can hold a billion worlds to their appointed courses must be nothing less than Divine.

"The heavens declare the glory of God: and the firmament sheweth his handywork.

"Day unto day uttereth speech, and night unto night sheweth knowledge.

"When I consider thy heavens, the work of thy fingers; the moon and the stars, which thou hast ordained;

"What is man, that thou art mindful of him? and the son of man, that thou visitest him?

"For thou hast made him a little lower than the angels, and hast crowned him with glory and honour.

"Thou madest him to have dominion over the works of thy hands: thou hast put all *things* under his feet."

—PSALMS 19:1-6.

More than a hundred years ago, an astronomer named Paley presented the case for God so clearly that I cannot do better than reproduce it here.

"I lay on the table before you a watch," said Paley, "a

complicated arrangement of wheels, springs, jewels, piv-
ots, and balances, all neatly combined in a case and covered with a crystal.

"I tell you that the watch had no maker; that out of the
bowels of the earth came iron and gold, and the elements
of glass; that they refined themselves, fashioned themselves
into springs and wheels and crystal, assembled themselves into this case, wound themselves up and started to
tick. I tell you all this and you tell me I am a fool. You
say that my story violates your reason; that the existence
of the watch is positive evidence of the pre-existence of a
watchmaker.

"And yet I show you a far more tremendous
mechanism—a watch whose parts are planets and stars,
suspended in limitless space, moving in unvarying orbits,
each perfectly adjusted to all the others—and you say: 'It
is a mystery beyond our understanding. It must have happened. There is no evidence of an Intelligence; no proof
of a Plan.'"

Your real scientist is in no doubt about the existence of
God. He never questions it. He has as much reverence and
respect for the Creator as you or I. It is your fledgling, your
dabbler in science that is so cocksure that the Prophets of
old, the Apostles—Jesus Himself—were mere tyros. He
knows more than they.

"A little learning is a dangerous thing," says Pope.

"Drink deep, or taste not the Pierian spring. There shallow drafts in-toxicate the brain, and drinking largely sobers us again."

Darwin never said that man was descended from the monkey. Read his *Origin of Species*. You will find no such statement in it. What he did say was that, from the study of all the facts known to science in his day, the conclusion that the monkey was a progenitor of man seemed to be a logical deduction. But—that was years ago—and science has made many new deductions since then.

"APE MAN THEORY NOW DISCARDED!"

That is the headline I read in the New York Herald-Tribune. At the convention of the American Philosophical Society, Dr. Henry F. Osborn, President of the American Museum of Natural History, branded the theory that man is descended from the ape as totally false and misleading. It should be banished from our literature, not on sentimental or religious grounds, but on purely scientific grounds.

"Of all incomprehensible things in the universe, man stands in the front rank," Dr. Osborn concluded, "and of all incomprehensible things in man the supreme difficulty centers in the human brain, intelligence, memory, aspirations, powers of discovery, research and the conquest of obstacles." In other words, something far higher than a monkey must have conceived the soul.

Science, in short, is back where it started from. With a little knowledge, it could tell all about man. But the more it learned, the less sure it became. Until now it frankly admits the origin of man to be incomprehensible—unless you accept the plain fact that as long as God was the origin of life, as long as He is the Directing Intelligence behind the universe, it would be no more wonderful—nor any more difficult—for Him to have evolved man complete and perfect as in the Scriptural accounts than to have brought him through all the different stages of development outlined by the scientists. In either case, we are back to the words of Job (33:4): "The Spirit of God hath made me, and the breath of the Almighty hath given me life."

Let us see where that brings us. Scientists are agreed, we find, that there is a God—though some prefer to call Him by some other name. They are agreed that He is the origin of life. The point on which they disagree is merely how He manifested that life—whether He created everything complete and perfect, or started in with the lowest form and from it gradually developed up to the highest.

Science and religion are not so far apart then, after all!

But how about the Bible? How about the Book upon which our whole religion is founded? What have they to say of it?

For a long time, many scientists had only disparaging things to say of it—that it was a mere collections of traditions, handed down from father to son through endless generations. That it was no more reliable than the Folk-lore of the Norsemen or the Mythology of the Greeks and Romans.

But for some years past, archaeologists have been exca-vating in Egypt and the Holy Land and throughout the territory covered by the Biblical records, and the facts they have dug up have established beyond question the histori-cal accuracy of many, at least, of the Scriptural chronicles.

To begin with, there undoubtedly was a flood. The record of it appears in the ancient writings of all the East-ern peoples. Tablets of clay and tablets of stone, writings of wax and rolls of papyrus, all bear witness to this great catastrophe.

On a tablet dug from the ruins of ancient Ninevah by George Smith of the British Museum and translated by Prof. Haupt of Johns Hopkins University, there is given a complete description of the Ark.

Professor Haupt's translation relates how Noah cut down trees in the jungle and laid the frame of his ark, which con-sisted of six decks, divided into seven compartments. After its cargo was taken aboard, Professor Haupt said, two-thirds of the ark was under water.

"For our food," read Professor Haupt's translation of the tablet, "I slaughtered oxen and killed sheep—day by day. With beer and brandy, oil and wine I filled large jars, as with the water of a river."

Then there is the Tower of Babel. In Ur of the Chaldeas,

excavators from the University of Pennsylvania uncovered what looked like a huge rubbish heap, but proved to be an immense pyramid temple, a staged tower 195 feet long, 150 feet wide and 60 feet high. To quote P. W. Wilson:

"It is what Chaldea meant by Babel. And a work so immense could only have been completed by a community politically united. The Scriptural statement, therefore, that the building was interrupted by a confusion of tongues— that is, by a divergence of race and culture—is rendered self-evident."

The mosque of Hebron covers a cave which corresponds exactly with that grotto of Machpelah which Abraham bought for the burial of his dead. And it contains the ancient coffins of that patriarchal family. One curious confirming fact, too. The coffin of Rachel is not there. Remember, in the Scriptural record, how she died suddenly and had to be buried at Ramah?

The finding of Moses has been sub-stantiated not only from tablets found in Sumeria, but an inscription discovered on a stone in the Sinai peninsula, on being translated by Prof. Grimme of Muenster University, was found to be a memorial from Moses to that Pharaoh's daughter who spied his baby ark in the bulrushes, where his mother had hidden it, as related in the second chapter of Exodus.

"I, Manasse," it reads, "mountain chief and head priest of the Temple, thank Pharaoh Hiachepsut for having drawn me out of the Nile and helped me to attain high distinction."

"Manasse" was a synonym for "Moses" in the Hebrew of that epoch.

Moreover, there is corroborative historical proof that a Queen Hiachepsut—the name is also written as Hatshepsut and Hatasu—reigned in Egypt at about the time of the Hebrew exodus. She was succeeded by Tutaos III, who destroyed all her kindred and all her monuments whenever either fell into his hands. What queen could there have been in Egypt who had dragged a Moses out of the Nile, except that same Pharaoh's daughter?

New light has also been thrown, according to an Associated Press despatch of Nov. 15 last, upon Old Testament scenes portrayed in the Books of Samuel and Chronicles, by excavations in Palestine of the University of Pennsylvania Musuem expedition at Beisan. Beisan, you know, is the Biblical "Beth-Shan."

A monument found there tells how Rameses, the Egyptian Pharaoh, put the Jews to work building cities.

The "House of Ashtaroth," mentioned in I Samuel 31:10, within which was hung the armor of Saul after his death, was also unearthed, together with the flame-scorched walls of the fortress of Beth-Shan, where the body of Saul had hung, for which King David in revenge put the fortress to the torch.

If you were told that a six-foot seam of coal underlay a large tract of land, and you wanted to verify the truth of the assertion, what would you do? Bore holes in a dozen different places down to the seam. If each of these showed six feet of coal, you would feel assured that a six-foot seam underlay the whole tract.

Well that, in effect, is what archaeologists have done to the Biblical records. They have dug down to them in a hundred places—and found a hundred different confirmations of their truth. More and more they are coming to believe that science, instead of being the enemy of religion, should be its greatest ally.

Even in the account of the creation in Genesis, there is nothing that need conflict with the latest discoveries of science. Suppose the world is a billion years old. Suppose man does go back 500,000 instead of 5,000 years. The days of creation are not days of 24 hours each. God does not measure time that way. "For a thousand years in Thy sight are but as yesterday when it is past, and as a watch in the night."—Psalms 90:4.

That doesn't sound as though the six days of creation were supposed to represent a lapse of actual time less than one of our weeks. Still less does this from II Peter 3:8, "But, beloved, be not ignorant of this one thing, that one day is with the Lord as a thousand years, and a thousand years as one day."

You believe in the Pharaohs, in Alexander, in Hannibal, in Caesar, in Cleopatra. Believe just as surely in Abraham, in Moses, in Elijah, in David and all the other Scriptural characters. We have stronger corroboration of the Scriptural record than we have of many great historical happenings.

And if you are going to accept the Scriptures at all, you must accept the most glorious part of them—their promises.

"O thou afflicted, tossed with tempest, and not comforted, behold, I will lay thy stones with fair colours, and lay thy foundations with sapphires.

"And I will make thy windows of agates, and thy gates of carbuncles, and all thy borders of pleasant stones.

"And all thy children shall be taught of the Lord; and great shall be the peace of thy children.

"In righteousness shalt thou be established: thou shalt be far from oppression; for thou shalt not fear: and from terror; for it shall not come near thee."

—ISAIAH 53:11-14.

X

THE GOLDEN CALF

"For this is the covenant that I will make with the house of Israel after those days, saith the Lord; I will put my laws into their mind, and write them in their hearts: and I will be to them a God, and they shall be to me a people:

"And they shall not teach every man his neighbour, and every man his brother, saying, Know the Lord: for all shall know me, from the least to the greatest."

—HEBREWS 8:10-11.

In ancient days there lived in the city of Sardis a King named Croesus. Croesus ruled over the country of the Lydians. He had conquered all of Asia that lies to the west-ward of the river Halys. And the wealth he had accumulated was so enormous that no man could even compute it. Gold and silver and precious stones he had in such quantity that they were stored like corn or wheat. Until Croesus reckoned that with all his riches to bulwark him, his throne would endure forever. He had gold to buy anything—even the favor of the Gods!

So when Cyrus, the King of Persia, became threatening, Croesus sent to the Oracle of Apollo at Delphi great stores of gold and silver, golden bowls, the golden statue of a woman and a great golden lion, thinking thus to buy the God's favor. And made inquiry of the Oracle as to whether he should make war against Cyrus. The Oracle answered, safely enough—"If Croesus make war against the Persians, he shall bring to the ground a great empire."

Croesus, thinking his gifts had done their work, immediately made all preparations for war. But the empire he brought to the ground was his own—not Cyrus'. And the first thing Cyrus did was to build a great funeral pyre upon which to burn Croesus. At the last, the Persian spared him, but 'twas the wisdom of the Greek Solon that moved him to compassion—and Solon was the man Croesus had driven from his court because of his contempt for its luxury!

So that all of Croesus' vast store of gold profited him not at all. Like so many men you see around you today, he worked and schemed, gathering it together only for some one stronger or cleverer than he to take it away again.

You know how often you have seen people who had slaved all their lives, pinched every penny, deprived themselves of every pleasure in order that they might put aside enough for their old age, lose all their life's savings in a bank crash or through some investment they had thought absolutely safe.

Why? Why does God permit such a malign fate? Why? Because they were putting their dependence not in Him— but in money. They had set it up as the idol which they worshipped, just as truly as had the Israelites in the desert with the golden calf. And the same fate had been meted out to them.

"And he spake a parable unto them, saying, The ground of a certain rich man brought forth plentifully:

"And he thought within himself, saying, What shall I do, because I have no room where to bestow my fruits?

"And he said, This will I do: I will pull down my barns, and build greater; and there will I bestow all my fruits and my goods.

"And I will say to my soul, Soul, thou hast much goods laid up for many years; take thine ease, eat, drink, and be merry.

"But God said unto him, *Thou fool*, this night thy soul shall be required of thee: then whose shall those things be, which thou hast provided?

"So is he that layeth up treasure for himself, and is not rich toward God."

—LUKE 12:16–21.

It is right and proper that you should be saving. It is right and proper that you should make reasonable provision for the future. But it is neither right nor proper that you should *rob* the present, which is all of time you will ever know, for a very problematical future.

To do that is to tell God, in effect, that He has managed pretty well thus far—with your help—but when the time comes that you are no longer able to lend a helping hand, you fear He will be powerless to provide for you. So you are going to put your dependence on man's *real* friend—money in the bank.

"If I have made gold my hope," said Job (31:24, 28), "or have said to the fine gold, Thou art my confidence; this, also were an iniquity to be punished by the judge; for I should have denied the God that is above."

Gold has been man's dependence for a good many thousand years. Let us see what it has profited him.

The American Bankers' Association took one hundred healthy average young men at twenty-five, and traced them to the age of sixty-five. All of these hundred, mind you, had been imbued from youth—even as you and I—with the idea that during their healthy, productive years, they must lay aside provision for their old age. But what do we find?

At the age of sixty-five, *five out of six were living on charity*—dependent upon others for food and shelter! Only one out of twenty was able to live on his own savings at sixty-five!

These hundred were healthy to start with. They were average young fellows, some from poor families, some from well-to-do. A certain percentage of them died off, of course, but of those who survived, only one in twenty had justified his faith in the money god.

"For riches are not forever; and doth the crown endure to every generation?"

Seems rather a poor outlook for most of us, don't you think? After thousands of years of sacrifice to him, if the money god can't do better than that for his votaries, it is time we threw down the golden calf and set up a temple to the Father instead.

"But my God shall supply all your need according to His riches, in glory by Jesus Christ."—Philippians 4:19.

"According to His riches"—and His riches, all will agree, are infinite.

If you had an earthly father who was vastly rich, if you knew that in five or ten years you were going to be so crippled or diseased or infirm as to be unable to provide for yourself, you would not immediately start grubbing, saving and scrimping to lay aside enough to care for yourself during your decrepitude. No—you would go on with your daily round, spending freely for what was necessary, putting aside only what you could without sacrifice to the present. You would know that, when the need arose, your father could be depended upon to supply whatever else might be necessary to care for you and yours.

If any ordinary earthly father can be depended upon for this, don't you think it is paying our Father above a poor compliment to think that He is less worthy of our confidence than one of us?

Remember the parable of the Prodigal Son? He had demanded of his father his share of the inheritance—just as we demand of the Father the meed of riches that go to youth and health and strength. And he had spent those riches in pleasure and riotous living—just as we do all too frequently. But then—instead of despairing, instead of pining away in misery, he had come back and thrown himself on his father's mercy. And his father, greatly compassionate, took him in, put a ring upon his finger, a fine cloak about him, killed the fatted calf for him. Is there any reason to think that the Father above will do any less for us—if we throw ourselves upon His mercy?

"In my Father's house," said Jesus in the parable, "there is bread enough and to spare."

Jesus did not come into the world to condemn it. He came to help it out of its misery. If he had purposed only to save souls for the hereafter, he might easily have done his preaching and his miracle-working for the rich and the powerful. Their souls needed saving far more than the poor man's. They were subject to greater temptations. And who can doubt that they would have welcomed this great Wonder-worker to their midst—and made his path a bed of roses instead of one of thorns?

But Jesus preached His Gospel to the poor man, because it was the poor man who needed His help right here on earth. He invited the poor and needy into the Kingdom of God, which He told them was *within them!* He came that He might reveal to them this Kingdom, filled with the richest treasures of Heaven—health and happiness, riches and love.

"The Kingdom of Heaven is at hand," He assured us. And again—"Fear not, little flock, for it is your Father's good pleasure to give you the Kingdom."—Luke 12:32.

His whole mission lay in discovering to us this Kingdom within. Throughout His earthly career, He kept referring to it continually. There are more references to it in His teachings than to almost any other theme. And lest we think it referred to some future state in the hereafter, he adjured us—"Seek ye not what ye shall eat or what ye shall drink. For all these things do the nations of the world seek after; and your Father knoweth that ye have need of these things. But rather seek ye the Kingdom of God; *and all these things shall be added unto you.*"—Luke 12:29-31.

Then where is this Kingdom? How shall we find it? How enter into it?

If you have ever been in a sailboat you know that you don't have to supply any motive power to make the boat go. All you need do is put your sail in the right position to catch the wind. It is the wind that makes the boat go.

So it is with heat, with running water, with electricity.

God creates the elemental forces. All we have to do is utilize them, put our boat or our water-wheel or our motor
in the right position.

And that is all you need to do to find the Kingdom of
God, to open up its riches—put yourself in position to
receive them. Express your desire. Pray. Give what service
you can. Then open up the channels with understanding
faith. "Let your loins be girded about, and your lights burning; and ye yourselves like unto men that wait for the Lord;
that when He cometh and knocketh, they may open to
Him immediately."—Luke 12: 35-36.

"Prayer," says Dr. W. F. Evans, "is the divine method
of opening the soul upward to receive what God is more
than willing to give."

And prayer, as we know, is no merely mouthing of
phrases, not "vain repetitions like the heathen do." Prayer
is the taking of our honest desires to God, just as we would
take them to an earthly father, in the secure knowledge
that we are His heirs, that all of good belongs to us and that
we have only to ask in perfect faith in order to receive anything that may be for our good.

Even the pagan philosopher Marcus Aurelius sensed this.
"If a thing is possible or proper to man," he said, "deem it
obtainable by thee."

There is no want or limitation in the Kingdom. If poverty and lack manifest themselves in your life, the trouble

is not with the supply—but with *you*. The abundance is there—but it is up to you to tap it.

What would you think of a man, owning a tract of land under which lay a vein of pure gold, who stopped trying to find it merely because his first feeble efforts had failed to locate the vein? Yet that is what most of us do when our prayers are not immediately answered, when our efforts to win health or riches or happiness are not at once successful.

How do we pray? Too often like the beggar asking for alms—doubting that he will get anything, expecting a rebuff, yet holding forth his hand in the forlorn hope that something may drop into it.

That is no way to ask the Father to give you the good things He has prepared for you, His son. How would you feel if your young son came to you that way, begging for shoes or coat or something to eat? You would feel insulted that he had not enough confidence in your love to know that it was a pleasure to provide these needs, that you required service and obedience from him only for his own good. Yet surely, you do not rate yourself as a better father than the One above?

You don't beg the sun for its rays. Neither need you beg God for His love—or for the evidences of that love. Years ago James Russell Lowell gave us the idea in *The Vision of Sir Launfal* when he said—"Heaven is given away, and God may be had for the asking."

"Thou shalt make thy prayer unto Him, and He shall hear thee, and thou shalt pay thy vows. Thou shalt also decree a thing, and it shall be established unto thee; and the light shall shine upon thy ways."

To say that "thou shalt also decree a thing" doesn't sound as though you were to take the attitude of a beggar when you ask anything of the Father.

If you were a great king and had many sons, which would you feel prouder of, which would you be more likely to reward with everything of good he might wish? One who cringed and whined and begged for every little thing, who grabbed each passing gift as though he feared there would never be another and even that one might be taken away from him, who mistrusted you and everyone around him? Or one who was proud of his high position, who knew that as your son he could expect all of good, and who, whenever a need arose, came to you with it in the serene confidence that if you thought it good, you would gladly satisfy it?

Then why act differently towards your Father above—the greatest King of all—whose "good pleasure it is to give you the Kingdom"?

You are not a beggar. You are not a slave. You are the Son of God!

"Thou madest him to have dominion over the works of Thy hand," said the Psalmist. "Thou hast put all things under his feet."

Dominion—decree—those are not the words of beggars

or slaves. Those words refer to Lords of the earth. And you are one of them!

Manifest your dominion. Decree the things you want. Never mind what your present circumstances may be. Never mind what you may lack now.

"Man's trust in God," says Albert C. Grier in *Truth's Cosmology,* "is measured largely by his ability to trust when he has no money. Trust in God is always in proportion to the amount of dependence we place upon the invisible—to the amount of poise and courage we maintain when there is nothing visible in the way of support."

Put your dependence—NOT on the material possessions you have amassed, but in the Father.

"Lay not up for yourselves treasures upon earth, where moth and rust doth corrupt, and where thieves break through and steal:

"But lay up for yourselves treasures in heaven, where neither moth nor rust doth corrupt, and where thieves do not break through nor steal:

"For where your treasure is, there will your heart be also."—Matthew 6:19-21.

From time immemorial, every generation, every year, every day has shown mankind how undependable are earthly possessions—here today, gone tomorrow. Fire may destroy them. Wind or flood sweep them away. Robbers steal them. But still we cling to them as the only security we know. Still we fall down and worship the Golden Calf, though that very minute may have proved to us how pow erless it is.

A ROOM HEAPED WITH GOLD

When the last of the Incas lay a prisoner in the dungeons of the Spaniard Pizarro, he proposed to his captors: "Promise me freedom, and I will fill this chamber with gold. It shall be piled as high as I can reach on tiptoe, and I will fill a smaller room twice full with silver as well."

The Spaniards promised, and immediately Atahuallpa's couriers set forth. Over the steep trails of the Andes they raced, to the mines and treasure troves and temples of the People of the Sun. And soon there started a procession of heavy-laden Indians, each bearing on his back part of the golden ransom for the last Child of the Sun.

Gold to the value of fifteen and a half million of dollars they packed on their shoulders, piling the dungeon room higher and higher. And every back-breaking load brought joy to the heart of the Inca, thinking it meant one step nearer to freedom.

But alas for his dependence upon gold. When the room was almost full, and the Spaniards felt they could get but little more from him, they took him out and strangled him.

Contrast that with the story of Elisha, or of Jehoshaphat, or of Peter when he was imprisoned. "Hearken ye, thou king Jehoshaphat. Thus saith the Lord unto you. Be not afraid nor dismayed by reason of this great multitude; for the battle is not yours, but God's. Ye shall not need to fight in this battle. Set yourselves, stand ye still, and see the salvation of the Lord with you."—II Chronicles 20:15, 17.

That is where you have got to put your trust, if you are to be saved from sickness and want and a dependent old age. Not in the money god, not in the charity of friends or relatives, but in the love of the One who never fails us if we lean entirely on Him. Well may we say with the Psalmist of old: "My soul, wait thou only upon God; for my expectation is from Him."—Psalms 62:5.

WHAT THEN SHALL WE DO TO BE SAVED?

A certain rich young man came to Jesus with that same question. Jesus told him to sell all that he had, give the proceeds to the poor and follow Him.

And what did following Him entail? *Service.* Service first, last and all the time. "Whosoever shall be great among you shall be your minister, and whosoever of you will be the chiefest, shall be servant of all."—Matthew 20:26, 27.

Giving away his money was not the important part. The service was the all-important part. For Jesus knew how hard it is for any young man who has come into money without effort to realize the service he owes for that money.

Often men have written me asking why they should

leave money to their children, when more often than not that money ruins rather than helps them.

It is not the money that does the harm. Money is opportunity—for good or evil. The trouble is in man's attitude toward money. Men who earn it honestly realize that it is the meed of service, the reward of work well done. And they strive to find still greater service that it may do.

But men who acquire it without effort look upon it as something made solely to contribute to their sordid pleasures. They feel no responsibility to any Power for it. They propose to make no accounting for it. It is theirs—and they are going to do with it as they please.

That is the reason money is such a curse to the sons and daughters of the rich—they give nothing for it in return. They worship only the Golden Calf. They put all their dependence in it. Is it any wonder they lapse so quickly into penury, until "three generations from shirt-sleeves to shirt-sleeves" has become a proverb?

"Charge them that are rich in this world, that they be not high-minded, nor trust in uncertain riches, but in the living God, who giveth us richly all things to enjoy;

"That they do good, that they be rich in good works, ready to distribute, willing to communicate.

"Laying up in store for themselves a good foundation against the time to come, that they may lay hold on eternal life."—Timothy 5:17-19.

Jesus had all power. He could feed the multitude with five loaves and two fishes. He could call forth gold from the fish's mouth. He could call upon the Father for anything He wished. He gave this same power to his disciples. And He offered the rich young man place among these.

But the man turned away. He had more faith in the Golden Calf. Rather than give up his riches and his possessions, he passed up powers far greater. He passed up rewards undreamed of. And who can doubt that most sons of rich parents, in like case, would do the same today? Why? Because they have more faith in the money god than in the Father.

In Ancient days there lived a certain King of Phrygia named Midas. Legend has it that he did a favor for one of the Gods, and in return was granted any wish he might ask.

Like most men to this very day, Midas more than anything else loved riches, and the greatest wish he could conceive of was that he might be able to turn everything he touched into gold. Given the same opportunity, how many men today would ask the same!

The Gods consented, though regretting that he had not made better use of his wish.

So Midas went his way, rejoicing in his new-found power, which he could scarce wait to put to the test. He broke a twig off an oak tree—and lo and behold, it turned to gold in his hands. He picked up a stone—and it turned into gold. He pulled a blade of grass—it did the same. He took an apple from a tree—immediately it became an apple of gold.

Midas' joy knew no bounds. He hastened homeward and directed his servants to prepare a great feast, the while he turned all the dishes, the chairs, the table, even the walls into gold. Then he sat down with his friends and courtiers to celebrate his power.

Imagine his dismay, when every piece of food he put into his mouth turned immediately into gold! Whether it was bread or meat or wine that he touched—no sooner had it reached his lips than it hardened into gold. To add the final touch of misery, his little daughter tried to embrace him—and at once was changed into a figure of gold!

A fairy tale, of course. But how much of truth there is in it! Men turn their thoughts, all their creative faculties, into the search for gold. And when they get it, it turns bitter in their mouths. They find that it has ruined health and home and happiness. Many a millionaire would cheerfully give all his gold for a good stomach, for the love of wife and children that he lost in his mad scramble for wealth. How much better the choice of Solomon than that of Midas.

"In that night did God appear unto Solomon, and said unto him, Ask what I shall give thee.

"And Solomon said unto God, Give me now wisdom

and knowledge, that I may go out and come in before this people: for who can judge this thy people, that is so great?

"And God said to Solomon, Because this was in thine heart, and thou hast not asked riches, wealth, or honour, nor the life of thine enemies, neither yet hast asked long life; but hast asked wisdom and knowledge for thyself, that thou mayest judge my people, over whom I have made thee king:

"Wisdom and knowledge is granted unto thee; and I will give thee riches, and wealth, and honour, such as none of the kings have had that have been before thee, neither shall there any after thee have the like."—II Chronicles 1:7, 10, 11, 12.

For here is the greatest of all wisdom—that understanding, that service, bring their own reward. You cannot serve without reaping a commensurate reward. And not commensurate only, but heaping full and running over.

"Seek ye first the Kingdom of God." Do you know what is the Kingdom of God? *The Kingdom of God is the Kingdom of Service.* "And all things else shall be added unto you."

You could easily give your young son every toy he asks for, every desire of his heart, and require nothing in return. Many rich parents do. But where would that leave your child? Greedy, selfish, with no sense of responsibility towards you or his companions or the world. A self-centered youngster, of no value to anyone.

But enlist him in the Kingdom of Service and what happens? He takes a new lease on life. His interest is awakened. At once he is trying to find some better way, some bigger thing he may do. In short, he serves.

So it is with God and His children. He makes it necessary for them to learn to serve Then all things else are added unto them.

"And He said unto them, Verily I say unto you, there is no man that hath left house, or parents, or brother, or wife, or children, for the Kingdom of God's sake, who shall not receive manifold more in this present time, and in the world to come, life everlasting."—Luke 18:29-30.

XI

THE FOUR KEYS
TO SUCCESS

"Behold that which I have seen. It is good and comely for one to eat and drink and to enjoy the good of all his labours that he taketh under the sun all the days of his life, which God giveth him; for it is his portion.

"Every man also to whom God hath given riches and wealth, and hath given him power to eat thereof and to take his portion, and to rejoice in his labour. This is the gift of God."

—ECCLESIASTES 5:18, 19.

Back in 1921, when Wall Street was generally believed to have at last gotten a strangle-hold on Henry Ford, Bruce Barton asked him what he would do if he went broke.

"I'd find something that lots of people have to have," said Ford, "and I'd figure out some way to make it better and sell it cheaper than it had ever been made and sold before. I'd have another fortune before I died.

"Money isn't important," he added. "I can't spend much on myself. Nobody can. There are only two things in the world that are really important—work and faith."

Many people look upon Henry Ford as uneducated. Perhaps he is as books go. But in those few sentences he epitomized most that is worth while in business.

Whole libraries have been written upon the practice of business. Schools and colleges have been founded to teach it. But where in all the thousands of volumes printed on the subject, can you find its essentials more succinctly set forth?

1. Find a need.
2. Satisfy it better than anyone else and at a lower price.
3. Believe in your work and in yourself.
4. Work—with head as well as hand.

It matters not whether you are the owner of a great enterprise or the third assistant errand boy in the corner grocery. The same principles apply. In either case, it is *you* that is your business.

Men and money and factories and stores and offices are merely the tools of trade. They are your equipment. It is the way your mind plans the use of this equipment that spells success or failure for you.

And if the only equipment you have is your own hands and brains, then it is more important than ever (for you) that you use them to utmost advantage. You can discharge incompetent workers and get good ones. You can scrap poor machines and get better ones. But you can't discharge yourself. You can't scrap your body. So it is the more important that you use your powers to good purpose.

And the first thing to do is to look around you—and keep looking around—to find ways in which you can serve better. "I have six honest serving men," wrote Kipling, "they taught me all I know. Their names are What and Why and When and How and Where and Who."

Promotion—success—comes for one reason—and only one. That is doing things a little better than the other fellow.

When Nurhachu, founder of the Manchu dynasty, planned to attack the great wall of China, he picked his strongest rival to lead the attack. Remonstrated with by his followers for giving another the place of honor, he silenced them by saying—"Victory demands the best available weapon."

And after all, that is what most concerns are looking for—victory, success. Favoritism may rule in little things, but when it comes to important work, most executives will pick the man for it that they honestly believe best fitted.

"I will study and work," said Lincoln in his backwoods home, "and my chance will come."

Every man's chance comes—not once but a thousand

times. The trouble with most is they are so unready for it they do not even recognize it as a chance for them. The greater the opportunity, the more surely it passes them by.

"I went by the field of the slothful, and by the vineyard of the man void of understanding; and lo, it was all grown over with thorns, and nettles had covered the face thereof, and the stone wall thereof was broken down."—Proverbs 24:30,31.

Suppose the position above you were vacated tomorrow. Could you fill it? Could you jump right in and make good? Could you add anything new, anything better, than is now being put into the work? Or would the Big Boss have to pass you up because you lacked training, because you had failed to prepare yourself?

The man who is offered the big job is the man who has trained himself to hold it before it is offered to him. Don't take chances on being promoted. Don't gamble on making good when the opportunity comes. If you want a big job that carries responsibility and pays good money, get ready for it!

Pick out the job you want in the work you like best. Then start right now to get the training that will prepare you to hold it.

Prepare! Who knows but that it will be vacant tomorrow? And if not that one, then another just as good—with your concern or some other. Be ready for your opportunity when it comes.

And one of the best ways of making ready is to learn to do one thing at a time.

I know an executive who has just been let go by a fast-growing, progressive concern—and he hasn't the remotest idea why. He had been with them for years. He had worked hard. But they dropped him and put a man in his place with not half the experience.

The reason? Not favoritism. Not prejudice. But the outgoing executive could never concentrate his attention on one thing at a time. He used a shotgun where business requires a rifle.

His desk was always piled high. He jumped from one thing to another, never finishing, never letting go of any. His mind was a turmoil. The new man has the essential quality he lacked—ability to stick to one thing until he finishes it.

Do one thing at a time. Concentrate your whole thought upon it. Only thus can you bring to your help the Spirit within. Finish it—*and forget it*. Then pass on to the next.

And in between times and all the time—study! Study first your own work. Study next the job ahead. But study always for the big job you are aiming for.

"So shall the knowledge of wisdom be unto thy soul. When thou hast found it, then there shall be a reward, and thy expectation shall not be cut off.—Proverbs 24:14.

In one of the interesting bulletins gotten out by the Ford Motor Company, there was this advice:

"Every man in this organization should be doing three things:

1. Giving the greatest possible satisfaction on the job he holds.
2. Preparing himself to fill the next job above; and
3. Training another man to fill his present place when he is ready to leave it for a higher one.

"When you have done one thing perfectly, you are big enough to try a bigger thing. Then is the time to prepare yourself for the bigger thing and train the man under you to take your place so as to free yourself when the opportunity comes for the job you are aiming at."

BETTER PAY—MORE MONEY

One of the successful Correspondence School advertisements pictures a man and his wife poring over the month's bills. "I simply must make more money," he exclaims. "Yes," she agrees, "but you never *do* anything about it."

And all too often, that is true. There are more opportunities for good men today than there ever have been. The man with ambition has only to fit himself for bigger things, and if the opportunity to use his knowledge does not come along of itself, he can *make* it.

I know of a man who was sent to the penitentiary for

life for killing another. For most people, that would spell the end of things. But his was one of those indomitable souls that adversity cannot down.

He learned to write letters—letters that would sell things. First he used them to sell the spare-time products of the prison workshop to buy little comforts for the prisoners. Then, as his fame spread, he began to write letters for business firms outside. In a few years his work was so well and favorably known that organizations with nation-wide membership began to appeal for his pardon.

Today he is free—holding down a big and responsible position—drawing a salary that few in his line can equal.

"Seest thou a man diligent in his business? He shall stand before kings."—Proverbs 22:29.

Just as the physician may read medicine, just as the lawyer may read law, just so may a man now read business— the science of the game which enables some men to succeed where hosts of others fail. It is no longer enveloped in mystery and darkness.

Take yourself now. You get more pay for each working hour now than you did the first day you worked. Why? Because you put more value into each hour of your time. You have developed your knowledge, your experience, your judgment.

Your value to your business is gauged by your ideas, and these come from your business knowledge and experience. If you enrich your own knowledge with the tested and proven experience of other men, you save yourself valuable time and the needless labor of studying out that which is already known. You avoid useless and expensive experiment. You make yourself a many-brain-power man.

Every man wants to get out of the rut, to grow, to develop into something better. Yet who is the man who wins promotion? Is it the clerk whose work is limited to his own routine of details? No, it is the man who has enriched his knowledge with the proven results of successful men's experience.

How does a lawyer learn the law? Not by cramming his head full of rules and systems and routine. That was the old way—the discarded way.

Nowadays a man studying for the bar is given the salient points of cases that have actually happened, and then shown how they were worked out, where to find the law pertaining to them.

Admiral Lord Nelson used the same effective plan in naval warfare. He was a genius in naval tactics. But he was more. He was a *maker of geniuses!* In the great battle of Trafalgar, which put a definite end to Napoleon's ambition to invade England, while the tactics used were Nelson's, they were used not so much by him as *by the Captains under his command!*

These lines from an old book describing his methods (*Jeffries' Manual*) might well be made the keynote for all business management, and set up as a guide for every man in business:

> "It was not in greater ability to direct his ships in action that Nelson's genius lay, so much as in this:
>
> "That his method was to *school* his Captains in his *principles* of fleet attack and defense, that in the hour of action each might *know the mind* of his Admiral without direct instruction from him. Indeed, no greater rebuke could Nelson administer to any Captain under his command than to order him to do this or to do that.
>
> "Even in his final great battle, an engagement of such magnitude, confusion and violence as to stagger the imagination, *signals were scarcely necessary nor but little used.*"

There is no limit upon you—except the limit you put upon yourself. You don't need to worry about your rivals, your business competitors. Indeed, you should be thankful for them. If it were not for them, you would lack the incentive for effort and soon be as dead as a Government bureau. Without contest, without competition, you would lapse into a grind. Competition, difficulties, obstacles, are the alarm clocks of business. They wake you up. They make you exercise your muscles—mental as well as physical.

Through them, you grow bigger and stronger, your vision is broadened, you are made to forge ahead.

Few great discoveries in science or chemistry would ever be made but for difficulties, obstacles. We see the end of one source of supply and we fear it means the end of our business. But we work, we use our ingenuity—and along comes something better far than the thing we feared to lose.

In *Advertising & Selling,* Floyd Parsons predicts the time in the very near future when synthetic rubber, made from petroleum or some other cheap source such as the soy bean, will largely replace the real article. When wood will be so valuable in the hands of the chemist that we will stop burning it for fuel, thereby increasing the market for coal a hundred million tons a year. When artificial stone, or other composition material will be cheaper and no less durable than natural rock, and the furnishings of our homes will be made largely of bakelite, artificial leather and artificial silk.

He sees millions of dollars being saved yearly by substituting non-corroding metal alloys for copper, lead, zinc, tin and antimony. Furniture that is fire-proof and resistant to decay being made out of resinoids and other wood derivatives, just as rayon, celluloid and artificial leather are now made.

Why, it is just a little while ago that someone discovered that the chip and wood waste which sawmills and lubermen have been throwing away or burning for so many years can be exploded into fibres and then pressed into boards or sheets in many cases better than regular hardwood boards!

Then there is oil. Oil underlay just as much of our lands a hundred or a thousand years ago as it does today. But it was never "discovered"—because the world was not ready for it.

"The simple truth appears to be," says the Harriman National Bank in a recent advertisement, "that when, in the history of the world, it became necessary for these firmly-fastened storehouses of oil to be uncovered, they were uncovered. Nature had held them for untold thousands of years for just this emergency. The discovery of oil in the earth was one of the most remarkable and instructive revelations of the age. It has shown that, whenever human necessity demands anything of the world of matter, the demand will be honored. Nature has always risen up grandly to meet every occasion for new resources. After she has presented mankind with her gift, it is up to mankind to harness it. We are treading every day upon the lids of great secrets that await the wants of the larger style and finer type of life that lie before us. Discovery has just begun and there is no end of it; yet the world is a thing to be weighed and measured. It is so many miles around it, and so many miles through it. It has more in it than humanity can exhaust."

"Ye shall seek me, and find me, when ye shall search for me with all your hearts."—Jeremiah 29:13.

And yet scienists are constantly worrying about the exhaustion of this or that source of supply. The fact is that we have not even begun to tap the resources of Nature.

Just listen:

Fifty years ago, three rabbits were taken to Australia, where rabbits were unknown. Forty years later, 96,000,000 rabbit skins and 25,000,000 frozen rabbits were shipped back from Australia to Europe!

We marvel at such increase. We use the skins and some of the flesh. But some day science is going to put that increase to real use.

Take the insects. Their birth rate is tremendous, many species laying a half million eggs in a single hatch. The stylonchia alone has a birth rate so high that if it were not for its almost equally high death rate, it would in a single week's time produce a mass of insects larger than the earth itself!

As things are now, one of our great problems is how to annihilate these insect pests, just as the greatest problem with our rivers only a few years ago was how to get quickly rid of their surplus waters.

Now these surplus waters are largely used for irrigation, for generating power, for a hundred and one useful purposes. And the time will come when the vast reproductive power of the insect world, which now is such a curse, will be turned to some good purpose.

In the town of Enterprise, Ala., there is a monument erected by its citizens for services done them. And you could never guess to whom it is dedicated. To the Boll Weevil!

Until a few years ago, the planters living thereabouts raised only cotton. When cotton boomed, business boomed. When the cotton market was off—or the crop proved poor—business suffered correspondingly.

Then came the Boll Weevil. And instead of merely a poor crop, left no crop at all. The Boll Weevil ruined everything. Debt and discouragement were all it left in its wake.

But the men of that town must have been lineal descendants of those hardy fighters who stuck to the bitter end in that long-drawn-out struggle between North and South. They got together and decided that what their town and their section needed was to stop putting all their eggs into one basket.

Instead of standing or falling by the cotton crop, diversify their products! Plant a dozen different kinds of crops. Even though one did fail, even though the market for two or three products happened to be off, the average would always be good.

Correct in theory, certainly. But, as one of their number pointed out, how were the planters to start? They were over their heads in debt already. It would take money for seeds and equipment, to say nothing of the fact that they had to live until the new crops came in.

So the townsfolk raised the money—at the Lord only knows what personal sacrifices—and financed the planters.

The result? Such increased prosperity that they erected a monument to the Boll Weevil, and on it they put this inscription:

"In profound appreciation of the Boll Weevil, this monument is erected by the citizens of Enterprise, Coffee Co., Ala."

Many a man can look back and see where some Boll Weevil—some catastrophe that seemed tragic at the time—was the basis of his whole success in life. Certainly that has been the case with one man I know.

When he was a tot of five, he fell into a fountain and all but drowned. A passing workman pulled him out as he was going down for the last time. The water in his lungs brought on asthma, which, as the years went on, kept growing worse and worse, until the doctors announced that death was only a matter of months. Meantime, he couldn't run, he couldn't play like other children, he couldn't even climb the stairs!

A sufficiently tragic outlook, one would say. Yet out of it came the key to fortune and success.

Since he could not play with the other children, he

early developed a taste for reading. And as it seemed so certain that he could never do anything worth while for himself, what more natural than that he should long to read the deeds of men who had done great things. Starting with the usual boy heroes, he came to have a particular fondness for true stories of such men as Lincoln, Edison, Carnegie, Hill and Ford—men who started out as poor boys, without any special qualifications or advantages, and built up great names solely by their own energy and grit and determination.

Eventually he cured himself completely of his asthma—but that is another chapter. The part that is pertinent to this tale is that from the time he could first read, until he was seventeen, he was dependent for amusement almost entirely upon books. And from his reading of the stories of men who had made successes, he acquired not only the ambition to make a like success himself, but the basic principles on which to build it.

Today, as a monument to his Boll Weevil, there stands a constantly growing, successful business, worth millions, with a vast list of customers that swear by—not at—its founder.

And he is still a young man, healthy, active, putting in eight or ten hours at work every day, an enthusiastic horseman, a lover of all sports.

But I don't need to go even as far afield as that to prove the truth of Shakespeare's oft-quoted maxim—"When

Fortune means to men most good, she looks upon them with a threatening eye." I know one of the best things that ever happened to me was to lose a position which I thought was mine for the rest of my days.

I had done good work. I had taken over a job at which six high-priced men had tried their hands, and failed. And I had put it across. I had succeeded. So I felt terribly abused when, in a reorganization a few months later, I was dropped.

It angered me—but it also woke me up. I went out and did for another concern what I could have done for the first one—just to show what I could do. But—and here is the thing that first concern saw and I did not—I had done one big thing. And I was inclined to rest on that. Like the soldier who fights one battle, I wanted to live on the glory of it the rest of my days. But the man at the head of that concern was like Napoleon when an officer came to him and told him of the wonderful thing he had accomplished. "Yes, yes," said Napoleon, "that was fine. But what did you do next day?"

Business is always in the present. A machine may have turned out wonderful work in the past, but when it ceases to be useful it goes to the scrap heap and a new one takes its place.

So it is with men—but with this difference. A machine, in the nature of things, is bound to wear out or get out of date. A man need not. Every cell, every organ in your body is daily being rebuilt. Every eleven months you have a brand new model. So why should youth displace you? There is not a thing about any other man younger or fresher or more vigorous than you. And you have the vast advantage of years of experience, than which nothing is more valuable in business. Provided it is backed by initiative, by enterprise.

"Be not as the horse or mule, whose mouth must be held by bit or bridle."—Psalms.

Age, poverty, ill-health—none of these things can hold back the really determined soul. To him they are merely stepping stones to success—spurs that urge him on to greater things. There is no limit upon you—except the one you put upon yourself.

> *"Ships sail east, and ships sail west,*
> *By the very same breezes that blow;*
> *It's the set of the sails,*
> *And not the gales,*
> *That determine where they go."*

Men thought they had silenced John Bunyan when they threw him into prison. But he produced "Pilgrim's Progress" on twisted paper used as a cork for the milk jug.

Men thought that blind Milton was done. But he dictated "Paradise Lost."

Like the revolutionist of whom Tolstoy wrote—"You can imprison my body, but you cannot so much as approach my ideas."

You cannot build walls around a thought. You cannot imprison an idea. You cannot cage the energy, the enthusiasm, the enterprise of an ambitious spirit.

This it is that distinguishes us from the animals. This it is that makes us in very truth Sons of God.

"MANANA"—TOMORROW!

But procrastination kills many an ambition.

The habit of indecision is responsible for countless failures. Every moment is a moment of decision. Form the habit of making those decisions promptly. Take care of these little questions that momentarily come up, and the big ones will take care of themselves. The man that cannot decide for himself is always subordinating his opinion and judgment to others. And his position naturally follows suit.

"The fault, dear Brutus, lies not in our stars, but in ourselves, if we are underlings."

You have twenty-four hours a day, three hundred and sixty-five days a year. What do you do with them all? Eight hours is enough for sleep; you probably work nine hours; what becomes of the other seven? Your future is determined as much by what you do out of working hours, as by what you do during working hours. I believe in recreation; every man should have it, and plenty of it. But there's at least an hour a day that every man can study.

Some men are born forty-four caliber or more; some are born twenty-two caliber or less.

The first sign of a forty-four caliber man is eagerness for knowledge. If you equip the forty-four caliber man with organized business knowledge, he soon becomes a power in the business world. "Nothing is too small to know. Nothing is too big to attempt."

But knowledge alone will get you nowhere—educated brains are as much of a drug on the market as uneducated brawn. It is the way you use your knowledge that counts.

Everywhere you turn you find some program for self-education urged upon you. One says—"Be a law student"; another—"Be an expert accountant"; a third—"Train your memory." All these are good things in themselves, but without initiative, without enterprise, without the energy and the courage to start things, they are valueless. The best educated man I know earns only $25 a week. The man with the best memory I ever heard of holds down the job of coatroom checker.

You cannot build up a human being by merely cramming him full of knowledge or feeding him up on business facts. It is what he puts to active *use* that counts—not what he knows. The best education is that which teaches him a thing one day, and then shows him how to *apply* it to his everyday work the next. Education, in short, is in learning to DO things.

"Who is wise, and he shall understand these things? Prudent, and he shall know them? For the ways of the Lord are right, and the just shall walk in them."—Hosea, 14:9.

You can have anything you want in life—for a price. The first payment on that price is effort Nothing worth while is ever accomplished without it. The rules for business success are simple enough.

1. Get the Idea—the need you are going to supply, the service you are going to render.
2. Learn the Method—study the best way to go about supplying that need, so as to be able to give the utmost value at the lowest cost.
3. Keep your Faith—believe in yourself, in your work, in the Divine Plan behind it all.
4. Use your Energy—start things, work head and hand to give the finest product, the best service you or anyone is capable of.

"There is that scattereth, and yet increaseth; and there is that withholdeth more than is meet, but it tendeth to poverty. The liberal soul shall be made fat; and he that watereth shall be watered also himself."—Proverbs, 11:24, 25.

There are 260,000 words in the English language, but

they are all dependent on the 26 fundamentals we call the alphabet. There are thousands of businesses you can start, hundreds of jobs you can try for—but they are all dependent upon the four fundamentals cited above.

Men will tell you they never had a chance, that fate dealt them a poor hand, that they were so handicapped they couldn't get a start.

What would you think of a baseball player who complained that the pitcher put so much speed behind his balls, or served him such twisters, that he never had a chance to make a hit? You'd laugh at him for a quitter. You'd tell him that was the pitcher's job. You'd point out the fellows that knocked home runs in spite of all the pitcher could do. You'd adjure him to stand up to the plate and whale the next fast ball that came along with all he had in him. And if he was made of the right stuff, he'd do it!

Business is just as much a game as is baseball. You can get as much fun out of it if you go at it in the spirit of fair play, of do-or-die, as you get at a good game of ball.

The pitcher has difficult curves. He has speed. But some men hit him all over the lot. And you can too if you will stand up to the plate and put everything you have into every swing.

Don't whine—"If so-and-so had done such-and-such, I'd be a big man today." So-and-so is just a little extra twister the pitcher put on the ball. You have got to look out for a few of those. You never hear your Big League pinch-hitter complain that if the pitcher hadn't put a curve on that last ball, he would have knocked a home run. Yet that would be no more ridiculous than for you to say that if fate had not put a few obstacles in your way, you would have been President of the firm.

That is what makes success worth while—the difficulties you must overcome to win it. If there were no obstacles, there would be no success, for everybody could have what he wanted for the taking.

Suppose Lindbergh had started to compare his meager equipment with the fine outfit and three-motored Fokker of Commander Byrd. Suppose he had become discouraged when his plane had difficulty in lifting from the muddy field. Suppose he had turned back when his weather reports proved unreliable, when his instruments failed him; when he ran into storms of rain and sleet where he looked for fair weather. Where would he be now? Do you think New York would have turned out en masse to welcome him? Do you think his name would be acclaimed the world over?

Nothing worth while is ever accomplished without struggle. No goal is ever won without overcoming obstacles. The important thing is to remember that back of all the toil and struggle, underneath the dust and the smoke, are the arms of the Father—guiding, guarding, supporting. Whatever you lack, He has. Whatever you need, He can supply. Whatever obstacle presents itself, the Father in you can overcome. "So near is God to man," wrote Emerson, "when duty whispers low, *thou must*, the youth replies, *I can!*"

"The Lord is nigh unto all them that call upon Him, to all that call upon Him in truth.

"He will fulfill the desire of them that fear Him. He also will hear their cry, and will save them."—Psalms 145:18-19.

XII

THE FORWARD LOOK

"Trust in the Lord and do good; so

Shalt thou dwell in the land and verily

Thou shalt be fed. Delight thyself also in the Lord;

And He shall give thee the desires of thy heart. Commit thy way unto the Lord;

Trust also in Him; and He shall

Bring it to pass."

—PSALMS 37:3-5.

Three hundred and forty years ago, there sailed from Spain the mightiest fleet the world had ever known. Spanish galleasses, Portuguese caracks, Florentine caravels, huge hulks from other countries—floating fortresses, mounting tier upon tier of mighty cannon—140 great ships in all, manned to the full with sailors and soldiers and gentlemen adventurers.

The treasure of the Incas, the Plunder of the Aztec, had gone into the building and outfitting of this vast Armada. No wonder Spain looked upon it as invincible. No wonder England feared it. For this was the Armada that was to invade England and carry fire and sword through town and countryside. This was the Armada that was to punish these impudent Britons for the "piratical" raids of Sir Francis Drake, Morgan and all those hardy seamen who had dared death and slavery to pull down treasure ships on the Spanish Main.

The iron hand of Philip II of Spain rested heavily upon the Netherlands. It dominated all of Europe. Now he confidently looked forward to the time when England, too, would groan beneath its weight.

But he reckoned without one thing—faith! He put in charge of this invincible Armada, the Duke of Medina Sidonia, a man who had no faith in himself, no faith in his ability, no faith in his men. And when he did that, he blunted the point of every pike; he dulled the cutting edge of every sword; he took the mightiest naval weapon ever forged, and deliberately drew its sting.

Am I putting it too strongly? Just listen. Here is the letter the Duke wrote to the King, upon being notified of his appointment to the command:

> "My health is bad and from my small experience of the water I know that I am always seasick. . . . The expedition is on such a scale and the object is of such high importance that the person at the head of it ought to understand navigation and sea fighting, and I know nothing of either. . . . The Adelantado of Castile would do better than I. The Lord would help him, he is a good Christian and has fought in naval battles. If you send me, depend upon it, I shall have a bad account to render of my trust."

He had everything to succeed with—everything but faith in himself. He expected failure—and disastrous failure met him at every turn.

One hundred and forty mighty ships—the greatest ever built. And England, to meet that splendid Armada, had only 30 small ships of war and a few merchant ships outfitted and manned by private gentlemen. Yet England, while alarmed, was yet courageous and hopeful. For had not England Sir

Francis Drake? And Lord Charles Howard? And a dozen other mighty fighters who had met and bested the Spaniards a score of times on the Spanish Main? And could they not do the same again?

So said England, believing in her leaders. And her leaders echoed that sentiment. Are not English sailors the hardiest seamen and finest fighters afloat, they asked. And believed in their men.

The English had 30 or 40 little ships against the Spaniards' 140 mighty men-of-war. The English had scarce two days' powder aboard—so penurious was their Queen—while the Spanish were outfitted with everything a ship-of-war could ask.

But Howard and Drake were not depending upon any Queen to fight their battles. They were not worrying about the size of the enemy. They were thinking—"There are the Spaniards. Here are we. We have fought them and whipped them a dozen times before. We can do it now. So let's get at them!"

They went out expecting victory. And victory met them at every turn.

From the Lizard in Cornwall to Portland, where Don Pedro de Valdes and his mighty ship were left; from Portland to Calais, where Spain lost Hugo de Moncado with the galleys which he captained; from Calais, out of sight of England, around Scotland and Ireland, beaten and shuffled together, that mighty Armada was chased, until finally the broken remnants drifted back to Spain.

With all their vast squadron, they had not taken one ship or bark or pinnace of England. With all those thousands of soldiers, they had not landed one man but those killed or taken prisoner.

Three-fourths of their number lost or captured, their mighty fleet destroyed. And why? Because one man lacked faith. Spanish soldiers were proving on a dozen fields that no braver fighters lived anywhere. The "Spanish Square" had withstood infantry, cavalry, artillery—then carried all before it. Yet these same soldiers, afloat in their huge fortresses, were utterly defeated by less than a fourth their number.

And the reason? Because they were a spear without a head—an army without a leader—riches and power without faith. Was ever a better example of the power of belief?

"The Lord is with you, while ye be with Him. And if ye seek Him, He will be found by you. Be ye strong, therefore, and let not your hands be weak, for your work shall be rewarded."—II Chronicles 15:2, 7.

Men go all through life like the Duke of Medina Sidonia—looking ever for the dark side of things, expecting trouble at every turn—and usually finding it. They call it caution. It is really lack of courage—courage to try for great things, courage to dare disappointment and ridicule to accomplish a worthy end. Have you ever sat in a train and watched another train passing you? You can look right on through its windows to the green fields and pleasant vistas beyond. Or you can gaze at the partitions between the windows and see nothing but their dingy drabness. So it is with everything in life. You can look for the good, the joyful and happy—and not merely see only these but manifest them in your daily life. Or you can look for trouble, for sickness and sorrow—and find them awaiting you around every corner.

Pessimists call this the "Pollyanna Age" and ridicule such ideas as this. But ridicule or not, it works—in one's personal life as in business—and thousands can testify to its efficacy.

"The eyes of all wait upon Thee, and Thou givest them their meat in due season: Thou openest Thine hand, and satisfiest the desire of every living thing."—Psalm 145:15,16.

Perhaps one of the best examples of the difference that outlook makes is in the lives of Emerson and Thoreau. Emerson's philosophy of living can best be expressed in his own words—"Nerve us with incessant affirmatives. Don't bark against the bad, but chant the beauties of the good." And his tranquil and serene life reflected that attitude throughout.

Thoreau, on the other hand, was constantly searching out and denouncing evil. With motives every whit as high as Emerson's, he believed in attacking the problem from the opposite angle, with the result that he was constantly in hot water, yet accomplished not a tenth part of the good that

Emerson did. Like the man in d'Annunzio's play, *La Citta Morta*—"Fascinated by the tombs, he forgot the beauty of the sky."

It is necessary at times to clean up evil conditions in order to start afresh. It is necessary to hunt out the source of pollution in order to purify a stream. But it should be merely a means to an end. And the end should always be—not negative like the mere destruction of evil, but the positive replacing of evil with good.

If you have ever walked across a high trestle, you know that it doesn't pay to look down. That way dizziness and destruction lie. You have got to look forward, picking out the ties you are going to step on ten or twenty feet ahead, if you are to progress.

Business is just such a trestle. And looking downward too much is like to make one lose his balance, stumble and fall. You've got to gaze ever forward in order to keep your perspective.

I know one great organization which went on the rocks solely because the man responsible for its policies lost his perspective by too much looking downward. Its founder had built it up to be the biggest in its line. But he had done it by keeping always one jump ahead of the field.

The man who succeeded to its management was put there because of his fervent reverence for the founders' methods and ideas. And to this day he sticks literally and

exactly to those methods of twenty years ago, never realizing that the genius who could build such a business would
have been the first to discard those methods the moment
they became outworn. "Remember ye not the former
things," said Isaiah (43:18), "neither consider the things of
old." And that advice might well be posted in the office of
every business executive over 45 years old.

Ten years after the founder's death, all his great fortune
had been swept away. The business was reorganized and
millions more put into it. And still it is headed for the
rocks, for the same Duke of Medina Sidonia sits at its helm.

While his policies last, there is no hope for it. But his
policies, to the men back of it, represent conservatism. And
conservatism, according to many, is the prime requisite of
every head of a great organization.

Conservatism! How many sins have been committed
in thy name!

Go back over the names that have made history—
Genghis Khan, Alexander, Hannibal, Caesar, Napoleon,
Nelson—was ever a conservative among them? Was Wash-
ington conservative when he crossed the Delaware? Was
Hannibal or Napoleon conservative when he crossed the
Alps? Was Jackson conservative? Or Perry? Or Farragut?
Was Foch a conservative when he sent this terse message
to Joffre in the first battle of the Marne: "My right has
been driven in. My left has been driven back. So with

all that is left of my center, I shall attack!" All the world knows the result of that gallant attack—yet the conservative thing would have been to retreat—and leave Germany the victor.

Conservatism—it is the refuge of lazy men and cowards. When one is too inept or too lazy to go vigorously after what he wants: when one would rather let an opportunity slip through his fingers than stand up and fight for it, then is when he takes refuge in "Conservatism." Conservatism let Lee escape after Antietam, though he fought with a river at his back. Conservatism let the German fleet escape at Jutland, though even the German reports admit that they were all but done for. Conservatism withdrew the British fleet from the Dardanelles at the very moment of victory—when the Turkish forts were down to their last shell.

In peace, as in war, the maxim of Foch is the only safe one. "The best defensive is a strong offensive."

"Behold, I will do a new thing; now it shall spring forth; shall ye not know it? I will even make a way in the wilderness, and rivers in the desert."—Isaiah 43:19.

THE THINGS THAT CAN'T BE DONE

There's a little poem by Edgar Guest[*] that exemplifies the idea correctly:

---

[*]From "The Path to Home." The Reilly & Lee Co.

"Somebody said that it couldn't be done,
But he with a chuckle replied
That 'maybe it couldn't,' but he would be one
Who wouldn't say so till he'd tried.
So he buckled right in with the trace of a grin
On his face. If he worried he hid it.
He started to sing as he tackled the thing
That couldn't be done, and he did it."

Most of the world's progress has been made by just such men as that. Men like Watt, who didn't know that steam could not be made to accomplish any useful purpose, and so invented the steam engine. Men like Fulton, who didn't know it was foolish to try to propel a boat with wheels— and so invented the steamboat.

Men like Bell, Edison, Wright, who didn't know how foolish it was to attempt the impossible—and so went ahead and did it.

"For God's sake, give me the young man who has brains enough to make a fool of himself!" cried Stevenson. And when they succeed, the whole world echoes that cry. "Then shall thy light break forth as the morning, and thy health shall spring forth speedily; the glory of the Lord shall be thy reward."—Isaiah 58:8.

There is no limit upon you—except the limit you put upon yourself. You are like the birds—your thoughts can fly across all barriers, unless you tie them down or cage them or clip their wings by the limitations you put upon them.

There is nothing that can defeat you—except yourself. You are one with the Father. And the Father knows everything you will ever need to know on any subject.

Why then, try to repress any right desire, any high ambition. Why not put behind it every ounce of energy, every bit of enthusiasm, of which you are capable?

"I will lift up mine eyes unto the hills, from whence cometh my help. My help cometh from the Lord, which made heaven and earth."—Psalms 121:1, 2.

Mahomet established a larger empire than that of Rome on nothing but enthusiasm. And Mahomet was but a poor camel-driver. What then can *you* not do?

Men repress their power for good, their capacity for success by accepting suggestions of inferiority; by their timidity or self-consciousness; by fear; by conservatism.

Never mind what others think of you. It is what *you* think that counts. Never let another's poor opinion of you influence your decisions. Rather, resolve to show him how unfounded is his opinion.

People thought so poorly of Oliver Cromwell that he could not win permission to emigrate to the Colonies. When he raised his regiment of cavalry, that afterwards won the name of "Ironsides" because of its practical invincibility, the old soldiers and the dandies of the day laughed

at it. Seldom had a lot of more awkward-looking countrymen been gathered together.

Any soldier might have trained them. But the thing
that made them invincible, the thing that enabled them to
ride over and through all the legions of King Charles, was
not their training, but their fervent belief in the justice of
their cause, in their leader and in their God.

"Hymn-singing hypocrites," their enemies called them.
But here were no hypocrites. Here were men who were
animated by a common faith that God was with them as
with the Israelites of old—and that with God on their side,
nothing could withstand them.

That was the faith of Cromwell. And he instilled that
faith into every man in his regiment.

And while Cromwell lived to keep that faith alive,
nothing *did* withstand them. They made the man who
was not good enough to emigrate to America, Ruler of
England!

"For as the heavens are higher than the earth, so are my
ways higher than your ways, and my thoughts than your
thoughts."—Isaiah 55-9.

Nothing worth while ever has been accomplished
without faith. Nothing worth while ever will.

Why do so many great organizations go to pieces after
their founder's death? Why do they fail to outlive him by
more than a few years?

Because the ones who take up his work lack the forward look, the faith, to carry on. His idea was one of service—theirs is to continue paying dividends. His thought was to build ever greater and greater—theirs to hold what he won.

"The best defensive is a strong offensive." You can't just hold your own. You can't stand still. You've got to go forward—or backward!

Which is it with you? If forward, then avoid the pessimist as you would the plague. Enthusiasm, optimism, may make mistakes—but it will learn from them and progress. Pessimism, conservatism, caution, will die of dry rot, if it is not sooner lost in the forward march of things.

So be an optimist. Cultivate the forward look.

"The Optimist and Pessimist,
The difference is droll,
The Optimist sees the doughnut,
The Pessimist—the hole!"

The good is always there—if you look for it hard enough. But you must look for *it*. You can't be content to take merely what happens to come into your line of vision. You have got to refuse to accept anything short of good. Disclaim it! Say it is not yours. Say it—*and believe it*. Then keep a-seeking—and the first thing you know, the good you have been seeking will be found to have been right under your nose all the time.

"For as the rain cometh down, and the snow from heaven, and returneth not thither, but watereth the earth, and maketh it bring forth and bud, that it may give seed to the sower and bread to the eater:

"So shall my word be that goeth forth out of my mouth: it shall not return unto me void, but it shall accomplish that which I please, and it shall prosper in the thing whereto I sent it."—Isaiah 55: 10, 11.

What is the backbone of all business? Credit. And what is credit but faith—faith in your fellow-man—faith in his integrity—faith in his willingness and his ability to give you a square deal?

What do you base credit-faith upon? Upon hearsay—upon what your prospective customer has done for others, his promptness in paying them, his willingness to cooperate with them. In many cases you have never seen him—you can't be certain of your own personal knowledge that such a person exists—but you believe in him, you have FAITH. And having faith, your business grows and prospers.

If you can have such faith in a man you have never seen, as to trust large portions of your earthly goods in his hands, can you not put a little trust in the Father, too?

True, you have not seen Him—but you have far greater proof of His being than of that of your customer thousands of miles away. You have far greater proof of His reliability, of His regard for you, of His ability and His willingness at all times to come to your assistance in any right way you may ask. You don't need money with Him. You don't need high standing in your community. You don't need credit.

"Ho, everyone that thirsteth, come ye to the waters, and he that hath no money, come ye, buy, and eat; yea, come, buy wine and milk without money and without price."—Isaiah 55:2.

Then why do not more people "come to the waters?" Because they lack faith.

What is it makes a successful salesman? Faith in his house. Faith in the goods he is selling. Faith in the service they will render his customers. Faith in himself. Have you faith in your "house"—in your Father—in the manifold gifts He offers you so freely?

Men can sell for a little while solely on faith in their own ability, they can palm off anything that will show a profit to themselves. But they never make successful salesmen. The inevitable reaction comes. They grow cynical, lose all faith in others—and eventually lose faith in themselves as well. The successful salesman must have a four-fold faith—faith in his house, faith in his product, faith in the good it will do his customer, faith in himself. Given such a faith, he can sell anything. Given such a faith in the Father, you can do anything.

It wasn't superior courage or superior fighting ability that enabled Washington's half-trained army to beat the

British. English soldiers were showing all over the world that they were second to none in fighting qualities. And the American soldiers were, for the most part, from the same sturdy stock. It was their faith in a greater Power outside themselves.

What is it differentiates the banker from the pawn-broker? Both make loans. Both require security. But where the pawn-broker must have tangible, material property that he can resell before he will lend a cent, the really great banker bases his loans on something bigger than any security that may be offered him—his faith in the borrower.

America was built on faith. Those great railroad builders who spanned the continent knew when they did it that there was not enough business immediately available to make their investment profitable for a long time to come. But they had faith—a faith that was the making of our country.

That same faith is evident on every hand today. Men erect vast factories—in the faith that the public will find need for and buy their products. They build offices, apartments, homes—in the faith that their cities will grow up to the need of them. They put up public utilities capable of serving twice the number of people in their territories—in the faith that the demand will not only grow with the population, but the availability of the supply will help to create new demands.

Faith builds cities and businesses and men. In fact,

everything of good, everything constructive in this old world of ours is based on faith. So if you have it not, *grow it*—as the most important thing you can do. And if you have it, *tend it,* water it, cultivate it—for it is the most important thing in life.

"I give waters in the wilderness, and rivers in the desert, to give drink to my people, my chosen."—Isaiah 43:20.

"If they obey and serve Him, they shall spend their days in prosperity, their years in pleasures."—Job 36:11.

XIII

DISCOURAGEMENT

"Keep thy heart with all diligence, for

Out of it are the issues of life."

—PROVERBS 4:23.

Years ago I read a story about a man who had become so discouraged that he decided to commit suicide.

He had married a widow, and she not only made life a burden for him at home, but spent all his savings, ran him into debt and discredited him with his employers.

He could see only one way out—to jump into the river and end his troubles.

It was Saturday night, so, waiting until late, he slipped out of the house and down through the deserted streets to the bridge.

Imagine the grim humor of it when, from out of the

shadow of one of the great stone towers, a man with a gun stepped forth and commanded—"Hands up!"

Automatically, the discouraged man obeyed, then brought his hands down again as the humor of it gripped him. If this highwayman wanted to save him the trouble of killing himself, let him!

But the highwayman wasn't that obliging. Being a bigger man, he seized the other, held him tightly while he went through the pockets the wife had emptied hours before, then turned him loose and looked him over curiously.

"What's the joke?" he asked roughly, as the intended suicide yielded to another paroxysm of laughter.

Between gasps, the man told him.

"Hum," mused the highwayman, immediately interested, "you ought not to do that. Why don't you just leave the woman? Leave her and start fresh somewhere else."

But the other was too discouraged. His mind was made up. He was going to put an end to his troubles once and for all.

"Well, do this much, anyway," suggested the highwayman. "Give fate a chance. Don't just jump off the bridge, but climb up on the railing there and see how far you can walk. You'll fall over before you've gone far. If you fall on that side—all right, you're a goner and that's the end of it. But if you fall on this side, go back home and give life one more try.

The would-be suicide agreed—so the other boosted

him up on to the rail and he started. Before he had gone twenty feet, he was down—and glad enough, if the truth were told, to fall on the bridge side after looking so close into the jaws of death.

His new-found friend picked him up and helped him home, where Fate chose that opportune moment to show him that the greater the obstacle, the bigger stepping-stone to success it can be made.

But perhaps you will say that only happens in stories. Read the lives of the great and you will never say it again. The difference between failure and success is measured only by your patience and faith—sometimes by inches, sometimes by minutes, sometimes by the merest flash of time.

Take Lincoln. He went into the Black Hawk war a Captain—and came out a private. His store failed—and his surveyor's instruments, on which he depended to eke out a livelihood, were sold for part of the debts. He was defeated in his first try for the Legislature. Defeated in his first attempt for Congress. Defeated in his application for Commissioner of the General Land Office. Defeated for the Senate. Defeated for the nomination for the Vice Presidency in 1856. But did he let that long succession of defeats discourage him? Not he. He held the faith—and made perhaps the greatest President we have ever had.

"He shall not fail nor be discouraged," promised Isaiah (42:4, 6), "till he have set judgment in the earth; and the isles shall wait for his law. Thus saith God the Lord: I the

Lord have called thee in righteousness, and will hold thine hand, and will keep thee."

Then there was Grant. He failed of advancement in the army. Failed as a farmer. Failed as a business man. At 39, he was chopping and delivering cord-wood to keep body and soul together. Nine years later he was President of the United States and had won a martial renown second in this country only to Washington's.

Search the pages of history. You will find them dotted with the names of men whom the world had given up as failures, but who held on to their faith, who kept themselves prepared—and when their chance came they were ready and seized it with both hands.

Napoleon, Cromwell, Patrick Henry, Paul Jones— these are only a few out of thousands.

When Caesar was sent to conquer Gaul, his friends found him one day in a fit of utter despondency. Asked what the matter was, he told them he had just been comparing his accomplishments with Alexander's. At his age, Alexander had conquered the entire known world—and what had Caesar done to compare with that?

But he presently roused himself from his discouragement by resolving to make up as quickly as might be for his lost time. The result? He became the head of the Roman Empire.

"Behold, the Lord thy God hath set the land before

thee; go up and possess it, as the Lord God of thy fathers hath said unto thee; fear not, neither be discouraged."—Deuteronomy 1:21.

The records of business are crowded with the names of middle-aged nobodies who lived to build great fortunes, vast institutions. No man has failed as long as he has faith in the Father, faith in the great scheme of things, faith in himself.

But it takes the kind of simple faith that F. S. Shinn tells of in *The Game of Life and How to Play It.*

A woman was looking for an apartment in New York at the time when apartments were scarcely to be had for love or money.

Her friends told her she would have to store her furniture and live in a hotel. But she held on to her fath. She knew that somewhere was just the apartment she was seeking—and that the Father knew exactly where that apartment was. So she prayed to Him to open the way—prayed in the full confidence that there is a supply for every demand, that her eyes had only to be opened as were Hagar's in the desert.

She knew that if she found the apartment she was going to need new blankets for the winter. But caution said—wait until you find an apartment to put them in. Faith made answer—"Whatsoever ye ask for when ye pray, believe that *ye receive it!*"

What would the first thing be that she would do if she

had the right apartment? Buy blankets. All right, if she had Faith in the Father, she must show her belief. So she went out and bought the blankets.

Needless to say she got the apartment—in what F. S. Shinn describes as a "miraculous way" and in spite of the fact that there were 200 other applicants for the same apartment. She had shown her faith.

YESTERDAY ENDED LAST NIGHT

When Robert Bruce faced the English at the battle of Bannockburn, he had behind him years of failure years of fruitless efforts to drive the English out of Scotland, years of heart-breaking toil in trying to unite the warring elements among the Scotch themselves. True, at the moment a large part of Scotland was in his hands, but so had it been several times before, only to be wrested from him as soon as the English brought together a large enough army.

And now in front of him stood the greatest army England had ever gathered to her banners—hardy veterans from the French Provinces, all the great English nobles with their armored followers, wild Irish, Welsh bowmen—troops from all the dominions of Edward II, over 100,000 men.

To conquer whom Bruce had been able to muster but 30,000 men, brave and hardy, it is true, but lacking the training and discipline of the English.

Was Bruce discouraged? Not he. What though the English had the better archers. What though they were better armed, better trained, better disciplined. He was fighting for freedom—and he *believed* in himself, he believed in his men, he believed in the God of battles.

And, as always, weight, numbers, armament, proved of no avail when confronted with preparation and faith. The vast English host was completely defeated and dispersed. Bruce was firmly seated upon the throne of Scotland, and never more did an invading English army cross its borders.

In Joshua (6 and 7) the Scriptures tell how the Midianites and the Amalekites lay along in the valley like grasshoppers for multitude, and had driven the children of Israel into caves in the mountains. And how Gideon gathered the Israelites together to the number of 30,000 to fight them.

But the Lord said unto Gideon: "The people that are with thee are too many for me to give the Midianites into their hands, lest Israel vaunt themselves against me, saying, Mine own hand hath saved me."

So Gideon told all who were fearful and afraid to depart. And 20,000 left. But still there were too many. So Gideon put the 10,000 that remained to another test, until of the original 30,000, he had only 300 men!

"And the Lord said unto Gideon: By the three hundred will I save you, and deliver the Midianites into thine hand.

"And it came to pass the same night, that the Lord said unto him: Arise, get thee down unto the host; for I have delivered it into thine hand.

"And the three companies blew the trumpets, and brake the pitchers, and held the lamps in their left hands, and the trumpets in their right hands, to blow withal; and they cried, The Sword of the Lord and of Gideon.

"And they stood every man in his place around about the camp; and all the host ran, and cried, and fled."

Never mind how many defeats you have suffered in the past. Don't be concerned about how great the odds may be against you. Below put it well when he said—"It's not the size of the dog in the fight that counts, so much as the size of fight in the dog." And the size of fight in you depends upon your faith—your faith in yourself, in your Father and in your cause. Just remember that yesterday ended last night, and yesterday's defeats with it.

The power which counts is not wealth or weight or numbers or any power that comes from without—but the power that comes from within, the power of the Father. With Him arrayed on your side, you are always in the majority. You don't need to *become* a success—you *are* a success from the moment you become at one with the Father. "Acquaint now thyself with God and be at peace." Cast your burden upon the Father—and go free. He can carry it. In fact, from the moment you can truly cast it upon Him, it ceases to be a burden.

"Come to me, all ye that labor and are heavy laden, and I will give you rest."

Time after time throughout the Bible we are told that

the battle is not ours—but the Lord's. But like all children, we know so much better than the Father how our affairs should be handled that we insist upon running them ourselves.

Is it any wonder they get so tangled as to leave us in the depths of discouragement?

We insist upon having our birthright, and we go into a far country (away from the Father) and lose it. And then how few of us have the courage to come back to the Father, to own up that we have sinned and are unworthy to be called His sons. We would rather feed upon the husks of discouragement and despondency than come back and throw ourselves upon the Father's mercy, leaving the future in His hands, taking His yoke upon us. Yet he assures us—"My yoke is easy and my burden light."

Have you ever, as a child, got into mischief, tried to conceal it from your parents, then gotten in deeper and deeper until finally, in despair, you went to them and made a clean breast of the whole thing? Remember what a relief it was to transfer that load of worry and fear from your small shoulders to their strong ones? Remember how willing you were to assume any "yoke," to suffer any punishment they might inflict, in order to get rid of that crushing weight of worry?

The Father above is as loving, as tender, as merciful as any earthly parent can possibly be, so why not carry your worries to Him in the same spirit?

"INVITED GUESTS"

"A crowd of troubles passed him by
As he with courage waited,
He said: 'Where do you troubles fly
When you are thus belated?'
'We go,' they said, 'to those who mope,
Who look on life dejected.
Who meekly say good-bye to hope.
We go—where we're expected'!"

BY F. E. ALLISON.

When the Black Prince with his little army was penned in by Philip of France, most men would have felt discouraged. For the hosts of France seemed as numerous as the leaves on the trees. While the English were few, and mostly archers. And archers, in that day, were believed to stand no chance against such armored knights as rode behind the banners of Philip.

The French came forward in a great mass, thinking to ride right over that little band of English. But did the Black Prince give way? Not he. He showed the world that a new force had come into warfare, a force that would soon make the armored knight as extinct as the dodo. That force was the common soldier—the archer.

Just as the Scotch spearmen overthrew the chivalry of England on the field of Bannockburn, just as infantry have over-thrown both cavalry and artillery in many a later battle, so did the "common men" of England—the archers—decide the fate of the French at Crecy. From being despised and looked down upon by every young upstart with armor upon his back, the "common men"—the spearmen and archers—became the backbone of every successful army. And from what looked like certain annihilation, the Black Prince by his faith in himself and his men became one of the greatest conquerors of his day.

Troubles flocked to him, but he didn't recognize them as troubles—he thought them opportunities. And used them to raise himself and his soldiers to the pinnacle of success.

"Have I not commanded thee? Be strong and of a good courage; be not afraid, neither be thou dismayed; for the Lord thy God is with thee whithersoever thou goest."—Joshua 1:9.

There are just as many prizes in business as in war—just as many opportunities to turn seeming troubles into blessings. But those prizes go to the men like the Black Prince who don't know a trouble when they meet it—who welcome it, take it to their bosoms, and get from it their greatest blessings.

I know a man who was "stuck" with 50,000 traveling bags—and the bank was pressing him to repay the money it had loaned on them.

Did he weep? Did he get discouraged and quit? Not

he! He developed a brand new market, an entirely new list he had never even thought of before, and not only sold his 50,000, but a lot more besides.

I know another man who was selling a special kind of poultry feed shortly after the war. And poultry feed seemed so in demand that he contracted for ten carloads of it. A few months passed, and the bottom dropped out of the market—leaving him with a warehouse full of poultry feed, and five more cars to come!

Did he get discouraged and quit? Not he! He got up a prize contest, that so stimulated the interest in poultry feed that he sold not only all that he had, not alone the five cars on the way, but three additional carloads!

Nearly every man can look back—and not so far back either with most of us—and recall cases like that where, by facing seeming troubles determinedly, he opened up entirely new resources, turned seeming troubles into his greatest blessings.

You can treat ALL troubles that same way, if you will just hold the faith, resist discouragement, and call upon the Father for help.

But yield to discouragement, and even though good come of your trial, you will lose the key to it. You will be like the man who knew that somewhere along the ocean shore was a pebble that would turn iron into gold. He started out full of hope and enthusiasm, picking up pebbles and touching them to the iron bracelet he wore.

But after a time he became discouraged. He still walked on, picking up pebbles, touching them to the bracelet and throwing them down again, but he did it mechanically, paying no attention to what he was doing.

As the sun was setting, he glanced down at the bracelet—to find, to his astonishment, *that it was turned to gold!*

But, alas! The stone that did it was lost, somewhere back along his way. He had held it—used it—and thrown it away!

What is the use of holding on to life—unless you at the same time hold on to your faith? What is the use of going through the daily grind, the wearisome drudgery—if you have given up hoping for the rewards, and unseeing let them pass you by?

Suppose business and industry did that? How far would they get? It is simply by holding on hopefully, believing, watchfully—as Kipling put it: "Forcing heart and nerve and sinew to serve your turn long after they are gone, and so hold on when there is nothing in you except the will which says to them: 'Hold on'!"—that many a business man has worked out his salvation.

Take the metal mines, as an instance: Supposedly worthless mines have now become productive, slag heaps have suddenly become worth millions, all through a froth that was discovered almost by accident!

Writing in *The Compressed Air Magazine,* Gail Martin says: "Froth is raising millions of tons of minerals each year to a state of high commercial value. An oily, fluffy, dirty-grey froth is separating complex minerals into valuable products. Difficult smelting problems have been overcome; waste has been converted into profitable ore; and all through the discovery that froth can be made to accomplish what no other known agency will do as effectively. Three years ago, plants in Salt Lake Valley poured on their slag dumps daily about 100,000 pounds of zinc—$2,000,000 worth annually. Today, the greater part of this metal is saved."

But do you suppose it would ever have been saved if industry had simply sat back discouraged, or if, like the man on the seashore, its efforts had been merely mechanical?

It is not enough to work. The horse and the ox do that. And when we work without thought, without hope, we are no better than they. It is not enough to merely hold on. The poorest creatures often do that mechanically, for lack of the courage to let go.

If you are to gain the reward of your labors, if you are to find relief from your drudgery, you have got to hold on hopefully, believingly, confidently—knowing that the answer is in the great heart of the Father, knowing that He is not only willing but anxious to give it to you, the moment you have prepared yourself to receive it.

It is never the gifts that are lacking. It is never the Father who is backward in answering our desires. It is we who are unable to see, who fail to recognize the good, because our thoughts are all of discouragement and lack. We dwell on the evil we see around us—and troubles come a-flocking around our heads. When all we need to do is to disclaim the evil and look for the good that is rightfully ours—and the Father's good gifts will compass us about.

"This book of the law shall not depart out of thy mouth; but thou shalt meditate therein day and night, that thou mayest observe to do according to all that is written therein: for then thou shalt make thy way prosperous, and then thou shalt have good success."

—JOSHUA 1:8.

XIV

THE BLACK MOUNTAIN

"If thou faint in the day of adversity, thy strength is small."

PROVERBS 24:10.

"Let not him that wavereth think that he shall receive anything from the Lord."

—JAMES 1:7.

In ancient days, there was believed to lie far out in the South Seas an island on which stood a great black mountain. This mountain was so highly magnetized that if a ship approached within miles of it, the attraction of the mountain would draw to it all the iron work—even the nails—right out of the ship, with the result that the vessel would speedily fall to pieces.

The story goes that a certain Sultan Agib, setting sail with his fleet to explore those seas, was caught by a typhoon and blown far out of his course until, when the clouds lifted, he found himself and his ships headed straight for the Black Mountain.

Before they could change their course, the attraction of the mountain began to make itself felt. First their swords and spears and the loose pieces of iron round about the decks, then the nails and iron-work of the boats themselves, were picked up as by a magic hand and whirled toward the mountain, where they attached themselves with a resounding whang! In a few minutes the ships began to go to pieces, and the Sultan and his men found themselves struggling in the waves.

Agib managed to fasten himself to a plank, and with its aid after a desperate struggle reached the shore of the island.

Finding no other of his men there, he undertook to climb the mountain, which with much labor he succeeded in doing. At the top he discovered a great dome of brass, set up on brazen pillars. On it stood a horse and rider of brass, the rider bearing on his breast a leaden plate with talismanic characters engraved upon it.

Agib entered the dome, and casting himself upon his knees, gave fervent thanks to God for his deliverance. Then, worn out, he lay down and slept. In his sleep a gray-bearded old man appeared to him and bid him arise, dig up the ground at a certain spot, and he would there find a bow of brass and three arrows of lead. "Shoot the arrows," the old man commanded him, "at the lead plate on the statue's breast. If but one hit there, horse and rider will tumble over into the sea, and thereafter the Black Mountain will lose all power for evil."

Agib awoke and did as he had been commanded. With the third arrow he struck the leaden plate, and immediately horse and rider tumbled into the sea. Thereupon the sea began to rise until it completely covered the Black Mountain. Only the dome of brass was left above the waves. There the Sultan took refuge, until a boat came that way and carried him back toward his own dominions.

So ended the Black Mountain (or so the ancient legend has it).

Would that the Black Mountain of today were as easily disposed of. For there is a Black Mountain. And every craft that comes within its influence has all the iron (all the courage) drawn out of it.

Its name is FEAR.

What is it that makes the boa constrictor's prey so still and powerless—unable to save itself by flight?   *Fear.*

What is it sends the horse back into the burning barn to its death?   *Fear.*

What is it makes men helpless in emergencies, unnerves them, turns them into panic-stricken mobs in fires or disasters?   *Fear.*

Fear is the Black Mountain that robs those under its influence of manhood, of courage, of reason. And the Man of Brass who sits so proudly mounted on its dome is the Devil—the only Satan there is—the *Devil of Fear.*

But to every man is given a brass bow and three leaden arrows which can overthrow that devil. To every man is given a sea of courage which can drown the Black Mountain, once its ruler is overthrown. The brass bow is named Faith—faith in the Father. "For He hath said, I will never leave thee, nor forsake thee. So that we may boldly say, the Lord is my helper and I will not fear what man shall do unto me."—Hebrews 13:5-6.

The three leaden arrows are:

1st—The Arrow of Light—bringing the thing feared out into the light of day so it can be seen in all its nakedness. The psycho-analysts, with all their over-emphasis of sex, have brought out one valuable thing—the harm that repression causes. If they would study fear more and sex less, they would get further.

Take the shell-shocked veterans of the war. You will find some of them creeping miserably around the walls of the room, never daring to cross the open. Why? Trench fear. Fear of death in the open places.

Doctors have told me that many of those most successful in treating shell-shocked cases were not medical men at all, but sympathetic, understanding men and women from all walks of life who could win the soldiers' confidence, get them to talk, to confide in them, to tell them exactly *what it was they feared*.

Bringing the spectre out into the open destroyed it. They slew the Demon of Darkness with the Arrow of Light.

"God hath *not* given us the spirit of fear, but of *POWER* and of love and of a sound mind."—II Tim. 1:7.

2nd—Walking up to the thing you fear. Nine times out of ten you find it is stuffed—a scarecrow—an image of straw.

You have probably heard the story of the lame man and the bully. The bully had such a reputation that whenever he started after a man, the other ran. And, of course, the bully jumped on him from behind and had him whipped before the fight really began.

But one day he went after a lame man. And the lame man realized he couldn't get away by running. His only chance lay in fighting. So he stood his ground. And so desperately did he fight that it was the bully who ran.

One of the few genuine ghost stories I have heard was told me by an old Civil War veteran years ago. Jim Youell was his name. He had enlisted in the war as a drummer boy at sixteen and stayed in it for four years. When the war was over he went back to his West Virginia mountain home.

One night, calling on some friends, the talk drifted around to ghosts. Youell laughed at the idea. But it developed that a number of people in the neighborhood had seen a headless ghost near a little cemetery Youell would have to pass on his way home. So he promised them he would pay the ghost a call.

'Twas a blustery winter night, the ground covered with snow, the moonlight peeking out for brief intervals from behind the clouds.

Youell got as far as the cemetery, in a scoffing mood still, and stood looking down at the graves. Nothing there, certainly, that looked like a ghost. And he turned to start home. But the sight that met him froze him in his tracks!

Over among the trees, some fifty yards away, was something that moved silently toward him, pausing ever and again—but coming nearer and nearer. It was white, and it looked like the figure of a small man—without a head!

Youell was a brave man, but he could feel the hair on his head rising, and he had an almost irresistible impulse to turn and run. Almost he did it—but the thought of his scoffing friends held him back, and the courage gained in a dozen battles soon nerved him anew. He decided to stalk this ghost—but from the side, and from the shelter of the graveyard wall!

Gun in hand, he crept silently along until he felt sure he was behind and to the side of the phantom. Then looked cautiously out—and dropped his gun, swearing with heartfelt relief. The ghost was a white "muley" cow!

Jim Youell was well over sixty when I knew him—lean and wiry, yet tireless as a wolf. He had been foreman and mine superintendent for years in as lawless a country as ever made the West famous. He had worked his mines peacefully through a dozen feuds, when to hire a man from one side was to enlist every man on the other as your enemy. He carried a gun—and knew how to use it. Yet he never had to. Why? Because he believed in walking right up to every danger and facing it openly. And each, in turn, faded silently away.

One instance I saw. A man named Jenkins—a mountaineer, with a reputation for meanness, and a rifle that wasn't above shooting from ambush.

Jenkins had bluffed his way with so many mine foremen that he felt he could get anything he wanted—merely by being ugly enough about it. One day he tried it on Jim Youell—to find himself presently on his way home, out of a job.

He went into executive session with his wife and a jug of "white mule," and the upshot of the conference was that Youell must be removed.

Youell by then was far away in the depths of the mine, but late that afternoon a telephone call reached him. There was another exit a mile to the south of the tipple. Hadn't he better take it home that evening? Why? Because Jenkins was waiting at the tipple with his rifle, vowing to "get" him the moment he came down, and drunk enough not to care how he did it.

"Waiting for me, is he?" flared up the old man. "Well, you just keep him there for ten minutes. I'll show him all of me he'll ever want to see again." And made for the drift mouth and tipple as fast as he could go.

When the ten minutes were up, Youell was very much present, but the "bad man" had taken his rifle and his reputation and departed to parts unknown.

A man of straw—but he lorded it over those around him until one came along with the courage to walk up to the scarecrow and pull out the straw.

"And David said to Solomon, his son: Be strong and of good courage, and do it. Fear not, nor be dismayed. For the Lord God, even my God, will be with thee. He will not fail thee, nor forsake thee, until thou hast finished all the work for the service of the house of the Lord."— I Chronicles 28:20.

3rd—The last and the surest arrow is casting the burden upon the Father. There are times when the most fearless facing of our troubles, when talking them over most freely, still seems to leave them insuperable as before. Those are the times when we must use our last arrow—and go free!

Whether it be sickness, or lack, or trouble, there is always a way out for the determined soul. And casting the burden upon the Father opens that way out.

"You have won," wrote a subscriber in South Carolina a short time ago. "Your books came at a time when impatient creditors were pressing us on every side. I could see no way out, and I told myself that if your philosophy could solve the problem, it would have stood the acid test. So I shot my last arrow.

"The next morning the Referee in Bankruptcy was to hold the hearing.

"When I left to attend that meeting nothing had happened. Two hours later our local banker appeared at the meeting and announced that he would advance every penny necessary to pay urgent obligations and carry on the business—without a promise from us, without having examined our books, without taking any precautions for the security of his money!"

He stopped worrying. He felt that he had done everything humanly possible. He cast the burden upon the Father—*and went free!*

The greatest successes have been built upon such temporary failures as his—failure that still left people with every confidence in his integrity, his ability, his courage. At the very point of failure and discouragement, you are often nearest to success.

"January 1, 1926," writes another friend from Pasadena, "found me very nearly broke, with immediate requirements for money. I sat down by myself and realized that help was always available and would speedily come.

"At five o'clock one of my friends called. I had never mentioned my need to him. He dropped ten $100 bills and a check for $1,000 on my desk, saying—'It's the least I can do. I felt somehow that you could use it, and if it helps out any, I am glad.' That was all!"

All through Lindbergh's story of his amazing flight, you sense the fact that he was depending not merely on his inadequate instruments, not alone upon his mechanically perfect machine, but upon that higher Power that "who hath gathered the winds in His fists"—the Father. The "We" he so constantly referred to was not only the plane and he—but the Father, too.

It was through no accident that in the ancient story of the Black Mountain, the Sultan was shown as having missed with his first two arrows—but the third went true. It is the one arrow that never misses, that can always be depended upon to topple over the devil of fear.

"For I thy God will hold thy right hand, saying unto thee, fear not; I will help thee."—Isaiah 41:13.

I know a man who was faced with the threat of an expensive lawsuit. There seemed nothing he could do to prevent it, so he shot his third arrow. He put the situation in the Father's hands, realizing that there is only one Mind—not minds a-many—and that there can be no conflict in Divine Mind. And there he left it.

The case was settled out of court without the cost of a penny!

There is nothing to fear in life. It is "our own hand that smites us"—not the hand of God. Today can always be managed. It is because we pile the memory of past troubles and the fear of future ones upon our backs that our load seems heavy.

The purpose of this entire universe is the working out of the supreme good of every soul in it.

Just remember that when troubles assail you. It is all right. Keep your grip on that principle, and it will turn seeming evil into the most certain good. Say to every trouble that confronts you—"You may not be a very pleasant thing to look upon now, but I am going to turn you into one of the best little workers I have."

Then *use it*—use it to good purpose. Like Jacob and the angel, make it bless you.

A great American once said—"Get rid of your regrets. You are what you are because of the obstacles you have overcome. Rightly applied, even errors can be a blessing."

And one of the country's greatest neurologists says— "The three main classes of destructive moods are: 1 Harboring a grudge. 2 Dwelling upon the past. 3 Playing the martyr."

The past is dead and done with. Forget it! Forget its grudges and resentments as well as its regrets.

Mankind's journey through life is an exploring journey—a forward-looking journey. There will be obstacles in your way, there will be savage tribes to fight and conquer—but you have an impenetrable shield in the protection of the Father. "Fear not, I am thy shield and thy exceeding great reward."—Genesis 15:1. You have a weapon nothing can withstand in your bow of brass and three leaden arrows.

So never worry about the morrow. Live today to its fullest. Joy in it. Serve in it. Know that you cannot expect too much from the Father, for—"The Father loveth the son and hath given all things into his hands."—John 3:35.

Then shall you be like the Psalmist of old:

"Though an host should encamp against me, my heart shall not fear: though war should rise against me, in this will I be confident.

"One thing have I desired of the Lord, that will I seek after; that I may dwell in the house of the Lord all the days of my life, to behold the beauty of the Lord, and to inquire in his temple.

"For in the time of trouble he shall hide me in his pavilion: in the secret of his tabernacle shall he hide me: he shall set me up upon a rock."

—PSALMS 27:3-5.

XV

THE DRAGON'S TEETH

"Be strong and of good courage. Be not afraid, neither be thou dismayed. For the Lord thy God is with thee whithersoever thou goest."

—JOSHUA 1:9.

"Then shalt thou walk in thy way safely, and thy foot shall not stumble.

"When thou liest down, thou shalt not be afraid: yea, thou shalt lie down, and thy sleep shall be sweet.

"Be not afraid of sudden fear, neither of the desolation of the wicked, when it cometh."

—PROVERBS 3:23-25.

There was once a King's son named Cadmus. Sent forth on a certain mission by his father, he was so fortunate as to overcome a great dragon.

Prompted thereto then by a soothsayer, he cut out the dragon's teeth and sowed them in the ground. What was his astonishment to see these strange seeds spring up as full-armed warriors!

Espying him, they immediately started in his direction, and so threatening did they look that Cadmus ran and concealed himself among the trees. From that safe hiding place he threw stones among them until he started the warriors fighting among themselves, which they did so fiercely that they soon killed each other off.

Or so the ancient tale avers. But there is nothing ancient in the application of it. It belongs to you and me and all of us. For there is nothing we are more prone to than sowing dragon's teeth, to spring up and threaten ourselves.

When the Prophet of old told his people—"It is thine own hand that smiteth thee," he uttered a truth that is worldwide in its application.

Sounds unbelievable, I know, to say that the only evils we meet are those of our own making, but incredible as it may sound, it is nevertheless true. Emerson had the same idea when he wrote—"My children, on life's highway you will meet nothing worse than yourself."

How do we do it? By sowing the dragon's teeth of fear, by imaging disaster—fire and flood and sickness and want, by charging our mental magnets with thoughts of all the evil things that may happen to us and thus actually drawing them upon ourselves.

There are two worlds—the House of our Father, and the Far Country to which the Prodigal Son ventured. The one is the world that God created, the other is the one made by man. It is yours to choose which you shall live in.

The House of the Father is everywhere. In it is no sickness, no accident, no want. "In my Father's house there is bread and to spare." It extends everywhere. It protects under any circumstance. You can live in it, you can keep your loved ones secure under its roof.

The Far Country, too, is all around you. You have but to step outside the House of the Father to be in it. And there you can find all the excitement you may wish—fire and flood and accident, disease and poverty and want. There is riotous living there—and abject poverty. Sorrow and pleasure and trouble. But real happiness—no! There is no room for happiness because of the ever-present fear of loss.

Fear is the one universal visitant in that Far Country. It stalks through every shadow. It lurks in every corner. It is the skeleton at every feast.

Does a man meet good fortune? "Look out for the rainy day," whispers Fear. "It is just around the corner."

Is he strong, healthy, full of the joy of living? "The very kind that fall easiest victims to the most dread diseases," chuckles Fear at his elbow.

Has he a happy family, a loving wife, wonderful children? "Careful," admonishes Fear, "a lot of accidents these days. Something may happen to them any minute."

Fear keeps the people of that Far Country in daily, hourly dread. Yet, like the prisoner so accustomed to his chains that he hugs them to him and refuses to be released, many delight in it. They get a morbid pleasure from recounting their troubles, from dwelling upon them; they delight in reading all the intimate, gruesome details of the troubles of others, never realizing or perhaps not caring that they are thus insuring the continuance of their own difficulties, and often bringing upon themselves disasters similar to those they gloated over.

They read articles, they scan advertisements, they listen to long talks describing in detail every symptom, every characteristic, of the things they fear—and immediately think to see these Dragon's teeth springing up in their own bodies or those of their children. Words crystallize thought, you know. Words are great forces in the realm of life. Be careful of their use. Who talks of hate, of poverty, of sickness, but sets rife these very elements to mar his fate.

And yet—it is all so unnecessary. "In my Father's House there are many mansions," said Jesus. Plenty of room for all. Plenty of "bread." Plenty of protection. Plenty of life and health and happiness. Why not at least put our loved ones there, out of danger?

How to do it? How to win the blessings so lavishly promised in the Scriptures? The directions are plain:

"For he that will love life, and see good days, let him refrain his tongue from evil, and his lips that they speak no guile:

"Let him eschew evil, and do good; let him seek peace, and ensue it.

"For the eyes of the Lord *are* over the righteous, and his ears *are open* unto their prayers: but the face of the Lord *is* against them that do evil.

"And who *is* he that will harm you, if ye be followers of that which is good?"

—I PETER 2:10-13.

The most valuable characteristic of the mind is its ability to attract to itself whatever it is charged with. It is, in effect, a powerful magnet. But when you charge your mental magnet with thoughts or fears of evil, you turn that very power against yourself or your loved ones.

When sickness and epidemics are rampant, when "the devil, as a roaring lion, walketh about seeking whom he may devour," don't sow the Dragon's teeth of fear in your children, don't put them in the way of the "devil" by being fearful for them.

"It is not the will of your Father that one of these little ones should perish," said Jesus.—Matthew 18:14.

Have confidence in that promise. Put them in the Father's House. Know that He is in them, even as they are in Him, that they are dwelling "in the secret place of the Most High, abiding under the shadow of the Almighty," and that where He is, no evil—no devil—can remain. Then calmly rest in that faith, no matter what threatens.

"One prays," said Marcus Aurelius, "how shall I not lose my son? Do thou pray thus—how shall I not *fear* to lose him."

If the Pagan Emperor of the Romans, who could find no idol in which to trust, could sense the fact that it was the *fear of loss* which brought the loss about—how much more we, with "a God who carries us," should cast out fear, should place our children in the care of the Father, should give His angels charge over them—and calmly trust.

Your son or daughter has a definite place in the Father's plan. He didn't "just happen." He has certain work to do, which no other can do as well. He has a definite niche to fill, which will go empty if aught happens to him.

When the Father imaged him, He did it because He wanted him, He needed him. Don't you suppose, then, that He did all that was necessary to insure his safety until his work should be done? Don't you know that "He gave

His angels charge over him, to lead him and to keep him in all his ways?"

Remember David's adjuration to Solomon, his son. "Fear not, nor be dismayed. For the Lord God, even my God, will be with thee. He will not fail thee, not forsake thee, *until thou hast finished all the work for the service of the house of the Lord."*—I Chronicles 28:20.

Every good is for "the service of the house of the Lord," for the House of the Father is everywhere. The work your child has to do is just as important, in the Father's eyes, as was Solomon's. So have no fear for him. The Father will not fail him, nor forsake him, until he has finished it.

Why, then, do sickness and epidemics, fire and flood and accident, take such toll of children, of young men and women whose work is still all before them?

Why? Because we take them out of the Father's house, we refuse His care and protection, we sow the Dragon's Teeth of Fear all around them, and those Dragon's Teeth spring up and destroy them.

We can't serve two masters, you know. As Jesus said— "We hate the one and love the other."—Luke 16:13.

Of course, we would all vigorously deny that we hate the Father. But what better is it than hate when we put our trust in His opposite—Fear—the Devil? Did Fear ever bring us anything of good? Did Fear ever help us in danger? Did he ever fail to do us harm when we entertained him?

The Father, on the other hand—has He ever failed us when we really put our trust in Him? In fire, or storm, or accident, or disease—when we abandoned all dependence upon material means and put our trust utterly in Him, have you ever known Him to refuse His help?

> "And when the servant of the man of God was risen early, and gone forth, behold, an host compassed the city both with horses and chariots. And his servant said unto him, Alas, my master! how shall we do?
>
> "And he answered, Fear not: for they that be with us are more than they that be with them.
>
> "And Elisha prayed, and said, Lord, I pray thee, open his eyes, that he may see. And the Lord opened the eyes of the young man; and he saw: and, behold, the mountain was full of horses and chariots of fire round about Elisha."
>
> —II KINGS 6:15-17.

In the House of the Father, mankind has been given an absolute protection from all evil—from sickness, from disaster, from want. And the password that carries you into that house is Faith, utter faith in the Father within.

In olden times, such simple faith was common. Today the age is too sophisticated. It would rather depend upon the efficacy of a rabbit's foot to ward off evil—on pills, on the virus of diseased animals, on the hair of the dog that bites them.

It has substituted for the protection of the Father every device of man, forgetting that the devices of each generation are laughed at by succeeding ones, as being efficacious only insofar as they relieve the mind of fear.

Ten plagues were visited upon the Egyptians, but, though the Israelites were in and among them, not a single one of the plagues touched them. Why? Because they had placed themselves under the protection of the Father.

"And I will sever in that day the land of Goshen in which my people dwell, that no swarms of flies shall be there."—Exodus 8:22.

Plagues of blood, of toads, of lice, of flies, of boils, of murrain, of hail, of locusts, of darkness and of death—all these were visited upon Egypt—but all of these the chosen people escaped.

And though all the ten plagues were visited upon the world again today, those who enter into His house may just as surely escape.

"When he seeth the blood upon the lintel, and on the two side posts, the Lord will pass over the door, and will not suffer the destroyer to come in unto your houses to smite you."—Exodus 12:23.

"When God gave man life upon this earth," writes Albert C. Grier in *Truth's Cosmology*, "He gave him perfect protection against every one of its seeming evils. He gave him a kind of protection he does not need to go to the university to discover—he does not need to wait thousands of years for inventions to show it to him. God gave him the kind of protection a baby can and does have. He gave him the kind of protection the simplest mind in all the world can discern and the astutest mind might find difficulty in discovering. He gave him the power of absolute safety from every wind of adversity, from every form of disaster the world can bring upon him."

Why doesn't the Father forcibly prevent us from getting into evil? Because that way no progress lies. And man's mission here on earth is to progress, to prove his Sonship to God.

Just as the mother bird throws its young from the nest to make them learn to fly, so does the Father throw you upon your resources to make you learn how to live.

Just as the mother bird flutters around her young, watching over them, urging them on, so is the Father ever behind you, ready to lend a helping hand, asking you only to do your best—then lean on Him in perfect faith for anything else you may need. "The eternal God is thy refuge, and underneath are the everlasting arms."—Deuteronomy 33:27.

Go through the Bible from Genesis to Revelation and see how many pages you will have left if you tear out the records of men and nations that were protected by God in answer to their faith and prayer.

"They that trust in the Lord shall be as Mount

Zion, which cannot be removed, but abideth forever."—Psalms 125:1.

When evil threatens you, when everything looks dark and there seems no way out, enter into the House of the Father—put the situation in His hands and let go! Realize that He is all about you—in the very air you breathe—His arms beneath you, His hand at once your shield and your support. "Acquaint now thyself with Him, and be at peace; thereby good shall come unto thee." Job 22:21.

Realize that evil is not an entity in itself—merely the absence of good. You have lost your connection with the source of all good. So get back into the House of the Father, recognize and claim your sonship, ask of Him what you need, and auguries of evil will be turned into harbingers of good. The good is always there, if you will but recognize it. The evil has no power, except the power your belief and that of those around you give to it.

"Observe and hear all these words which I command thee, that it may go well with thee, and with thy children after thee forever, when thou doest that which is good and right in the sight of the Lord thy God."—Deuteronomy 12:28.

Cease from worrying about your health, about your affairs, about your children. Don't you know that your very fears and worries are responsible for the diseases and accidents and failures that come into your life? Don't you know that you are sowing Dragon's teeth? Fear pictures these conditions in the mental realm, and what you mold there is sooner or later objectified in your physical surroundings.

Know that the Father has an antidote for every poison, a panacea for every ill, an answer for every prayer. "There shall no evil befall thee, neither shall any plague come nigh thy dwelling."—Psalms 91:10.

But merely to know that *He* has the answer is not enough. You must visualize it—see it as YOURS in your own thoughts—KNOW THAT YOU HAVE IT in the realm of the REAL, the realm wherein you have all power, the realm that can be reached only on the wings of faith. Realize that you HAVE it there, and you will speedily find that your mental crucible has brought it into being in the realm of the physical as well.

When? *Now!* The very minute you can show perfect faith, *that* minute you can manifest the object of your desires. It matters not how remote they may seem, how hopeless they may appear to those around you. If it is right for you to have them, you can manifest them right there and now.

"Say not ye, there are yet four months and then cometh the harvest? Behold I say unto you, lift up your eyes and look in the fields. For they are white already to harvest."—John 4:35.

All of good is already yours in the House of the Father. Don't wait to claim it—enter there now on the wings of faith—enter and take possession as His son, His rightful heir.

"And Hezekiah wrought that which was good and right and true before the Lord his God.

"And in every work that he began in the service of the house of God, and in the law, and in the commandments, to seek his God, he did it with all his heart, and prospered.

"And Hezekiah had exceeding much riches and honour: and he made himself treasuries for silver, and for gold, and for precious stones, and for spices, and for shields, and for all manner of pleasant jewels;

"Storehouses also for the increase of corn, and wine, and oil; and stalls for all manner of beasts, and cotes for flocks.

"Moreover he provided him cities, and possessions of flocks and herds in abundance: for God had given him substance very much.

"This same Hezekiah also stopped the upper watercourse of Gihon, and brought it straight down to the west side of the city of David. And Hezekiah prospered in all his works."

—II CHRONICLES 31:20, 21; 32:27-30.

XVI

THE UNDYING FIRE— LOVE AND MARRIAGE

"There be three things which are too wonderful for me, yea, four which I know not:

"The way of an eagle in the air; the way of a serpent upon a rock; the way of the sea; and the way of a man with a maid."

—PROVERBS 30:18, 19.

Last Spring when the Mississippi was in flood and the government sent its warnings throughout the adjoining states, an old negro preacher in Louisiana conceived the idea that he was a second Noah. Calling his flock together, he told them that the flood was coming and he had been commissioned by God to build the ark that would save them.

So they set to work, constructing a great ark which should hold all their possessions, their cattle, their horses, everything that was theirs. When the waters drew near and relief boats came, they sent them contemptuously away. Embark on those old flat boats when they had an ark all their own? They laughed at the idea.

The waters came and the preacher and his flock withdrew into the ark—their cattle and their chickens and all that was theirs with them.

The waters rose, the while the relief boats stood anxiously by, but all went well—until the waves lapped the sides of the ark. Then that frightened flock discovered they had overlooked one important essential—they had failed to caulk the seams! The water poured in between them faster than it could be bailed out.

And so it often is with marriage. To the lonely man or maid, to one craving love or companionship, to those looking for a haven of refuge from a work-a-day world, marriage seems an Ark of Happiness.

But when rainy days come, when the waters of trouble and sickness and poverty rise around it, too often it is found that the seams have not been caulked. Instead of an ark, it was merely a few planks of self-gratification, nailed together by passion, and temporarily roofed over by mutual infatuation. A few heavy storms will unroof it, a few waves of adversity break it apart and set the two voyagers crying shrilly for the relief boat—"Divorce."

That is no way to build an ark that will carry you safely all through life.

It would be foolish to lay down rules for happiness, but there are four cardinal principles that every couple, young or old, can well bear in mind:

First, you must lay a keel of mutual respect. Without it, any high wind may upset your craft.

Second, you must have a framework of love. Not mere infatuation, mind you, not selfish passion only, but the kind of love that delights in *giving*—that seeks first the happiness and the good of the one loved.

Third, to make your craft water-tight, it should be boarded with planks of mutual tastes, of a liking for the same things—above all, similar views on religion. These make mental bonds of comradeship which reinforce the physical ones. But the whole must be caulked with the oakum of liberal-mindedness—of each recognizing the other's individuality and not trying to foist his ideas or opinions upon her.

Fourth, your craft should be decked over with generous appreciation on the part of each for everything about the other.

Neither these nor any other rules can be called sure guides to wedded bliss. For, like Greek verbs, there are more irregular than regular cases. But at least they offer you a seaworthy craft which, with ordinary care, will ride through any storm you may meet on life's way.

"And now abideth Faith, Hope, Love, these three; but the greatest of these is Love."—I Corinthians 13.

In an old newspaper clipping, I remember reading of a fire on the hearth of a farmhouse in Missouri, that has not been out for eighty years.

When the builder of that old homestead left Kentucky with his young bride eighty years before, he took with him some live coals from the home fireplace, swinging in an iron pot slung from the rear axle of his prairie schooner.

Matches were unknown in those days, and the making of fire from flint and steel was too uncertain. So all through the long trek from Kentucky to Missouri, he kept that little fire alive, finally transferring it to his new log cabin home.

There his children grew and prospered. There he lived and there he died—by the light and warmth of that living fire.

So it must be with love—an undying fire. There will be scorched fingers at times, of course. There will be gusts of anger that blow the embers in all directions, there will be tempests that seem to quench the flame entirely—but you must never let them be quenched. You must nurse them back into life with forgiveness, bring back the glow with forbearance, keep the fire alive with undying faith.

> *"Love suffereth long, and is kind;*
> *Love envieth not;*
> *Love vauntech not itself, is not puffed up.*
> *Doth not behave itself unseemly*

Seeketh not her own,
Is not easily provoked,
Thinketh no evil;
Rejoiceth not in iniquity, but rejoiceth in the truth;
Beareth all things; believeth all things,
Hopeth all things, endureth all things."

—I Corinthians 13:4-7.

Have you ever read the story of Procrustes? Procrustes was one of the most notorious robbers of olden days. He kept an inn into which he enticed the unwary traveler. In that inn was a certain bed which every traveler had to fit. Procrustes would tie the traveler in it and measure him. If he proved too short, that was unfortunate, for Procrustes would stretch him until he was the right length. If he were too long, that was still more unfortunate, for the robber would trim off either end of his person until he fitted.

Sounds gruesome, but is it any more so than the constant nagging some husbands and wives subject their partners to, in their efforts to make them fit their particular standards?

The ancient Greeks had a legend that all things were created by love. In the beginning, all men were happy. Love reigned supreme, and life was everywhere. Then one night while Love slept, Hate came—and everything became discordant, unhappy, dying.

Thereafter, when the sun of Love rose, life was renewed, happiness abounded. But when the night of Hate came, then came discord also, and sorrow and ashes.

And truly, without love, life would be dead—a thing of wormwood and death. Ask some of these selfish old bachelors, with none to share their loneliness, with none to care whether they live or die. No worse fate can befall a man than to live and grow old alone—unloved and unloving.

"Better a dinner of herbs where love is, than a stalled ox and hatred therewith."—Proverbs 15:16.

Why do you want to live tomorrow? Because there is someone you love—who loves you—whom you want to see, to be with, to watch and serve. To love much is to live much. To love forever is to live forever.

Easy enough to speak platitudes, I hear you say, but how shall we go about picking the right mate?

First, there must be some physical attraction. By that, I don't mean that the girl must be a reigning beauty, or the man an Apollo. Beauty, while an asset, is in no way an essential to desirability and charm. Girls do not win happiness by looks alone—they never have and never will.

The most fascinating women in history—Cleopatra, Helen of Troy, Catherine the Great, Queen Elizabeth, Madame de Pompadour—none of them had beautiful features. Cleopatra's nose was much too big—but that didn't keep her from holding the ruler of the then-known world under her thumb for ten long years, and after his death, subjugating Antony in his turn.

Of course, she had something else—as did all these famous women of history—something stronger, more subtle, more fascinating than beauty. She had charm—that enticing, bewildering thing called feminine charm. The same charm that is born in every daughter of Eve who has the brains to use it.

What is charm? Charm is that something in the glance of your eyes, the turn of your head, the touch of your hand, that sends an electric thrill through every fiber of the one man at whom it is directed. Charm is taking the gifts that God has given you and keeping them supernally young and fresh and vivid. Charm is being so exquisitely alive and buoyant, keeping the magnet within you so surcharged with the joy of life, that even poor features are lost sight of in the bewitching attraction of the whole.

James Montgomery Flagg once spoke of the age where every girl not sick or a cripple is lovely. Charm is keeping that loveliness all through life. It can be done—*is* being done every day.

"Though we travel the world over to find the beautiful," wrote Emerson, "we must carry it with us or we find it not." Charm is not to be bought in jars or bottles. Nor is beauty. Both must come from within. Both spring from that magnet of life which is in your subconscious mind.

There are women who seem to have been born tired—never exactly sick, never entirely well. They don't go out because they don't get any fun out of play. They are sallow, listless, having neither charm nor personality, because they have allowed the magnet of life within them to run down. To them I would say—renew your health first, renew your energy and vigor, renew your interest in those around you—*then* begin to look for a fit mate. For love, says Browning, is energy of life.

> *"For life, with all it yields of joy or woe*
> *And hope and fear,*
> *Is just our chance of the prize of learning love—*
> *How love might be, hath been indeed, and is."*

As for men, beauty of face or feature is even less important than with women. Character, strength, a cheeriness that shines through storm and cloud—these are the attributes that attract, these are the characteristics that most women admire. And mutual admiration, mutual attraction, are the first essentials of a happy marriage.

How to inspire that feeling in another? By first cultivating it in yourself. Love begets love, you know. Charge your mental magnet with thoughts of unselfish love and devotion, give to the loved one in your thoughts the admiration, the appreciation, the idealized service you would like to give in reality—and as you give, love will come back to you. It may not be the one you first admire, but it will be one with the very qualities you think to see in your first love.

Love is giving. Real love asks no return. It cannot be jealous, for it seeks only the good of the one loved.

Love such as that is never lost or wasted. It comes back as surely as the morrow's sun—oftentimes not from the one to whom you send it, but it comes back, nevertheless, blessed and amplified. As Barrie says—"Those who bring happiness into the lives of others, cannot keep it from themselves."

You read in the papers of some man or woman dragging the other through the filth of a sensational divorce, and then ending up by declaring that he still loves her—or she him. And the pitiful part is that in their way, they still do. But it is a sad way.

Love such as that is merely selfish desire. The difference between it and hate is measured by gratification or refusal. Neither side gives anything. Both are trying to gratify themselves. Is it any wonder they go on the rocks?

You cannot receive what you do not give. Give an unselfish love—and an unselfish, idealistic love will come back to you. Give only passion, and the ashes of passion are all that will be left to you.

"Though I speak with the tongue of men and angels, and have not Love, I am become as sounding brass, or a tinkling cymbal. And though I have the gift of prophecy, and understand all mysteries, and all knowledge; and though I have all faith, so that I could remove mountains, and have not Love, I am nothing. And though I bestow all my goods to feed the poor, and though I give my body to be burned and have not love, it profiteth me nothing."—I Corinthians 13:1-3.

To every man and woman there comes the opportunity for happiness. It is yours—yours by Divine right. Demand it! Know that somewhere there exists a perfect mate for you. "He is the half part of a blessed man, left to be finished by such as she; and she a fair devoted excellence, whose fulness of perfection lies in him."—Shakespeare.

The Spirit Within knows exactly where this mate is, so put it up to Him to bring you together. Know that He has the answer—know that He *is* supplying it—know that you HAVE it!

And when you have found your love, don't settle back like the man who has caught his car—and feel that you have done all that is required of you. That's only the beginning. To hold that love, you must work just as hard as you did to get it. When you stop giving, you will stop getting. There is no place where the Law of Compensation works more surely.

There is a story in *Cappers Weekly* of a small boy who was puzzled over the girl problem and so consulted his pal Joe.

"I've walked to school with her three times," he told Joe, "and carried her books. I bought her ice-cream sodas twicet. Now, do you think I ought to kiss her"?

"Naw, you don't need to," Joe decided after a moment of deep thought. "You've done enough for that girl already."

Too many of us think we have done enough for "that girl" when we provide her with food and lodging and a reasonable amount of clothes.

Man, man, that's only a start—and an unimportant start, at that. There is many a woman bedecked with jewels and fine clothing who would cheerfully change places with her cook if thereby she could win back the honest love and attention and thousand and one little evidences of affection her husband showed her when they first married.

Marriage is a business, and to win happiness from it, you have got to work at it just like any other business.

Your wife is your customer. You have sold her a certain machine which is you—a combination of radio and automobile and Don Juan and automatic provider. That machine has to keep running, doing all those things reasonably well that you promised in your sales talk it would do, else your customer will junk it or send it back.

And you, Mrs. Customer, you have certain duties too. It is a delicate machine that has been put in your charge. It needs the most constant care to perform at its best. It must be used continually to keep it from rusting. It must be wound regularly. It must be provided with the best fuel. Above all, it must be handled with the utmost care—never impatiently, never angrily—if you would keep its parts in order, if you would get the utmost of satisfaction and use from it.

At the Oklahoma Agricultural and Mechanical College, a new course has recently been inaugurated. Not only are the girls taught how to run a home, but the boys are learning how to appreciate all the work their mothers or wives do. And there is no better way of insuring a happy home than for each party to it to thoroughly appreciate all that the other contributes toward the making of that home.

A home is a partnership and it should be an equal partnership. No man expects to work all day and every day, without change and without rest. No more should he expect it of his wife.

Why do many married women grow old so quickly, lose their youthful lines and rounded cheeks, grow sallow and wan while their husbands are still in their prime?

Bearing children? I know hundreds of women with three and four and five children who still look as youthful as when they married.

Work? A reasonable amount of work is good for every woman.

Then what is the reason?

Strain—unending, unceasing strain. There is not a servant in this country that you could hire to work every day and all day, without any period of freedom, any day of rest. Yet many men think nothing of making their wives do it.

When Taylor, the great efficiency engineer, was called in to re-organize the work of a certain foundry, he found a number of men with wheel-barrows engaged in carting pig iron from the pile in the yard to the cupola. They worked continuously, without rest except for lunch, and careful checking showed that each man carted from twelve to fifteen tons of pig iron a day. At the end of the day they were worn out.

Taylor took one of the men (an entirely average man), stood over him with a watch, and had him work exactly in accordance with his directions. He would have him load his barrow with pig iron, wheel it over to the cupola, dump it—then sit down and rest, utterly relaxing for a minute or more. When the minute was up, he would go through the same performance—and again rest.

It took two or three days to figure out the best periods of rest, but at the end of the week, Taylor's man was carting forty-five tons of pig iron every day, where before he had carted twelve to fifteen! And at the end of the day he was still fresh, where before he had been worn out.

There is not an organ in the body that does not require and take its period of rest, from the heart and lungs to the stomach and digestive tracts. Yet many a wife and mother goes all day and every day with never a moment of relaxation, never a minute when her nerves are not taut with strain. Is it any wonder they grow old years before their time? Is it any wonder they are nervous and irritable, unhappy themselves and making those around them depressed and unhappy?

To every such mother, I would say, first—relax! Sit down, lie down, every chance you get—*and just let go!* Don't listen for the baby—don't worry about dinner. Just blissfully relax—even if only for five minutes at a time. If you can multiply those five minutes by a dozen times a day, you will be surprised how much better you feel when night comes.

And for the husbands of those tired mothers, I have this word of advice: Give your wife a few hours' vacation at least once a week. The poorest domestic gets that much. Make her go out, away from the children, away from all the cares of the household, where her mind can rest, where her nerves can be renewed. If you can get no one else to help out for that rest period, take charge yourself. It won't hurt you, and you will be rewarded a dozen times over in the good it will do your wife.

Marriage is a give and take affair, you know. The more you give, the less you will have to take. You may consider it undignified to do these little menial jobs around the house, but to the really great soul, nothing is undignified. It is your little man who is worried about his dignity.

The story is told of a soldier on leave in Paris, longing for a smoke, but without a match. Spying another soldier walking ahead smoking a cigar, he caught up to him, slapped him on the shoulder and accosted him with— "Gimme a light, will you, buddie?" The other obligingly held out his cigar, and the first soldier puffed his cigarette alight. What was his horror, on looking up to thank his friend, to see on his collar the star of a General. He started to sputter apologies and cigarette smoke, but the General patted him reassuringly on the shoulder. "It's all right son," he said. "No harm done. But thank your lucky stars I'm not a second lieutenant."

THE DECALOGUE

To advise those whose wedded life has already gone on the rocks is, for the most part, playing Job's comforter. When Empedocles, the Greek statesman, sought a separation from his wife, his friends gathered about to advise him against undue haste. Empedocles said nothing, but took off his sandal and handed it to them. "Can any of you," he asked, "tell me where this sandal pinches?"

But to those who have merely met with storms and rough sailing, let me offer this:

See your mate in your mind's eye as the ideal husband or wife you would have him to be. See him doing all those things you would most like him to do—and whenever he does one of those things, praise him for it, thank him, give it a prominence out of all proportion to its importance.

Pick the one or more respects in which he does shine and hold these ever before him (and before yourself), using them as a framework or foundation upon which to graft other good qualities. Then slowly, persistently build—and all the while hold the faith. Know that he *has* all the qualities of a perfect mate—know that it is up to you merely to bring them out. And by telling him (and yourself) that he HAS them, you will be adopting the surest means of bringing them out.

Judge Joseph Burke of the Court of Domestic Relations in Chicago has had so much experience in patching up domestic quarrels that the decalogue he gives for husband and for wife merits more than passing attention. Here it is:

FOR HUSBANDS:

1. Don't hesitate to admit you are in the wrong. It is a matter of small importance and the reward is great.
2. Don't nag.
3. Only the very rich can buy good liquor. The other stuff renders you blind, deaf and dumb—perhaps forever. Let it alone.
4. Make it a rule in your home never to let the day

close unhappily. Wipe out the score before you go to sleep.

5. Prolonged arguments are horrible. There is no torture like the one which lasts for years.

6. Indulge liberally in compliments. They raise a wife's spirits, make her a better cook, a finer mother, and a more loving companion.

7. If your wife had the money for clothes that the other woman spends she would probably make her look like a dowd. Remember that.

8. Give your wife a diversion from domestic routine. Take her to a show, often if possible.

9. Tell your wife the exact amount of your income. Plan together how to spend it. Be fair about it.

10. Lock petty business troubles in your office at night. Talk over the big troubles with your wife.

FOR WIVES:

1. In an argument it softens the husband to tell him you were wrong, especially when you know you are not.

2. Don't nag.

3. Don't drink with your husband and then complain that he drinks too much. It never fills a man with admiration to see a woman drink.

4. Don't go to sleep at night with an aching heart.

Ask forgiveness. Women do that much easier than men.

5. Arguments are distasteful and destructive. Men have too many of them at work to enjoy them when they get home.

6. If your husband has money, insist upon dressing well. If he hasn't don't make life miserable for him scolding about it.

7. Don't refuse to go out with your husband. It is your duty to improve your disposition by relief from drudgery now and then.

8. Don't waste money. Have a budget system in your home.

9. Don't bother your husband with petty household annoyances at night.

10. Tell him he is the world's greatest husband, *and he will be.*

About Rule 4: Every Psychologist will tell you that the old Biblical adjuration—"Let not the sun go down upon your wrath"—Ephesians 4:26—is the finest psychology there is.

For anger and fear impress themselves on the subconscious more surely than any other emotion. And for a husband or wife to go to sleep thinking angry thoughts of the other, means that the subconscious will go on working over those thoughts all night long, with the result that the conscious mind will awaken ready to quarrel all over again, and more disgruntled and sore than ever.

WONDER OF GOD

But enough of the unhappy marriages. We read so much of these in the daily news that we forget the vast majority of marriages that come as near to heaven on earth as ordinary man could ask.

Have you ever read O. Henry's "Gift of the Magi" or Jack London's "Wonder of God"? Simple love stories, both of them, but they show the heights to which ordinary men and women will rise for love of a man for a maid, or maid for a man.

"What is thy love more than another beloved"? asked the daughter of Jerusalem of the bride. "My beloved is mine," she answered quite sufficiently, "and I am his."— Songs of Solomon 1:9, 16.

That is all that really counts—love. "Love is the fulfilling of the law," said Paul. Possessions are relatively unimportant. They are as nothing to love and health and cheerfulness and comradeship. They frequently help, but the only love worth while is the love that comes in spite of possessions or the lack of them. Happiness is not in having or in getting—but in *giving*.

The story is told of an Eastern potentate whose son seemed wasting away with melancholia. The soothsayers and doctors, on being consulted, announced that the only cure for him was to find a really happy man, take his shirt and put it upon the Prince.

So the search started. And at last, after many months, a really happy man was found. But alas—*he had no shirt!*

Many a happy marriage has started with but little more. Yet happiness and reasonable success usually go hand in hand. For happiness is based on mutual love, mutual esteem, and no man can fail when some loved one sees him successful. Love knows that there is some talent or ability in the loved one which, given a chance for expression, will carry him up the ladder of success.

Love never seeks the easy way. Love is always looking for the best way to help the loved one, regardless of the cost to itself. Love is like a magnet—it draws the loved one into and makes it one with itself. It is like a flower—it opens and expands in the sunlight of love and grows towards the sun. Love never fails.

"And Ruth said, Intreat me not to leave thee, or to return from following after thee: for whither thou goest, I will go; and where thou lodgest, I will lodge; thy people shall be my people, and thy God my God:

"Where thou diest, will I die, and there will I be buried: the Lord do so to me, and more also, if aught but death part thee and me."—Ruth 1:16, 17.

Viscount Cowdray, oil and industrial magnate of Great Britain, who has been characterized as the world's greatest contractor and the man who by repute might have been King of Albania had he accepted an offer of that romantic throne, in his last speech gave his wife credit for his success in life.

"Of all the influences which shape one's life," he said, "nothing comes into the same category with the great crowning influence which man possesses in that perfect partner—a well-mated wife.

"To have one by you who shares with head and heart successes and failures; who gives due encouragement, but has the courage to administer home truth, unpalatable but necessary some times; who is never afraid of responsibility, but is prepared to start life afresh should the need arise—such a partner is beyond praise or price.

"She is simply one's needed life blood and I make no apology for this due tribute to mine."

And science bears him out. Every man has had the experience of going to his work downhearted, discouraged, after a quarrel or misunderstanding with his wife. Every man remembers how irritable he was that day, how little worthwhile work he accomplished.

Contrast that with the days he goes down happy and cheerful, with the belief in himself that moves mountains—and credit the difference to a good wife.

"Above all things," says Peter (I Peter 4:8) "have fervent love among yourselves."

The earth moves eighteen miles each second, yet we are

never conscious of any strain, any effort. Neither is there any effort, any strain, when a man loves—and is loved. He cannot remain inert, useless. He must do something for others. He must serve. He feels the irresistible urge to do big things. He must progress. He must show his loved one what her love means to him. And therein lies the hope of the world.

"I shall pass through this world but once. Any good thing therefore that I can do, or any kindness that I can show to any human being, let me do it now. Let me not defer it or neglect it, for I shall not pass this way again."

Two thousand years ago, for the first time in the world's history, a religion was founded based not on fear, not on harrowing fetish or priestly ceremonial, but on *love*. "A new commandment I give unto thee—that ye love one another."—John 13:34.

Countless generations have broidered their forms upon that religion, but again we are coming back to the simple teaching of the Master—a religion of Love, a life of Service to our fellow men.

"Diversity of worship has divided mankind into seventy-two nations," wrote Omar Khayyam. "From all their dogmas I have selected but one—Divine Love."

"I pray the prayer the Easterns do,
May the peace of Allah abide with you.
Wherever you stop—wherever you go—

May the beautiful palms of Allah grow;
Thru days of love and nights of rest
May the love of sweet Allah make you blest.
I touch my heart as the Easterns do
May the love of Allah abide with you."

XVII

THE MOULTING PERIOD

"I hate, I despise your feast days, and I will not smell in your solemn assemblies.

"Though ye offer me burnt offerings and your meat offerings, I will not accept them: neither will I regard the peace offerings of your fat beasts.

"Take thou away from me the noise of thy songs; for I will not hear the melody of thy viols.

"But let judgment run down as waters, and righteousness as mighty stream."

—AMOS 5:21-24.

Forty million people in these enlightened United States do not belong to any Church. Most of them never attend any form of religious service.

Atheist societies have been organized in twenty of our biggest Universities. A national Atheist Association has been legally chartered and is now operating with the avowed intention of destroying every form of religion. Make no mistake—this is not a joke! It is a countrywide movement that is making rapid strides, especially among the younger element who aspire to be regared as of the "Intelligentsia."

What is the reason for this sudden wave of unbelief?

There have been athestic movements before, but never anything like this. If we knew what was behind this one, perhaps we could supply the remedy.

To find the answer, it is necessary to go back to the beginnings of religious teaching, among the early peoples. One of man's primary impulses is the search for the Supreme Being. Even the most savage peoples, the most degraded races, believe in God, and in their fashion offer sacrifice to Him.

But in primitive times, as in savage communities today, the shadow that stalked ever at man's elbow was the spectre of fear. Fear of wild beast, fear of savage neighbor, fear of lightning and wind and cold, fear of hunger and thirst. We who live in well-heated homes, protected by every device that modern ingenuity can contrive, have no conception of the fear that abode in the hearts of our savage ancestors. To them, the unknown was something to be afraid of. To them, the Hand that sent the lightning, the wind and the hail, was a Power to be feared, to be appeased at any cost.

So they offered to Him whatever was most desirable in their eyes—the fruits of the trees, the products of the chase—even their own children! Gladly would they have given Him anything to ward off His supposed wrath as evidenced in the uncontrolled elements.

After a time, some of the most prized fruits and animals came to be considered the especial property of God, to be used only as sacrifices to Him. They were called "taboo"—marked for God—and to appropriate any of them to one's own use was to bring down the wrath of God upon oneself and possibly upon one's whole tribe. While to sacrifice them regularly to the Power above would keep Him appeased and perhaps induce Him not to unloose the fury of His elements.

But sometimes it wasn't possible or convenient to sacrifice. Sometimes one journeyed far from the home over which one had bought God's protection. How protect oneself then? By taking along a charm in which dwelt some of the good properties of the Power above—a stone whose markings happened to attract the eye—an amulet containing some part of a tabooed animal, anything which by any stretch of the imagination could be supposed to contain magic properties.

Thus began the traffic in "fetishes"—charms and amulets to keep off evil spirits.

Fed upon fear, naturally it grew. And with it grew up a class known as shamans or medicine men. Their original province was to drive out evil spirits, to make and sell amulets and the like to ward off evil; but gradually, as their power grew, their shrewdness increased also, and soon they undertook not only to drive the evil spirits out of those who had purchased their help, but to drive them *into* their enemies!

Around this shaman, the whole cult of worship grew. The more fearful and awe-inspiring he could make it, the greater he seemed in the eyes of his tribe. Until presently even the boldest chief hesitated to make a move without the sanction and approval of his witch-doctor.

And because people needed some tangible evidence of the reality of their gods, the witch-doctors erected idols—fierce and terror-inspiring creatures, all of them—housed them on islands or in temples and made their habitations "taboo." No one but the shaman could commune personally with their god—to all others it was sure death.

Others might see him on the occasion of public festival, but only after going through certain ritual, only after being "purified" and introduced by the witch-doctor.

Thus did primitive religion grow. And as shaman followed shaman, each intent on his own aggrandizement but all united on the one idea of keeping their class supreme, there gradually grew up a ritual so involved that none but regularly "Qualified" witch-doctors could acquire it, so awe-inspiring that common folk could not but be impressed by the ceremonial which even his shamans must go through before they could approach their tribal god.

A god so unapproachable must be a terrible creature, one to be appeased at every turn. And it was thus that most ancient peoples regarded Him. They made no move without first casting furtive glances around to see if the "Powers" were still well disposed towards them. They lived in constant fear. They prayed to a god of fear. And their priestcraft, realizing that their power was built upon fear, cultivated it in every way they knew. Religion became a matter of forms—and woe betide the man who failed to observe those forms! You might get away with robbing your neighbor, you might win the witch-doctor's intercession for having killed a man, but there was no pardon for the man who scorned his gods by failing to observe the ritual his priests had laid down. Cursed he would be in his waking, cursed in his sleeping. Cursed he should be until his death (which was soon and sudden if the witch-doctors laid hands on him or his food), and thrice accursed after his death, for there the "Devourers" would get him and rend him limb from limb through all eternity.

A pleasant religion—truly. And yet, with the exception of a small strip of Palestine, most of the world struggled along under some such religion as that for thousands of years. A religion of fear. A religion of taboos and fetishes. A religion of rituals and forms.

The record of the Old Testament is the record of the progress of a people in grasping the true idea of God.

Beginning with the idea of the One God—unseen and not to be worshipped through idols—its conception of His natures and quality rose from that of a God who had to be persuaded by argument and sacrifices, first to a God of Justice, then to a God of Mercy, and finally in Jesus to a God of Love.

Two thousand years ago, there came to this earth a Man who taught a religion unhedged by fetish or taboo—a Religion of Love. His was no God of wrath, to placate whom it was necessary to sacrifice cattle or doves or treasure. No—His was a joyous, happy Father-God, whose good pleasure it is to give His children the Kingdom.

He required no ritual, no ceremonial. When He "called" His disciples, He did not even require them to be baptized. He taught in the Temple, or on the street corners or on the mountain—for Him the House of God was everywhere, and he condemned as "whited sepulchres" the ritual-loving priestcraft of that day, upright in the sight of men, adhering strictly to the letter of the law, but rotten and foul within. Their precious ritual was less acceptable in the sight of God, He told them, than the cry for mercy of the untaught publican.

The religion that Jesus taught was a religion of service, of love. His God was a God of Love—not locked up in a house, approachable only through certain men and certain forms—but everywhere and in all mankind!

"As ye have done unto the least of my brethren," He taught, "ye have done unto me."—Matthew 25:40.

No need of ritual or priest for that. You can serve God anywhere, anytime, merely by serving your neighbor.

"Whosoever shall give a cup of water in my name shall not lose his reward."—Mark 9:41.

Service, service—always service. "Whatsoever will be great among you shall be your minister; and whosoever of you will be the chiefest, shall be servant of all."—Mark 10:43, 44.

Imagine what the chief priests of Jupiter or of Ishtar would have had to say of that. Imagine how the High Priest Caiaphas must have taken it. The idea—for him to become servant to the common people—'twould be laughable if it were not so dangerous. This Man must be stopped—at any cost!

And then—His idea of prayer. What would become of established religion if everyone followed His teaching? The Temple would be ruined!

"Thou, when thou prayest, enter into thy closet, and when thou hast shut the door, pray to thy Father which is in secret, and thy Father which seeth in secret, shall reward thee openly."—Matthew 6:6.

In short, when you want anything of the Father, you need only go commune with Him in secret—ask of Him as you would ask of any loving earthly Father! No intermediary necessary. No charms. No magic.

Everything simple, easy—a religion that any child could understand. Altogether too simple, too easy, for those in authority. Anyone could practice it. If the common people were to look up to the Temple followers, there must be more to religion than that. There must be some things priests could do that no one else could. There must be special powers vested in them—special favors from the Almighty that could be gained only through their intercession.

And so, as Christianity grew older, as it grew in power and the inevitable desire for personal gain and glory animated some of its followers, certain of the old Jewish and pagan ritual was grafted upon it, certain forms and ceremonial used until they came to be considered a necessary part of it.

Then in the days of Constantine, Christianity became the state religion of the entire Roman Empire. And to popularize it among peoples who knew nothing of Jesus' teachings and were accustomed only to forms and rituals, still other ceremonials were added until some branches of it have become as thoroughly ritualized as were ever the pagan rites of the Egyptians or Romans.

But today people no longer believe that the lightning is the wrath of God, searching them out for their sins.

They no longer believe they are surrounded by evil spirits, just waiting to pounce upon them, kept off only by virtue of the amulet or fetish that they wear. People understand the forces of nature. They have harnessed many of them to be their servants. They confidently look forward to the time when they shall harness all of them.

So the day of a religion of fear is past. People can't be frightened into church. They cannot be fetished or ta-booed into doing right. They can see through the empty forms and ceremonials.

But—and here, I think, is the reason for so many empty churches—while people have become better educated, while they have advanced far past the stage of fetishes and taboos, many well-intentioned but narrow-minded ministers are still back in the Middle Ages as far as their teaching of religion is concerned. Hell and damnation, fire and brimstone, seem to be the only terms they know. Naturally the young scoff at that. Naturally they think that if this is all religion has to offer, religion is not for them.

Revivals? Of course. You can work people into a religious hysteria. You can trade upon their fears until they "profess religion." But have you ever checked up how long that "religion" stays with them? I have—and I wouldn't give the snap of a finger for that sort of convert.

There is nothing radically wrong with the younger generation. They are in no essential different from the young people of your day or of mine. They are more accustomed to look at facts—that's all. They are not interested in forms or ritual. They have no reverence for a thing simply because it is old.

It may shock you to learn that your young son or daughter has joined the ranks of the "Devil's Angels" or some such wild-sounding order. But it need not alarm you. It is just their method of rebelling against the shams and taboos of established religion. And youth, you know, always goes to extremes.

In reality, they are going through the "moulting period" that every man of sincere convictions must go through. They have seen through the ritual and forms with which the simple teachings of Jesus have become beclouded. They have not yet worked out for themselves a satisfying belief of their own. And being without "feathers," without the solace, of any belief, they want company. They want companionship in their misery. Hence these societies of "Damned Souls," of "God's Black Sheep" and the like. They think they are very wicked, very cynical, but give them half an excuse and they will flock back like moulting chickens to their mother hen.

Perhaps the best explanation of what is wrong with them is contained in an interview with the 18-year-old National Secretary of the Junior Atheist League, on her trip to New York to enlist school infidels: "I have never really studied the Bible," she acknowledged, "but I have read enough of it to feel that it is false, *and I want to enlighten other people."*

Ridiculous enough, of course—but not half as ridiculous as the author of some of our recent "best sellers" who got up in the pulpit one Sunday, and defied God to strike him dead! A noble gesture—truly. Because God did not strike him dead, there is no God. Like the man who announced triumphantly that he had searched the entire heavens with a telescope and found no God there—therefore there was no God.

Can you imagine on Napoleon's march into Russia, some little child running in front of him and defying him in such wise? Can't you almost see the pitying smile on the face of the Emperor of the French as he motions some soldier to gently remove the child from his path?

THE STRAIGHT LINE TO GOD

When Peter the Great planned to build a road from Moscow to St. Petersburg, his engineers spent long hours in wordy discussions as to whether it should take in this town, or go out of the way to stop at that town. When they finished plotting it, the result was a zigzag that wandered over most of Russia.

Peter gave it one glance—then called for a map. Laying a ruler upon it, he drew a straight line from Moscow to St.

Petersburg. "The object of this road," he told his engineers drily, "is not to explore Russia, but to get from Moscow to St. Petersburg and back. There is the line of your road. Now build it!"

What is the object of religion? Not merely to keep up the Churches or to support men of God. Those things are incidental. The object of religion is to enable all men to get in touch with the Father-God—in the straightest and easiest way.

Priests and Ministers are a help, but except in teaching the young and the ignorant, they are in no wise essential.

Churches are a help, but they too are in no way essential. Jesus more often worshipped outdoors than in the Temple. His greatest sermons were delivered outdoors. He used no ritual. He required no ceremonial. Reminded by the woman of Samaria that "Our fathers worshipped in this mountain, and ye say that in Jerusalem is the place where men ought to worship," He told her:

"Woman, believe me, the hour cometh, when ye shall neither in this mountain, nor yet at Jerusalem worship the Father.

"God is a Spirit: and they that worship Him must worship Him in spirit and in truth."—John 4:20, 24.

Then what is the straightest path to God? The straightest way to the Father above is exactly the same as the straightest way to any earthly father—to take our hopes and our fears and our desires directly to Him, to take Him

entirely into our confidence, to ask Him confidently, believingly, for anything of good we may wish.

The word religion is derived from the Latin—re and
ligo—to bind together, to bring the soul into union with
God. And the principal value of a Church is just that—
to bind its members together in a common cause, for a
common purpose, for, as Jesus said: "Again I say unto you,
that if two of you shall agree on earth as touching anything that they shall ask, it shall be done for them of my
Father which is in Heaven. For where two or three are
gathered together in my name, there am I in the midst of
them."—Matthew 18:19-20.

The original Apostles and Ministers of Christianity
were teachers—teachers and *demonstrators* of the healing
power of the Truth. They showed their followers definite
results—definite answers to prayer.

And what Churches are making progress in this country today? What Churches are largely increasing their
membership?

According to the report of the Inter-church Conference, the Protestant communions are facing appalling
losses, nearly half a million people yearly leaving the
Church, many of them "passing out of the back door."
Only one large denomination is showing consistent gains.

Why? What is there about it that sets it apart from the
others?

Just one thing—it offers its members help, not merely in some future state, but right here and now.

It offers health, relief from sickness, surcease from bodily pain. It offers harmony in the home and business life. It says to each man—I give you a new conception of your body, the perfect conception of it that is in Divine Mind. I give you a new idea of your surroundings—the peace and plenty so often promised you in the Scriptures.

Against these, what do most Churches offer? Salvation in the hereafter—and in exchange for it, a rough, hard road here below, beset with thorns and briars, every cross-road marked "Danger!", every sickness and tribulation just a cross sent by the Father to chasten you and prepare you for the hereafter.

Is it any wonder that people prefer to grasp what pleasures they can here below rather than wait for it in such a problematical future state, especially when they are taught that even after a whole lifetime of careful plodding, they may be eternally damned by one false step at the end?

With such a theology as that, it is not surprising that the Bishop of Ripon should be asking the scientists to take a ten-year holiday so that the world might catch up with them. It is not the world that needs to catch up. It is some of the Churches—or, rather, some of their Ministers.

Religion has never needed to ask any favors of science. The greatest scientists have been and are the most sincere believers in God. Newton, Faraday, Pasteur, Kelvin—can you think of any greater names in the annals of science? Yet they were every one sincerely religious men—intense believers in God.

"There is a world filled with spiritual realities," says Professor Pupin, who last year was President of the Association for the Advancement of Science, "to the deeper understanding of whose meaning the new Physical revelations will contribute. So it is not the scientist but the fool, as was written in ancient wisdom, who says in his heart that there is no God."

"The fool hath said in his heart, There is no God. The Lord looked down from Heaven upon the children of man, to see if there were any that did understand and seek God.

"Have all the workers of iniquity no knowledge? Who eat up my people as they eat bread, and call not upon the Lord."—Psalms 14:1, 2, 4.

Listen to most sermons and what do you hear? Dogma—ritual—"Was Jesus born of a virgin?" "Should one be baptized by sprinkling or by immersion?" "Are unbaptized children eternally damned?"

Reminds one of the debates that stirred the theologians of mediaeval days. "How many angels can stand on the head of a pin?" was one of the favorite subjects, and the heat and rancor that could be aroused over so academic a question were wonderful to behold.

Did you ever read of Jesus preaching upon such a subject? When He enlisted Matthew among the disciples, did He first ask him if he believed in the Virgin birth? No—it was to get away from dogma, from ritual, from unnecessary forms that He enlisted simple fishermen, tax-gatherers and the like to spread His gospel.

He didn't worry about slight differences of creed. One of the disciples found a man doing good in Jesus' name, but he was an outsider and not one of their number, so they hastened proudly to Jesus to tell Him of it. "And John answered Him, saying, Master, we saw one casting out devils in Thy name, and he followed not us; and we forbade him, because he followed not us."

"But Jesus said, Forbid him not; for there is no man which shall do a miracle in my name, that can lightly speak evil of me.

"For he that is not against us, is on our part."—Mark 9:38-40.

Small comfort there for the bigoted or narrow minded credist. *"He went about doing good."* There is the story of His life. There is the example He left for all who would be His Ministers to follow.

"Have we not all one Father? Hath not one God created us? Why do we deal treacherously every man against his brother, by profaning the covenant of our fathers?"—Malachi 2:10.

The feeling with which one leaves after many a sermon is much like that which Demosthenes imputed to his great rival orator Aeschines. "You," said Demosthenes, "make them say—'How well he speaks.' I make them say—'Let us march against Philip!'" Whereas what one goes to Church to hear is how to find the straightest road to the Father. When that is more often taught, when Jesus' example is more generally followed, there will be no need to worry about atheism or agnosticism, for everyone—even the most confirmed infidel—*wants* to believe, wants something, someone, on which to hang his faith.

Go back to the simple teachings of Jesus. Go back to His life, His works.

Go to the Father in the way that He directed. You will never again lack faith. You will never again listen to any religion of fear.

"At the same time came the disciples unto Jesus saying, Who is the greatest in the Kingdom of Heaven?

"And Jesus called a little child unto Him, and set him in the midst of them.

"And said, Verily, I say unto you, except ye be converted (turned about), and become as little children, ye shall not enter into the Kingdom of Heaven."—Matthew 18:1-3.

And what does being "converted" entail? Becoming baptized? Joining the Church? Not necessarily. That in itself will not make you "as a little child." A child's most common characteristic is faith, trust—utter dependence upon its father, utter faith in him, utter love for him.

Those are the traits you must "turn about" and cultivate if you would enter into the Kingdom of Heaven—
utter dependence upon your Father above, utter faith in
Him, utter love for Him.

When Athens was still a village, Rome not even dreamed
of, all of Europe nothing better than a savage playground,
China was already a highly civilized country.

People rode in carriages, lived in well-built houses,
dressed in silks, wore leather shoes, sat at tables to eat food
from plates, measured time by sundials, even had umbrellas!

And the reason?

Because China, alone among all the earlier nations, had
developed a religion without fear and without priests. Every
man was free to progress in whatever way offered the greatest opportunity. Every man could call upon his Maker in
his own way. There were no taboos, no fetishes to hold
him back.

But then suddenly all progress stopped. For 2,000 years,
China stood still while all the world passed her by. Today
she stands—a tragic figure—one of the most backward of
nations, the football of the Powers.

Why?

Because that fearless, forward-looking religion of hers
was turned backward—*was ritualized!* It became a religion
of forms and ceremonies. "Three hundred points of ceremony and three thousand points of behavior"—instead

of means, these became the aims and ends of life. Every action, under every circumstance, was worked out in advance. No initiative, no individual thinking was wanted or tolerated. Men became merely animated figures.

No longer was the common man encouraged to better his condition. On the contrary, he was told by China's "greatest" religious teacher that there was no grosser guilt than to be discontented with his lot.

No longer was the ambitious youth permitted to experiment, to progress; he was assured by China's most orthodox teacher that all change was injurious—that salvation was to be attained only if none tried to disturb the religious, social or political order that was already established! Whatever had been, whatever their ancestors had done—was good. Whatever was new, untried, novel—was bad.

Imagine the effect of such teachings, inculcated into the young of the nation for more than 2,000 years! A wonderful thing for those already rich, already in authority—yes. But how about the others? Is it any wonder China is backward? Is it any wonder she lacks a leader?

Orthodoxy, ritualism, carried to its logical conclusion—that is China. And it is just such orthodoxy, just such ritualism, that is now meeting its death in the Christian Churches of today. Should we mourn it? Should we try to delay its quick demise? Should we not rather hasten it, that we may the sooner replace it with the real Christianity that Jesus lived and taught?

"He hath shewed thee, O man, what is good; and what doth the Lord require of thee, but to do justly, and to love mercy, and to walk humbly with thy God?"

—MICAH 5:8.

"Withhold not good from them to whom it is due, when it is in the power of thine hand to do it.

"Say not unto thy neighbor, Go, and come again, and tomorrow I will give; when thou hast it by thee.

"Devise not evil against thy neighbor, seeing he dwelleth securely by thee.

"Strive not with a man without cause, if he have done thee no harm."

—PROVERBS 3:27–30.

XVIII

WHAT ARE WE HERE FOR?

"Arise, shine; for thy light is come, and the glory of the Lord is risen upon thee."

—ISAIAH 60:1.

One of the early Christian missionaries to Britain was addressing a conclave of the tribes, gathered at night in a rude hall, made of branches covered with skins and open at each end.

He spoke eloquently of the one God. He told them of the Saviour. He pictured the joys of a future life.

As he finished, suddenly out of the night there swooped a great bird, fluttered for a moment over their heads, then disappeared into the blackness beyond.

All were silent—awed, impressed. Then an old Chief arose.

"You tell us of one God," he said.

"We believe in another. You tell us of a Heaven where the just and the meek go. We believe in a Valhalla for the brave and the fair. But who has ever come back from beyond to say which is right?

"Life is like that bird which flew through here. It comes from none knows whence. It stays with us an all too brief moment, then goes none knows whither. Tell me if you can—what is it all about? What are we here for?"

That is the old, old question. What are we here for? Philosophers have wrangled over it since time began. And few indeed have been the acceptable answers.

But one thing we can be sure of—we are put on this earth to progress. All through history, all through nature, all through life, we can see evidences of this on every side. Whenever a nation becomes too self-satisfied, whenever a man or an institution walls himself around to shut out new ideas, whenever a plant stops growing—it is a sure sign of decay and death. We must go forward—or die. We can't stand still. Time is ever moving. We must keep up with it—or perish.

Professor Michael Pupin, famous scientist, in an interview published in the *American Magazine*, says: "Science finds that everything is a continuously developing process. It reveals man as a being with a soul which is progressing more and more toward Divinity.

"Here's my opinion. . . our Physical life is only a stage in the existence of the soul. . . . The human soul goes on existing—*and developing*—after death."

What do you live for? You might ask nine-tenths of the

people in the world, and all they could tell you would be: to work to buy food and clothing and shelter, so I may gain strength to work tomorrow to buy more food and clothing and shelter. And that is as far as most of them ever get. The endless round of work and eat and sleep, and work and eat and sleep. Is that worth living for? Is that any preparation for a future life?

Suppose you sent your son to a preparatory school that was to make him ready for College. And instead of giving him the studies necessary for his College entrance, the school taught him only carpentering, or bricklaying, or plastering, or common day labor. What would you think of it as a preparatory school for College?

If our life here is anything, it is a preparation for the life to come. It is a preparatory school. You are taught Greek in school—not because you expect ever to speak it, not even because some of our words are derived from Greek roots, but because of the valuable mental training its study gives you. Every College student must learn higher mathematics, even though not one in a hundred ever will use anything but the plainest arithmetic. Why? For mental training.

We go through experiences here on earth which apparently have no purpose, no good in them. We are given obstacles to overcome, trials and tribulations to fight our way through. Why? To give us something we may take with us to the other side—Character.

"It is written in the Prophets, and they shall be all taught of God."—John 6:45. To quote Dr. Pupin again— "Everything that happens in this great universe is for a purpose; and that purpose is the development of the human soul."

Accounting, engineering, mechanics, law, business— none of these in itself is going to do us any good over there. It is what the *use* of it adds to our *perceptive faculties* that counts.

It is an unknown country "over there." There are no telephones, no electric lights, no automobiles, no courts, no factories, no stores. To regard our ordinary avocations as preparation for the hereafter is as though a man with a perfect knowledge of typewriters—and nothing else— were set down in the middle of the Amazon jungle and left there to live or die. Unless he had learned something else from his tinkering with typewriters besides mechanics, he would be in a bad way.

But tinkering with typewriters—or any other job— does teach higher things to the man ready or willing to receive them. It teaches patience, perseverance, honesty, pride in work well done. All the attributes that, summed up, spell S-E-R-V-I-C-E.

That is something which is as welcome in the Brazilian wilds as here. It is something which pays dividends on the other side of the River Styx just as surely as on this—the attitude of mind which is always looking for the best way, the most effective way to SERVE others—to make the world a better place for his having been in it.

"And they that be wise shall shine as the brightness of the firmament; and they that turn many to righteousness as the stars forever."—Daniel 12:3.

Stewart Edward White had a story in the May *American* of a man who, to all intents, had died. And in that hazy limbo between the new world and this, the thing that worried him was his utter nakedness—his complete lack of any trait he might carry over from our world into the beyond.

To quote in part the character in the story—

"Here is how it seemed to me:

"There I was, temporarily inactive, but convinced that sooner or later I would participate in whatever there was. And I knew there was something to participate in. There was an environment. I couldn't become cognizant of it because I had not the proper development to possess senses that would take it in. I had no equipment. I was like a baby.

"It came to me with rather a shock of illumination that my appreciation of even this much was due solely to the fact that I had gotten something spiritual out of my earth life.

"Perception was one of them. And I realized with a kind of sinking feeling that if I had not brought over that much, I would probably be unconscious—perhaps just dormant like a seed, waiting for something to germinate me."

"Waiting for something to germinate me." Isn't that the way most of us are even here—waiting for some force outside ourselves to come along and start us into action? Are we going to carry that same inactivity, that same lack of initiative over to the other side? We will unless we speedily learn to bestir ourselves.

A noted criminal judge once said that he had yet to meet the man who had not some good in him, some redeeming trait. He thought once he had found him—a man hard as iron, a murderer and a thief. Yet out in the chain gang, working on the roads, that man risked crippling or death to save a little child!

So we all take something with us across the Great Divide, something that, with sufficient exercise and help, may germinate there and enable us to grow in time to the stature of God's children. But how much we have to start on and how fast we grow, depends upon the faculties we acquire here that are of use on the other side.

In the gold rush to the Klondike in the Fall of '98, no man was allowed across the Chilkoot Pass unless he carried with him $1,000 and a ton of provisions. The Canadian authorities wanted no "foolish virgins" on their hands to provide for. Each man must carry with him the requisite money and provisions to supply him through the winter—or go back home.

Death is the Chilkoot Pass across which each soul must

travel to reach the Land of Promise beyond. But there are no Northwest Mounted Police to turn you back if you cross without provisions and without equipment. You are allowed to go through—but not to the Promised Land. To Hell instead.

That Hell is not a place of fire and brimstone. Rather it is one of darkness and loneliness. Those in it have failed to carry over any perceptive faculties, and without them they cannot find their way to the Promised Land.

Do you know what "Hell" means? The word used for it in the New Testament is "Gehenna," and it comes from the Vale of Hinnom, which was a dump-heap outside the city walls of Jerusalem.

Hell is the place for waste and useless material. Hell is the place for those who cross the Great Divide without anything that can make them useful on the other side. Hell is the dump-heap of useless souls.

At a little wayside station up in Northern Michigan, a lumber jack was waiting, an old grain sack over his shoulder with his spare clothes and belongings in it. Seeing a fellow traveler eyeing the meager load, he explained tersely—"This old sack holds all I've been able to accumulate in sixty-two years."

What is in your sack? What have you that you can take with you over the Great Divide? Blue blood won't help, you know. Nor a bank account. Eloquence or mechanical skill or salesmanship count for nothing in the country beyond.

What have you added to the world's knowledge? What have you done to help your fellow man? What noble thoughts have you added to your mental store, what kindly deeds, what unselfish service?

Those are the things that count "over there." Those are the riches you can take with you to clothe your nakedness, to start you in your new life, to give you that faculty of "Perception" which shall enable you to see your way to the Promised Land.

"He that findeth his life shall lose it; and he that loseth his life for my sake shall find it."—Matthew 10:39. In other words, he that works only for his own aggrandizement shall lose all that he makes. But he that loses all thought of self in the service of others shall thereby serve himself, too!

What is that you say? You have been one of God's poor all your life? What good is that? The poor have no better chance over there than have the rich. The ceaseless grind for a bare livelihood is as stunting to the soul as the ceaseless grind for wealth. There must be more to your life than that. There must be a ceaseless search for the wealth of the soul, a ceaseless reaching out to God, a ceaseless effort for understanding and knowledge of the Father. "Acquaint now thyself with Him and be at peace. Thereby good shall come unto thee."—Job 22:21.

The Father is not poor. He is not sick or weak or afflicted. And He is not proud of any of His children who
boast of such gifts as coming from Him.

The Father has all riches, all power, all life, and those
who "acquaint themselves with Him" share in His gifts.
When you live in the Father, it will make little difference
to you whether you live in Him on this plane of existence
or another. When you depend on His bountiful law of supply for your subsistence, on His love and protection for your
happiness, you will know that "My God shall supply all
your needs, according to His riches."—Philippians 4:19.

I read the other day of a mother whose daughter was
killed in an automobile accident, just after she had begun
a wonderfully useful work. Did the mother repine? Did
she sit down and waste away with grief?

No—she decided that the way she could best help her
daughter was to carry on her work for her. She would take
her daughter's place. In spirit, in planning, in everything
she did, she tried to put all her daughter's energy and her
daughter's efforts into the work, with the result that not
only is the work itself a complete success, but the mother
is a new woman—rejuvenated and happy. Her daughter
lives again in her.

And if there is any way that the souls of the departed
can be helped, if the faculties they have carried over with
them can be made to germinate from without, that is the

way—to carry on for them here the work that would have developed those very faculties.

When father or mother or loved one dies, prayer may help them, but far better than wordy petitions is to send them riches they can use in the world beyond—the riches of service you are doing in this world in their name.

When Marshall Field died he left the bulk of his fortune to his children. But it was not to be given them at once. Part they were to receive immediately. The rest only as they proved themselves ready and worthy. When they did so-and-so, they were to receive such-and-such.

The Father above left a far vaster fortune to each of us than that acquired by Marshall Field. But He put the same restrictions upon it. All are given a certain amount without effort, but thereafter, we receive only as we prove the law. There is no limit to the amount of the fortune. The only limit is in our ability to prove ourselves ready to receive it.

THE KINGDOM OF HEAVEN

The glory of life is in our mastery of it. We are put here to prove ourselves—to wash away the dross, to refine the gold in the fire—and to the extent that we prove ourselves, to that extent we win to the Kingdom of Heaven, here and hereafter.

For the Kingdom of Heaven is not some occult place

we can enter only through the gates of death. On the contrary, unless we can win to some measure of it here, we shall find it a long, hard trail to win to it in the hereafter.

"The Kingdom of Heaven is within you," said Jesus. Until He came, mankind had been taught that circumstances were the result of causes outside ourselves. Jesus showed that all circumstances are within our own control. Instead of being under the control of some malign fate, under the influence of some natal star, the reverse is true. "And he that overcometh and Keepeth my works unto the end, to him will I give power over the nations, and I will give him the morning star."—Revelations 2:26-28.

But granting that the Kingdom of Heaven is within us, *what* is it? "The Kingdom of God is as if a man should cast seed into the ground," said Jesus, "and the seed should spring and grow up, he knoweth not how. For the earth bringeth forth fruit of herself: first the blade, then the ear, and after that the full corn in the ear."—Mark 4:26-28.

To go back to the man in White's story: "I used to know a man who suffered a stroke of paralysis. All he could move was two fingers in his left hand. Instead of getting discouraged, he said to himself: 'Well, all right, I'll move those two fingers!' So he did. And by and by he found he could move the next finger. Today he's almost as good as ever.

"That's the way I felt. I got a sudden glowing conviction that if I exercised what faculties I had, I'd speedily develop more faculties."

The seed of the Kingdom of Heaven is love—unselfish love. The stalk is service. The golden grain is riches and happiness. The stronger the stalk—the more ears of golden grain.

"Seek ye first the Kingdom of Heaven, and all those things shall be added unto you," said Jesus.—Matthew 7:33. Seek first the seed of love, plant it in the soil of work, water it with genuine interest in your fellow man, and the stalk of service will speedily spring up, to bring forth golden grains of reward.

"The Kingdom of Heaven is like unto a treasure hid in a field, the which when a man hath found, he hideth, and for joy thereof goeth and selleth all that he hath, and buyeth that field."—Matthew 13:44.

When a man learns the joy of genuine service, he will gladly give up all that he has for it. He will guard it jealously as his dearest treasure.

Henry Ford was offered a billion dollars for the Ford Company. He refused it. Not because he wanted to make more money—a billion dollars are more than any man can spend in one lifetime, more than he wants to leave to his children—but because that company represented to him the most valuable thing in life, his means of service to his fellow-man.

Hundreds of men have refused the most generous offers for their businesses—for the same reason. To the extent to which you find that reason—to that same extent you have justified your existence, to that same extent you have discovered the Kingdom of God.

Hold on to it, for as much of it as you take with you across the Great Divide—that much will serve you as seed to plant on the other side, seed that will germinate and grow and bring forth an evermore abundant harvest.

Don't let it slip from your fingers merely because you have already reaped a golden harvest. That is the very time you can sow most surely for the future. You no longer need to worry about money. Now you can sow for happiness.

So, you millionaires and successful men about to retire—take heed! There is no retiring. You must keep going forward—or lose what you have. Perhaps not in money, but in that which is far more valuable than money—the seed you are to take to the other side.

That seed decays with disuse. Keep sowing it—and reaping it—and what you no longer need to sow for riches, sow for happiness instead. You will find that harvest not only more bountiful, but more satisfying and more easily carried over the Great Divide. It is not necessary that you stick at your desk. It is not even necessary that you stick at your business. But it is necessary that you hold on to the idea of service to your fellow men.

What are we here for? To discover the Kingdom of Heaven—to carry its seed with us into the next great phase of existence.

"I am Alpha and Omega, the beginning and the end. I will give unto him that is athirst of the fountain of the water of life freely. He that over-cometh shall inherit all things."

—REVELATION 21: 6, 7.

"And behold, I come quickly; and my reward is with me, to give every man according as his work shall be."

—REVELATION 22:12.

XIX

PRAYER

*"Thou shalt make thy prayer unto Him, and He shall
hear thee, and thou shalt pay thy vows.*

*"Thou shalt also decree a thing, and it shall be established
unto thee: and the light shall shine upon thy ways.*

*"When men are cast down, then thou shalt say, there is
lifting up; and he shall save the humble person."*

—JOB 22:27-29.

Daddy," said the little boy as he knelt for his
prayers one evening, "please pray that Detroit is
the capital of Vermont."

"Why," exclaimed the father, "what on earth do you
want to pray that for?"

"Because," came the naive answer, "that's the way I put
it in my geography examination today."

And that, truly, is the way many grown-ups pray. Then they wonder why their prayers are not answered, and go off scoffing at the idea of any prayer bringing an answer. "Ye ask and receive not because ye ask amiss."—James 4:3.

Prayer is not a mere petition. Prayer is communion with the Father. Prayer is realizing that He has all good, including all riches, all honor, all success, all happiness, and that as His children we are heirs to these. Prayer is manifesting the good the Father long ago gave to us. As Phillips Brooks reminds us—"Prayer is not forcing God's reluctance: it is taking hold of God's willingness."

Our God is Love. Our Father the personification of goodness and mercy. We are His children. He has given us dominion over all things. Can we ask for more?

We *have* all of good. We *have* all of power. Prayer is realizing this—*manifesting it.*

"Ask ye of the Lord rain in the time of the latter rain. So the Lord shall make bright clouds: and give them showers of rain, to every one grass in the field."—Zechariah 10:1.

Most of us are like a man who owns a fertile valley, surrounded by reservoirs of water. But rather than make the effort of clearing out his ditches and opening the sluice gates, he stands around hoping for rain. Prayer is simply an opening of our receiving channels. There is water enough and to spare. How much you will receive is limited only by how much you can use. More than that will do you harm.

"Concerning the works of my hands, command ye me."—Isaiah 45:11.

How then shall we pray? How manifest all this good which is ours?

How would you do if you had the fertile valley? First, prepare your ground to receive the water, would you not? Till it, then plant your seed in the secure confidence that you could turn on the water as soon as you were ready for it.

Just so you must do when you pray—make ready to receive the thing asked for.

Jesus gave us specific directions for prayer, and first and most important of them was: "What things soever ye desire, when ye pray, believe that ye *receive* them and ye shall have them."—Mark 11:24.

If we truly "believe that we receive," then we will make ready for the accomplishment of our prayer just as surely as if we ourselves were going to turn on the water. Failing in this, the conditions that Jesus laid down for successful prayer are not fulfilled. The seed falls upon stony ground and quickly withers away.

"He that wavereth is like the wave of the sea driven by the wind and tossed: let not that man think that he shall receive anything of the Lord."—James 1: 6,7.

A country congregation was praying for rain. Three evenings they had besought the Lord, yet the skies remained clear as crystal. "What's the use?" they began to ask one another. "Here we've been praying and praying, and not a drop has it brought us. We've done our part. Why can't the Lord do His?"

But the Pastor of that little flock had a clearer view. "You've done your part, have you?" he asked. "Well, tell me, one of you, what is the first essential that Jesus laid down for successful prayer? Belief aright. 'Believe that ye receive it.' You say you have that belief. You have come here three nights and prayed for rain. Yet I ask you—how many of you have brought umbrellas?"

The only obstacle that stands between you and the greatest desire of your heart is doubt and fear. When you can pray without doubting, wish without worrying, the good does not exist which you cannot win through prayer.

But having made your prayer, you must BELIEVE THAT YOU RECEIVE IT. The great minds are those that can wait undaunted, even though the answer seems long delayed, secure in the promise of the Father.

"In due season we shall reap if we faint not." —Galatians 6:9.

Your prayer is never lost until you stop praying. No man is defeated until he acknowledges defeat. Jesus lying in the tomb refused to acknowledge the finality of death, and the resurrection was his triumphant answer.

Never try to force results. Put your desires in the hands

of the Father, serenely, believingly. Then—"Be still and know that I am God."—Psalms 46:10. Hold the faith. Hold the thought. There is no stronger faith than that which can go ahead, making all preparations for the thing it wants, even though there be not the slightest sign of its coming. "Trust in Him, and He shall bring it to pass."—Psalms 37:5.

The reason that the answer to our prayers is so often delayed until the eleventh hour is that only then do we truly let go—clear the brushwood of restraint out of our channels and let the Father work through us unhindered.

"Ask and it shall be given you. Seek and ye shall find. Knock and it shall be openeth unto you."—Matthew 7:7.

When the Baptist Temple that now stands on the corner of Broad and Berk streets in Philadelphia was first proposed, the fund in hand for the lot and the building was exactly 57 cents. But it happened that the Scriptural text for that morning was the story of the five barley loaves and the two fishes. So instead of asking—"What can we do with 57 cents?"—the Minister blessed them and asked the Father to take those few pennies and with them build a worthy Church.

Did He build it? Go look at the Church! The old Baptist Temple was very small and its congregation was poor. Yet they multiplied that 57 cents to well over a hundred thousand dollars. And if you ask them how, they will tell you—"Through prayer."

Prayer built the Baptist Temple. Prayer supplied its furnishings. Prayer bought it an organ. Not a move was made—not a thing undertaken—without earnest prayer. Many a time when it seemed as though that little congregation had reached the end of its resources, prayer found the way out.

"My word shall not return unto me void, but shall accomplish that where-unto it is sent."—Isaiah 55:11.

And once they had found the efficacy of prayer, the congregation used it in their homes, in their businessess, with just as great success.

A doctor, utterly baffled in the treatment of a serious case, prayed for light and was shown the hidden cause of his patient's trouble. A workman out of a job prayed for work and before he left the Church, was brought into touch with an employer who had just been praying for such a man as he. A servant girl prayed for a dress, and was given three by a friend of her mistress. A young man prayed for the opportunity to study for the Ministry, and near him sat the principal of such a school praying for a suitable man to do certain work in return for his board and tuition. They were promptly brought together to the profit and satisfaction of both.

A woman prayed for a purchaser of her land. A student that he might pass his examinations. A farmer to learn what seed to use. A girl that her parents might join her. A law-

yer for some lost evidence. A business man for guidance.
And each and every one promptly received the answer to
his prayers.

"And ye shall seek me, and find me, when ye shall
search for me with all your heart."—Jeremiah 29:13.

Too many of us pray only under pressure. Like the small
boy who goes home only when he is hungry or in trouble.
Of course, it is better to pray then than not at all, but to get
consistent results from prayer, we must pray consistently.

"Watch and pray," was the admonition of Jesus.
"Watch"—be on your guard against those things that
may interfere with your happiness or well-being or success. "Pray"—take your business, take your home life, take
everything you are interested in to the Father for His advice, His help, His protection.

For praying does not mean petitioning God to change
His will towards us. Rather, praying is asking the Father
to point out the path of good. The right way always leads to
good—no matter what the obstacles, no matter what troubles wall us 'round. There is always a way out—and prayer
finds that way.

"Again I say unto you, that if two of you shall agree on
earth as touching anything that they shall ask, it shall be
done for them of my Father, which is in Heaven. For where
two or three are gathered together in my name, there am
I in the midst of them."—Matthew 18:19-20.

THE PILLAR OF FIRE

When the Midianites and the Amalekites and other children of the East descended upon the Israelites of old, God chose Gideon to save Israel from its invaders. But Gideon was a modest soul and could not see why the Lord should pick him out of all the hosts of the Isräelites. So he prayed for guidance, he asked for a sign:

> "And Gideon said unto God, if thou wilt save Israel by mine hand, as Thou hast said,
>
> "Behold, I will put a fleece of wool in the floor; and if the dew be on the fleece only, and it be dry upon all the earth beside, then shall I know that Thou wilt save Israel by mine hand, as Thou hast said.
>
> "And it was so; for he rose up early on the morrow, and thrust the fleece together, and wringed the dew out of the fleece, a bowl full of water.
>
> "And Gideon said unto God, Let not thine anger to be hot against me, and I will speak but this once: let me prove, I pray Thee, but this once with the fleece; let it now be dry only upon the fleece, and upon all the ground let there be dew.
>
> "And God did so that night: for it was dry upon the fleece only, and there was dew on all the ground."
>
> —JOSHUA 7:36-40.

On another occasion, when Moses was called of God to lead the children of Israel out of Egypt, he shrank back appalled at the magnitude of the task. He was slow of speech, he objected, and anyway the people would not listen to him. What sign could he show them—what proof give them?

> "And the Lord said unto him, What is that in thine hand? And he said, a rod.
>
> "And He said, Cast it on the ground. And he cast it on the ground, and it became a serpent; and Moses fled before it.
>
> "And the Lord said unto Moses, Put forth thine hand, and take it by the tail. And he put forth his hand, and caught it, and it became a rod in his hand."
>
> —EXODUS 4:2-4.

When Pharoah proved obdurate, there were signs a-many to show the still doubting Israelites that the Lord was on their side.

And when at last they started on their way out of the land of Egypt—"The Lord went before them by day in a pillar of cloud, to lead them the way; and by night in a pillar of fire, to give them light; to go by day and night."—Exodus 13:21.

All through their years in the desert—the years of their

purging from idolatry and slavery—that pillar of cloud and pillar of fire was their guide.

Throughout the Old Testament, you will find evidence of just such leading. And through it, again and again from direst straits the Israelites were brought forth triumphant and unharmed.

It was not when their numbers were small that they were overwhelmed by their powerful neighbors. It was when they grew so rich and strong that they depended upon their own fighting ability rather than upon the Lord. Let them stop and pray, let them ask for guidance through their Prophets—and they were victorious. Let them depend upon the strength of their own arms, and their enemies overran them.

"Then why," many will ask, "does no leading come to me? I pray—but I get no answer to my prayers."

Possibly it is because you are never still long enough to hear the answer. You don't wait for it. You pray—then go ahead in the way *you* think best, without waiting for guidance. "Man's dreary desires are answered drearily, and his impatient desires long delayed or violently fulfilled."

There must be time for concentration, time to strengthen the structure of your belief, time to clear away the static of petty thoughts, of doubts and fears, so you can hear the still, small voice beneath. Remember how the Lord led the Israelites into the Promised Land:

"At the commandment of the Lord the children of Israel journeyed, and at the commandment of the Lord they pitched: as long as the cloud abode upon the tabernacle, they rested in their tents.

"And when the cloud tarried long upon the tabernacle many days, then the children of Israel kept the charge of the Lord, and journeyed not.

"Or whether it were two days, or a month, or a year, that the cloud tarried upon the tabernacle, remaining thereon, the children of Israel abode in their tents, and journeyed not: but when it was taken up, they journeyed.

"At the commandment of the Lord they rested in the tents, and at the commandment of the Lord they journeyed: they kept the charge of the Lord, at the commandment of the Lord by the hand of Moses."

—NUMBERS 9:18-19-22-23.

Like a successful business, prayer needs the right amount of attention and the right kind of neglect. It pays at times, when difficult problems confront you in business, to shut down your desk and go off and play. It gives your subconscious mind a chance to work them out without the petty distractions of ordinary routine. In the same way, once you have made your prayer, once you have the structure of your belief right, it pays at times to forget it—in the serene knowledge that the burden is now the Father's, that you have done your part and He can be trusted to do the rest. "I will pray with the Spirit, and I will pray with the understanding also."—I Corinthians 14:15.

Prayer can do anything. Prayer can fight battles. Prayer can win games. Prayer can bring success in any right undertaking.

Not lip prayers—not the kind of prayer that is a mere mouthing of phrases—"Use not vain repetitions, as the heathen do, for they think that they shall be heard for their much speaking."—Matthew 6:7. But prayer from the heart. Prayer that goes to God as a loving Father, takes its desires to Him, realizes that He loves nothing better than to grant any right desire—*and then accepts it as granted,* in short, "BELIEVES THAT HE RECEIVES IT."

When the vast English host of more than a hundred thousand descended upon the Scots at Bannockburn, the Scots sank to their knees in their ranks and sent up heartfelt prayers to the God of Battles that He might save their country.

"See," cried the English King exultantly to a militant Bishop near, "they give in! They are on their knees to me already."

"They are on their knees, sire," answered the Bishop, "but to a greater King than you. They pray for victory. 'Twould be well, sire, did we do the same."

But Edward, secure in his hundred thousand veterans, laughed at the need of higher help. And before the day was done, met the most crushing defeat ever suffered by English arms!

Instances of successful prayer are so many and so well authenticated that whole volumes could be filled with them. In the home, in the Church, in business, in every phase of life. Perhaps the field in which prayers seem least often used is in games, yet we have it on the authority of Tim Lowry, Northwestern University football star, that prayer belongs to the football field as much as to the pulpit, and the record of his team stands as a tribute to its efficacy.

E. C. Garbisch, for two years captain of the West Point football team, established the custom of having the team join with him in earnest prayer, and the remarkable success of the team during his two years of leadership attracted worldwide attention.

Coach McDonald of the University of North Carolina established the practice of prayer on his basketball team years ago—not only before entering the game but between halves. "Prayer has inspired teamwork and morale," he says, "and has enabled the 'Tar Heels' to win time and again when defeat seemed certain."

I know many an actor who has obtained the part he longed for through prayer. I know others who have found producers for their plays, manufacturers for their inventions, publishers for their books. To illustrate, here is an item cut from a Boston paper of March 12, 1927.

"Ted McLean, actor, playright, esthete, lay on his bed one night recently and sobbed. He had neither food, clothing to brave the icy gales of winter, nor money to pay back rent for his room. From the bed he slipped to his knees on the floor and prayed.

"It was no prayer by rote, no mumbled prayer he had learned to repeat. It was a fervent supplication for aid in his distress.

"Next morning the telephone rang and there was a producer on the other end of the line. He was accepting one of McLean's plays and offering plenty of advance royalties for it.

"Luck? Ned believes it was the prayer, the first he had prayed in years."

I know scores of people who have found the right position through prayer. I know men and women who have been brought together to their mutual happiness through prayer. In fact, I know of nothing good that cannot be gained through sincere prayer.

"For verily I say unto you, That whosoever shall say unto this mountain, Be thou removed, and be thou cast into the sea; and shall not doubt in his heart, but shall believe that those things which he saith shall come to pass; he shall have whatsoever he saith."—Mark 11:23.

CASTING BREAD UPON THE WATERS

In days of old, when the Jews knelt in prayer, they had a custom of sacrificing to the Lord the finest lamb from the flock—as an "offering." In the beginning, it had started with the old idea of fear—they offered the best of the flock to the Fear-God in the hope that he would spare the rest.

But as the idea of a God of Justice and Mercy became more prevalent, the spirit in which the offering was made changed. Instead of a sacrifice of fear, it became one of gratitude and love. God had blessed the flocks. He had sent His increase. Therefore the finest of this increase should be given to His service.

Giving such as that is easy. Anyone can show gratitude *after* he has received largely. The sort of giving that is not so easy is to give *before* you can see any evidence of the answer to your prayers. That sort of giving requires faith. But because it is so sincere an evidence of faith, it is the sort of giving that comes back amplified an hundredfold.

Mere belief is often passive. Faith is active. Faith must do something to *show* its belief. Faith BELIEVES THAT IT RECEIVES, and evidences that belief by a "Thank Offering" to the Father even before there is any physical sign of the answer to its prayers.

"What doth it profit, my brethren, though a man say he hath faith, and have not works? Can faith save him?

"If a brother or sister be naked, and destitute of daily food,

"And one of you say unto them, Depart in peace, be ye warmed and filled; not-withstanding ye give them not those things which are needful to the body; what doth it profit?

"Even so faith, if it hath not works, is dead, being alone."—James 2:14-17.

In *Effective Prayer*, Russell Conwell tells how making an "offering" to God was used by his congregation when the Baptist Temple was being built. To quote him:

"The prayers made that day were made immediately before the offering was taken. The question was afterward put to the audience twice to ascertain if anyone who made a special offering on that particular day had not been answered, and there was no exception in the mass of testimony to the efficiency of each prayer that day. The recitals of the marvels which followed that prayerful offering were too startling for general belief. The people had complied with the conditions, and God had answered clearly according to His promise. They had brought the tithes into the storehouse, and the Lord had poured out the blessings as an infallible result.

"Cases of sudden and instantaneous recovery of the sick were related by hundreds. One poor man whose child was insane prayed for her recovery. That afternoon when he went to the sanitarium, she met him in her right mind.

"A lady sold her jewelry and brought the proceeds as an offering as she prayed for healing from sciatic rheumatism. She fell going from the Church, and arose to find the rheumatism gone.

"One old gentleman involved in a ruinous lawsuit brought all the profits of the previous week and deposited them as he prayed for a just outcome. Within the week, the suit was withdrawn.

"A woman with an overdue mortgage on her home determined to risk all on one prayer, and gave all she had as she prayed. When plumbers came to repair a leak the following week, they discovered a loose board in the floor under which her father had hidden all his money. The sum was more than enough to pay off the mortgage in its entirety.

"There were probably fifty such cases."

They had faith. And to show that faith, they gave thanks—they made their offering—as soon as they had prayed. They BELIEVED THAT THEY RECEIVED, so without waiting for more tangible proof of the answer to their prayers, they offered their thanks. "I have planted, Apollos watered; but God gave the increase."—I Corinthians 3:6. Do your part, and God will never fail you with the increase.

But don't think you can work Him like a slot machine—putting in a nickel and taking out a dollar. Your offering must be made—NOT in the hope of getting back more than you give, but as a thank-offering for what you HAVE RECEIVED! You have received abundantly—therefore you cheerfully give abundantly. You have asked for and are receiving infinite riches—therefore you cheerfully give of those you already had. Your giving must be a sincere act of faith. Unless you can make it such, keep your money. It will do you more good where it is.

And when you offer it, don't offer it on the first altar that presents itself. Don't just GIVE. Give to a cause you know to be good. If possible, give to the ultimate consumer, to some particular man you know who needs help, for—"As you have done it unto the least of these my brethren, you have done it unto me."—Matthew 25:40.

To give merely to some organization or Church without regard to the cause is lazy. Every man knows cases right in his own neighborhood that are as worthy as any ever cared for by an organization. Hunt these up. Give them a helping hand—and what is far more than the money you offer, give them the friendly, neighborly interest which restores their faith in God and man.

That kind of giving is never wasted. That kind is never lost. You can bless such gifts and look for them to return to you an hundred times over.

"No man gives to himself but himself. No man takes away from himself but himself."

Every bit of help and sympathy you give to others, you are really giving to yourself. Every time you lend a helping hand to lift another, you are really boosting yourself. So *give*—give though you see no evidences of return—and as you give, so it will come back to you, only amplified, a thousand times amplified.

"Trust in the LORD, and do good: so shalt thou dwell in the land, and verily thou shalt be fed.

"Delight thyself also in the LORD; and he shall give thee the desires of thine heart.

"Commit thy way unto the LORD; trust also in him, and he shall bring it to pass."—Psalms 37:3-5.

KEEPING THE TRACKS CLEAR

A few years ago, when the Grand Central Terminal in New York was being built, traffic there was fearfully congested. Thousands of trains coming in—thousands of others going out—tracks to be laid, building to be done, space to be found for vast quantities of material—and all the while the din of building, building.

Naturally, trains were delayed. Naturally, passengers were complaining. Naturally, good business was being lost to competing roads.

And then a strange thing was noticed. Incoming trains were late—five minutes, ten minutes, half an hour and more, on every division *but one*. On that one division, practically every train *came in on time!*

They checked up to find the reason. Trainmen smiled

when they asked them—"Nothing in their way," they explained, "so they brought their trains in on schedule."

They traced it to the Superintendent in charge of that division—and there they found the answer. "Why," he told them, "it's simple enough. You can't bring trains in unless you first send out those that came in ahead of them. I just keep my tracks clear, that's all."

And for keeping his tracks clear they made him Vice-President and put him in charge of the whole Terminal.

Men write asking me how they can tap the Universal Supply that is all about them, how they can get the money they require for some worthy enterprise or need.

How do you tap the supply of electrical current from the power house near you? Not merely by connecting your wires to the main current. That puts power into your wires, but of itself it serves no useful purpose. Before you can actually tap the source of electrical power, you have to *find an outlet for it!* You have to use what is in your house wires before more can come to you. The moment you stop the outflow—that moment the incoming current stops, too.

What is the surest way to bring business into a store? To first give out something—give out advertising, give out samples, give out special service.

What is the surest way to bring more water from the common reservoir into your pipes? To first draw out the water that is in them.

What is the surest way to draw upon the Universal Supply for more money? To first use to good advantage that which you have.

You don't depend upon the water in your pipes for your bath. You cheerfully use it to clean the tub, knowing there is plenty more behind, pushing its way forward, waiting to be used.

No more must you depend upon the money in your pocketbook or your bank account. Use it cheerfully, freely, for any good purpose, knowing there is infinitely more where that came from, merely waiting for you to make room for it.

The other day a friend told me of a time when he was in urgent need of a thousand dollars. All he had to his name was a $10 bill. And he found himself holding on to that $10 like a drowning man to a straw. For days he kept it, fearing to break it lest he should be lost entirely.

Then it suddenly occurred to him that he was pinning his faith to a lone $10 bill instead of to the Source of all supply—that he was damming the flow of money by keeping that little obstruction in the faucet.

He sat down at once and to show his faith, he mailed that $10 to the first worthy charity that came to his mind.

Immediately his faucet opened and the supply flowed through abundantly, and never since has it failed to respond to the same treatment.

"There is that scattereth, and increaseth yet more. And there is that withholdeth more than is meet, but it tendeth to poverty.

"The liberal soul shall be made fat; and he that watereth, shall be watered also himself."

—PROVERBS 11:24, 25.

EXERCISE

Out in California, away back in 1847, there lived a man who owned a ranch located upon a little stream.

The news came to him that down in the south of the state, men had discovered gold. All afire with the thirst for it, he sold his ranch and hurried south.

The man who bought the ranch, Colonel Sutter, built a mill and settled down with his family. One day his little girl brought some of the wet sand from the spillway into the house and that evening, playing before the fire, she sifted it through her fingers.

Here and there in the falling sand the firelight caught bright yellow glints and a visitor, watching them, recognized them for glints of gold. Since that evening, $38,000,000 in gold has been dug out of those few acres!

For thousands of years the gold lay there. For all that time, untold wealth was right beneath the feet of any chance wanderer. It remained for a little child to find it—

for a chance visitor to make the contact which turned this dormant wealth into dynamic riches.

All about you is electrical energy—in fact, many great scientists believe that this whole world, the heavens, the planets, all are nothing more than vast aggregations of protons and electrons. But the most of it is static. You have to put it to work—give it a job to do before it becomes dynamic.

In the realm of Mind, there are ideas worth more than all the gold ever dug out of the sands of California, all the diamonds ever taken from African mines. There are ways of harnessing the tides, of utilizing the power of the atom, of manipulating the steam in the tornado, of turning to account the full power of the sunlight. Why, right now, in the oldest section of the world known to man—the Land of Palestine—there have been uncovered riches greater than any gold or diamond mine ever dug, the riches of the Dead Sea! In this great body of water, which men have passed contemptuously by for thousands of years, it is estimated that there are recoverable salts worth a thousand billion dollars! But it required the power of mind to uncover them, to show men how to extract these vast riches.

In the Universal Mind, the God-Mind all about us, is the answer to thousands of even greater problems.

There is nothing you seek—neither wealth nor happiness, nor well-being nor success—that you cannot find in Mind.

How to do it? How make the contact? The Bible tells us—"Ye shall seek Me, and find Me, when ye shall search for Me with all your heart."—Jeremiah 29:13.

And how shall we search for Him?

The first essential is to have a definite work in which you want His help. Go through the Old Testament. When did God actively interfere with the ordinary processes of nature in behalf of the Israelites? Only when they had definite needs which must be met.

When did He divide the Red Sea? When did He send the pillar of cloud by day and the pillar of fire by night? When did He give water to the three Kings in the desert? When did He find the well for Hagar, send the manna for the Israelites, feed the Prophet through the ravens? Only when they sought Him and searched for Him with all their hearts.

Find the need. Find a cause worthy of all that Mind can give. Then give of your best—work head and heart and hand—and when you have done all that is humanly possible, have faith in the great God-Mind for the rest.

The first essential is a definite task. The second is perfect faith.

If the task be likened to a bulb which the electric current is to light or a motor which it is to turn, faith may be called the wire which brings the current from the power house. There can be no connection without the wire. There can be no results without faith.

Faith forms the contact between Universal Supply and your immediate need. The supply is always there, ready, able, willing to fill any need. But it is merely static supply as far as you are concerned—until you make it dynamic through faith.

How acquire such a faith? Read your Bible. Read of the many times the Israelites were saved by faith. Read the promises of the Scriptures, promises that offer you any and all things if only you will have the faith. Just listen:

"For the eyes of the Lord are over the righteous, and his ears are open unto their prayers; but the face of the Lord is against them that do evil."

—I PETER III:12.

"And it came to pass, as she continued praying before the Lord, that Eli marked her mouth."

—I SAM. I:12.

"And whiles I was speaking, and praying, and confessing my sin and the sin of my people Israel, and presenting my supplication before the Lord my God for the holy mountain of my God; Yea, whiles I was speaking in prayer, even the man Gabriel, whom I had seen in the vision at the beginning, being caused

to fly swiftly, touched me about the time of the evening oblation." —DAN. IX:20-21.

"Hear me when I call, O God of my righteousness;
thou hast enlarged me when I was in distress; have
mercy upon me, and hear my prayer."

—PSALM IV:1.

"My voice shalt thou hear in the morning, O Lord;
in the morning will I direct my prayer unto thee,
and will look up." —PSALM V:3.

"The Lord hath heard my supplication; the Lord
will receive my prayer." —PSALM VI:9.

"And when ye stand praying, forgive, if ye have
ought against any; that your Father, also which is in
heaven, may forgive you your trespasses."

—MARK XI:25.

"Now when all the people were baptized, it came to
pass that Jesus also being baptized, and praying, the
heaven opened." —LUKE III:21.

"I was in a city of Joppa praying: and in a trance I
saw a vision, a certain vessel descend, as it had been

a great sheet, let down from heaven by four corners; and it came even to me."   —ACTS XII:5.

"I will pray with the spirit, and I will pray with the understanding also; I will sing with the spirit, and I will sing with the understanding also."

—I COR. XIV:15.

"Thou shalt make thy prayer unto him, and he shall hear thee, and thou shalt pay thy vows."

—JOB XXII:27.

"He will regard the prayer of the destitute, and not despise their prayer."   —PSALM CII:17.

"The sacrifice of the wicked is an abomination to the Lord; but the prayer of the upright is his delight."

—PROV. XV:8.

. . . . "and nothing shall be impossible unto you. Howbeit this kind goeth not out but by prayer and fasting."   —MATT. XVII:21.

"Be anxious for nothing; but in everything by prayer and supplication with thanksgiving let your requests be made known unto God.

"And the peace of God, which passeth all understanding, shall keep your hearts and minds through Christ Jesus." —PHIL. IV:6-7.

"And the prayer of faith shall save the sick, and the Lord shall raise him up; and if he have committed sins, they shall be forgiven him." —JAMES V:15.

"Confess your faults one to another, and pray one for another, that ye may be healed. The effectual forvent prayer of a righteous man availeth much."
—JAMES V:16.

"Then what prayer or what supplication soever shall be made of any man, or of all thy people Israel, when every one shall know his own sore and his own grief, and shall spread forth his hands in this house;

"Then hear thou from heaven thy dwelling place, and forgive, and render unto every man according unto all his ways, whose heart thou knowest (for thou only knowest the hearts of the children of men" . . .) —II CHRON. VI:29-30.

"And at midnight Paul and Silas prayed, and sang praises unto God; and the prisoners heard them."
—ACTS XVI:25.

"Thinkest thou that I cannot now pray to my Father, and he shall presently give me more than twelve legions of angels." —MATT. XXVI:53.

"Therefore I say unto you, what things soever ye desire, when ye pray, believe that ye receive them, and ye shall have them." —MARK XI:24.

"And he spake a parable unto them to this end, that men ought always to pray, and not to faint." —LUKE XVIII:1.

"I pray for them: I pray not for the world, but for them which thou hast given me; for they are thine.

"I pray not that thou shouldest take them out of the world, but that thou shouldest keep them from the evil.

"Neither pray I for these alone, but for them also which shall believe on me through their word."

—ST. JOHN XVII:9, 15, 20.

"Likewise the Spirit also helpeth our infirmities; for we know not what we should pray for as we ought; but the Spirit itself maketh intercession for us with groanings which cannot be uttered."

—ROM. VIII:26.

"And the very God of peace sanctify you wholly; and I pray God your whole spirit and soul and body be preserved blameless unto the coming of our Lord Jesus Christ." —THESS. V:23.

"Wherefore also we pray always for you, that our God would count you worthy of this calling, and fulfill all the good pleasure of his goodness, and the work of faith with power."

—II THESS. I:11.

"And whatsoever we ask, we receive of him, because we keep his commandments, and do those things which are pleasing in his sight."

—I JOHN III:22.

"And this is the confidence that we have in him, that, if we ask any thing according to his will, he heareth us;

"And if we know that he hear us, whatsoever we ask, we know that we have the petitions that we desired of him." —II JOHN V:14-15.

"But I know, that even now, whatsoever thou wilt ask of God, God will give it thee."

—ST. JOHN XI:22.

"And whatsoever ye shall ask in my name, that will I do, that the Father may be glorified in the Son."   —ST. JOHN XIV:13.

"If ye shall ask any thing in my name, I will do it."   —ST. JOHN XIV:14.

"If any of you lack wisdom, let him ask of God, that giveth to all men liberally, and up-braideth not; and it shall be given him.

"But let him ask in faith, nothing wavering."
                                   —JAMES I:15-6.

"Now unto him that is able to keep you from fall-ing, and to present you faultless before the presence of his glory with exceeding joy."   —JUDE 1-24.

"But when ye pray, use not vain repetition, as the heathen do; for they think that they shall be heard for their much speaking.

"Be not ye therefore like unto them; for your Father knoweth what things ye have need of, before ye ask him.

"After this manner therefore pray ye: Our Father which art in heaven, Hallowed by thy name.

"Thy kingdom come. Thy will be done on earth, as it is in heaven.

"Give us this day our daily bread.

"And forgive us our debts, as we forgive our debtors.

"And lead us not into temptation, but deliver us from evil; for thine is the kingdom, and the power, and the glory, for ever, Amen."   —MATT. VI-7-13.

"Trust in the Lord, and do good; so shalt thou dwell in the land, and verily thou shalt be fed."

—PSALM XXXVII:3.

"Commit thy way unto the Lord; trust also in him; and he shall bring it to pass."   —PSALM XXXVII:5.

"Rest in the Lord, and wait patiently for him."

—PSALM XXXVII:7.

"The Lord is my shepherd; I shall not want."

—PSALM XXIII:1.

"Yea, though I walk through the valley of the shadow of death, I will fear no evil; for thou art with me; thy rod and thy staff they comfort me."

—PSALM XXIII:4.

"Give ear to my prayer, O God; and hide not thyself from my supplication."   —PSALM IV:1.

"Let my prayer be set forth before thee as incense; and the lifting up of my hands as the evening sacrifice." —PSALM CXLI:2.

"I exhort, therefore, that, first of all, supplications, prayers, intercessions, and giving of thanks, be made for all men." —TIM. II:I.

"Yet have thou respect unto the prayer of thy servant, and to his supplication, O Lord my God, to hearken unto the cry and to the prayer, which thy servant prayeth before thee today." —I KINGS VIII:28.

"And the whole multitude of the people were praying without at the time of incense." —LUKE I:IO.

"Praying always with all prayer and supplication in the Spirit, and watching thereunto with all perseverance and supplication." —EPH. VI:I8.

"Night and day praying exceedingly that we might see your face, and might perfect that which is lacking in your faith." —I THESS. III:IO.

"And hearken thou to the supplication of thy servant, and of thy people Israel, when they shall pray toward this place: and hear thou in heaven thy dwelling place: and when thou hearest, forgive."

—I KINGS VIII:30.

"Nevertheless, we made our prayer unto our God, and set a watch against them day and night, because of them." —NEH. IV:9.

"And I set my face unto the Lord God, to seek by prayer and supplications, with fasting, and sackcloth, and ashes." —DAN. IX:3.

"But we will give ourselves continually to prayer and to the ministry of the word." —ACTS VI:4.

"And on the Sabbath we went out of the city by a river side, where prayer was wont to be made; and we sat down, and spake unto the women which resorted thither." —ACTS XVI:13.

. . . . "be ye therefore sober, and watch unto prayer."

—I PETER IV:7.

XX

THE UNPARDONABLE SIN

"Wherefore I say unto you, All manner of sin and blasphemy shall be forgiven unto men: but the blasphemy against the Holy Ghost shall not be forgiven unto men.

"And whosoever speaketh a word against the Son of man, it shall be forgiven him: but whosoever speaketh against the Holy Ghost, it shall not be forgiven him, neither in this world, neither in the world to come."

MATTHEW 12:31-32.

There was once a young Prince so courted, so pampered and waited upon, that when he grew to manhood, his parents found he had not learned the first principle about acting or even thinking for himself.

Like most parents, the King and Queen could not understand the reason for such stupidity. Finally despairing of his ever learning enough at home to succeed to the throne, they decided to send him on a journey through foreign lands in the hope that thus he might learn to look out for himself—and eventually for his Kingdom.

The Prince rode gaily forth, for even to a Prince, a life where everything is done for you becomes monotonous.

Presently he came to a little man lying with his ear to the ground. "What are you doing?" asked the Prince. "Listening to all that goes on in the world," answered the little man. "I am called Hearing. For anyone who is interested in his fellow man, I could be an invaluable servant."

"Then come with me," directed the Prince. "I have use for such as you."

Coming to a little wood, they saw a very tall man on the other side of it—quite the tallest he had ever seen. "And who are you?" asked the Prince. "I am called Smell," the tall man said. "I can reach over tree-tops, or around corners or through cracks. I could clean up the world if I had a Master who knew how to use me. Can you use another servant?"

"That I can," replied the Prince, "just come with me."

Journeying along cheerfully together, they espied a man sitting in the sun, wrapped in blankets, yet shivering as though with the ague. "And what ails you, my good man?" asked the Prince.

"Alas," moaned the poor fellow, "I had a master who was always afraid of something. In cold weather it was overheating. In hot weather it was drafts. Until now that he has left me, I can't be comfortable in either. I am looking for a master who fears neither cold nor heat. Him I can serve happily and make happy. Pray can you tell me of such a one?"

"What is your name?" asked the Prince curiously. "My name is Feel," answered the miserable one. "Then come with me, Feel," said the Prince, "and I will make you happy."

Nearing the boundaries of the Prince's kingdom, they saw a huge oaf lying by the side of the road and stopped to talk with him. "Do you need another servant?" asked the fellow. "If I did," replied the Prince smilingly, "I don't know what I should do with such a huge fellow as you. What are you good for?"

"I can be the best servant in the world," answered the other. "My name is Taste, and I am so strong I can carry you all day long without tiring. It was only because my last employer let me become the master that you see me looking so fat and ugly. I rode him instead of carrying him. Now I am looking for someone who knows how to remain the master."

Once more they wended their way through wood and meadow, until they came to a high hill. On top of it they found a man gazing intently at all that went on below him.

"And who are you?" asked the Prince. "I am Sight," replied the other. "And I am watching all that goes on in the world. I can tell you the good and the bad, the needy and the shiftless. I can show you all that is wrong with the world. I can point out the way to make things right. But I will work only for one who will work with me. I want a master who is intelligent, who is industrious and who will use me for good. Pray tell me, do you know any such?"

"Come with me," said the Prince, "and I will try to be such a master."

That night the Prince and his five servants rested at a tavern, where Sight and Hearing pronounced the landlord honest, Smell picked out a clean room for the Prince to sleep, Taste ate circumspectly, as became the ideal servant he had promised to be, and Feel settled them all comfortably for the night.

The next day they reached the castle of Princess Happiness. The Princess greeted them so graciously and looked so charming that the Prince fell in love with her at once. But to win her, he was told that he must perform three herculean tasks—to fail in which would lose him not only the Princess, but his head.

How his five servants accomplished those tasks, how he won the Princess' hand and heart and bore her back in triumph to his parents, make a story too long to tell here.

The meat of it I know you have already grasped—that he who would win happiness must himself work for it to some worthy purpose—and that he who learns to master his five servants (senses) can get from them any good service he may ask.

Most of us are like the young Prince—good fellows,

cheerful, well-meaning, but without purpose. We let circumstances or people say what we shall do, what we shall be. We let others do our thinking for us. We let circumstances control our actions.

Like the heathen idols of old—"They have mouths, but they speak not: eyes have they, but they see not:

"They have ears, but they hear not: noses have they, but they smell not:

"They have hands, but they handle not: feet have they, but they walk not: neither speak they through their throat."—Psalms 115:5-7.

All knowledge is written in an open book before us— yet how much do we grasp? The little that others hand to us on a platter.

All power is put in our hands—yet how much do we use? The infinitesimal bit necessary to do our daily tasks.

All riches are spread out before us—yet how much do we take? Enough to buy our daily bread, to give us a few little comforts and necessities.

Like the little green loafers in the plant leaves, we waste 99 per cent. of the power, 90 per cent. of the raw material that is given us.

"The greater part of agriculture," says the *New York Herald-Tribune,* "is the job of persuading the small green slaves that do our fundamental agricultural work to labor a little more earnestly at their jobs."

"These small slaves are the most incorrigible loafers in

the world. They are those tiny green globules which any botanist's microscope will show you in the leaves of a green plant and which operate that enormously important process called photosynthesis, by which sunlight and air and water are converted into the bodies of living plants and into food for every living thing. The power that runs the green-leaf factory is sunlight. Of this power it is estimated that the leaf uses less than one-tenth of 1 per cent. The materials of the factory are water and air and the salts of the soil. Of these the factory wastes well over 90 per cent., usually more. A manufacturing enterprise that throws away 99 9-10 per cent. of its raw materials ought certainly to give its owner some disquiet. If the working habits of these granules could be bettered, farming would recover at one step the ground that it has lost to more mechanical crafts."

What is the Unpardonable Sin? It is to neglect the latent powers within yourself.

What is the sin against the Holy Ghost? It is to ignore the Holy Spirit within you. It is to use only your conscious energies, when the Holy Spirit is capable of a thousand times as much.

"Ye stiffnecked and uncircumcised in heart and ears, ye do always resist the Holy Ghost."—Acts 7:51.

You have been given a certain talent. Yet for lack of initiative or fear of loss, you keep that talent buried. What will you say when the accounting is demanded of you? Go read the parable of the talents. Go listen to what the Master had to say of the unprofitable servant.

The story is told of a great artist of several hundred years ago. His skill in mosaics was marvelous. He had a poor young assistant whose duty it was to keep the studio clean, to lift and carry and help around the place.

One day he asked the artist if he might have the little fragments of glass that fell from the latter's work bench. "Of course, of course," said the great man impatiently, "do what you like with them. They are of no value."

Over in a corner of the studio, behind tools and canvasses and the like, the young man studied and worked over his fragments during the long evenings after the artist had left. Through weeks and months he labored painstakingly, tirelessly.

Upon a time the artist, looking for a lost tool, happened into the corner and stood astounded. The face of glass that confronted him was the most beautiful thing he had ever seen!

He called the young man. "Who did this?" he asked. "I did, Master," the other explained, apologetically. "I used only those bits of glass you threw away."

Long and earnestly the other gazed. "It is wonderful," he said at last, "wonderful! Better than I, with all my fine materials, have ever done. It shall have the place of honor in the new Cathedral."

You say you have no opportunity to do big things?

Where do you suppose opportunity is—around the next corner, or hiding in the cellar? Opportunity is all around you. It is like the air you breathe. It is everywhere—and always.

A. T. Stewart, founder of the great Wanamaker's store in New York, began his merchandising career with $1.50. 87½ cents of it he invested in buttons and thread and needles. But they would not sell. He sat down to think this out. Buttons, thread, needles—they were necessities—it seemed to him they ought to sell. But people wouldn't buy them. Should he keep on trying until somebody would buy them, or should he—wonderful thought—should he first find out what people WANTED, invest the rest of his capital in that and sell it?

He decided on the latter—and the store he eventually sold to Wanamaker for millions was the result.

It is said that John Jacob Astor once took over a bankrupt millinery concern. He did not immediately conclude—as most seem to—that the buyer, or the manufacturer, or the sales people were at fault, and discharge them. Instead, he went out and stood on a corner which fashionable women were in the habit of passing. And whenever a particularly well dressed woman passed, he studied her hat. When he had it well in mind, he went back to the store, picked out one as nearly like it as possible, and put it in the window at a special price. Took all the other hats out of the window and left only that one.

Then he betook himself to the corner until he found another attractive style—and added it to the first one. And so on until he had learned what people wanted. He didn't try to sell people what they did not want—and then wonder why no business came his way. He took time to find out what people did want—and then gave it to them at a special price.

Emerson had the same thought when he wrote: "He who addresses himself to modes or wants that can be dispensed with, builds his house off the road. But he who addresses himself to problems that every man must come to solve, builds his house on the road, and every man must come to it."

There are opportunities to build your house by the road every day and everywhere. A man down in Washington, who was too poor to buy his kiddie toys, sat down one evening and carved out a "Kiddie Car"—just to satisfy the father-love in him for his own child.

But the "Kiddie Car" made such a hit that he was promptly besieged by every other child on the street for one like it. He grasped the idea that the toy which appeals to your own child is likely to appeal to all children of the same age—took his idea to a manufacturer and made millions out of it.

Capital? His material capital consisted of a pen-knife and a piece of wood.

Do you know how the mowing machine was invented?

A woman nailed a lot of scissors along the edge of a board, wired them together so they would all open at one pull of the wire, and close at another. And there was the principle of the mowing machine!

What do people want? What do people need? Those are the questions to ask—not how much capital or training or tools you have. Find the need—then work out the way to satisfy it. The capital will be easy to get.

Everything is useful. Everything has in it the seed of riches. Even the insects can be used for gain.

The other day I read in the paper that armies of English beetles and caterpillars are being picked at the experimental station at Harpendon in Hertfordshire to ship to New Zealand. Brambles and ragwort weed are getting beyond control out there, so the insects that feed specially on these are being sent out to keep them in check. And every farmer is familiar with the idea of encouraging the propagation of harmless insects to prey upon those that ruin trees or crops.

All about us is opportunity—so close under our noses that we cannot see it. Often the very obstacles in our path, the very things we fear most, are our greatest opportunities. Like Moses, our supporting staffs sometimes seem to change into serpents in our hands, but if we grasp them fearlessly, we find them just as strong to support us as of old.

"And the Lord said unto him, What is that in thine hand? And he said, a rod.

"And He said, Cast it on the ground. And he cast it on

the ground, and it became a serpent; and Moses fled from before it.

"And the Lord said unto Moses, Put forth thine hand, and take it by the tail. And he put forth his hand, and caught it, and it became a rod in his hand."

What is the correct way to pick up a snake whose fangs you fear? By the neck. Take it by the tail and it will twist around and fasten its fangs in you. Yet the Lord told Moses to grasp the serpent by the tail. Why? To make him first overcome his fear of it. When Moses grasped the serpent fearlessly, it turned into a supporting staff in his hand.

Have you ever heard the story of Tombstone, Ariz.?

A prospector, with all the faith of the true prospector, believed he could find gold in the mountains of Arizona. His friends laughed at him—ridiculed his dream of fortune—told him all he would ever find in those mountains was his tombstone.

He held on to his dream—he kept his faith—and discovered a mine worth millions. Then in kindly irony he named the town "Tombstone."

"Faith," said Paul, is "the substance of things hoped for, the evidence of things not seen." Faith must be up and doing. That prospector might have *believed* all his life that there was gold in those Arizona mountains, but it would have done him little good had he not had the active faith to pack up his tools and go get it.

The man who dreams, then works and prays to make his dreams come true, cannot help but succeed.

"Be ye doers of the word," says James (1:22), "and not hearers only, deceiving your own selves."

Pray—believe—then turn that belief into active faith by doing your part, even if that part be only the making of a "Thank Offering" for the granting of your prayer.

THE STEAM OF THE MIND

If there is any place more than another where we have neglected the power given us by the Holy Spirit, it is in controlling our thoughts.

What would you think of an engineer who kept his boilers coaled to capacity, but left his steam cock open so that as fast as it formed, the steam escaped?

Yet that is what most of us do a large part of the time. For thoughts are the steam of the mind, with a power far greater than any steam ever formed of water. Yet instead of using that steam to direct and control our destinies, we let it blow off through our mouths—through the steam cock of idle conversation.

Don't run to someone else with every new idea that comes to you. Keep it bottled up. Drop a bit of yeast into it and let it work. When it is ripe it will pop off of itself. Then you will have something worth while. But to take it and look at it, to show it to admiring friends, is like taking the hen off the nest every few minutes to see whether any eggs have hatched. After a while she loses interest and refuses to go back.

Your subconscious mind is your part of Divinity. Baptize it with understanding of your Divine sonship, confirm it with active faith, and it becomes the Holy Spirit within you that has all power, that can bring you anything of good.

Your subconscious is controlled—not by will power, but by your thoughts. Your real, secret, innermost beliefs. Whatever beliefs penetrate to the subconscious, it proceeds to bring into being in the material world.

In short, your thoughts register upon the subconscious much as sound registers upon the phonographic disc, to be given back to you in material manifestations just as surely as the seed in the soil brings forth the plant.

When John McCormick sings into the phonograph, you do not get back the sound of Galli Curci's voice. When your shout rings against the mountain side, the echo does not bring back the sound of another's voice. When you think thoughts of poverty, or sickness, or unhappiness, you do not get back evidences of riches or health or happiness. No— you get what you give. You see materialized the thought you have impressed upon your subconscious mind.

"As a man thinketh in his subconscious mind," we might well paraphrase the old saying, "so is he!"

Thought is the greatest power we have. It is the steam of the mind. It is the electricity that runs our mental dynamo. But just as the electric current can be used to electrocute or to serve you, so can your thoughts make you well or ill, rich or poor, happy and prosperous or miserable and needy.

What happens when electricity runs loose—when wires become crossed and the power of the volt scatters in all directions? What happens when steam pipes burst and the escaping steam suddenly finds itself uncontrolled? Fire—explosion—death—injury—these are the penalties of lack of direction in handling the mighty elemental forces of nature.

What happens when thought is uncontrolled, when it lacks direction? Sickness—poverty—crime—death—these are the penalties of lack of direction in handling the greatest force in the whole wide world, the force of thought.

What is the Unpardonable Sin? It is to waste this mighty energy the Father has given you. It is to fail to harness it to your needs, to your worthy desires.

What is the sin against the Holy Spirit? To ignore Him, to lack the initiative or the faith to call Him to your side, to go through life with never an inspiration, never a guiding hand from this Holy Spirit within.

"And whosoever shall speak a word against the Son of Man, it shall be forgiven him. But unto him that blasphemeth against the Holy Ghost, it shall not be forgiven."—Luke 12:10.

How do we blaspheme against Him? By scorning the power latent in Him, by ridiculing the idea that any good thing is within our reach if only we will seek His guiding Spirit.

There is no goal you can strive for that He cannot guide you to. There is nothing you can ask for—believingly— that He cannot show you the way to obtain.

Do obstacles bar your way? Baptize them—baptize them stepping-stones to your goal—in the name of the Father, the Son and the Holy Ghost. Then confidently, believingly use them as stepping-stones. The Holy Spirit will show you the way.

The important thing to remember is that no sincere prayer is lost. Even though you pray for something it is not good for you to have. The effort is not wasted. If your prayer is offered in the right spirit, it will come back to you in good.

So pray for what you want—believing. Then enlist the Holy Spirit on your side by your active faith. Ask for a sign—ask for guidance. Then start, one step at a time, towards your goal. Any task is easy if you break it up into enough little tasks, and then do one at a time, finishing each before you start the next. The start is the hard part. To begin is to be half finished.

"For if any be a hearer of the word, and not a doer, he is like unto a man beholding his natural face in a glass:

"For he beholdeth himself, and goeth his way, and straight way forgetteth what manner of man he was.

"But who so looketh into the perfect law of liberty, and continueth therein, he being not a forgetful hearer, but a doer of the work, this man shall be blessed in his deed."

—JAMES 1:23–25.

XXI

THE COVENANT

*"And He said unto them; which of you shall have a
friend, and shall go unto him at midnight, and say unto
him, Friend, lend me three loaves; for a friend of mine
in his journey is come to me, and I have nothing to set
before him?*

*"And he from within shall answer and say. Trouble me
not; the door is now shut, and my children are with me
in bed; I cannot rise and give thee.*

*"I say unto you, though he will not rise and give him,
because he is his friend, yet because of his importunity he
will rise and give him as many as he needeth."*

LUKE 11:5-8.

If there is one riddle which more than any other has defied mankind's ingenuity, it is that of supply.

In a world full of unlimited riches, with mental powers whose limits have never yet been reached, a large part of the human race barely subsists, keeping scarcely a jump ahead of starvation.

Even here, in the richest country on earth, misery stalks through idle coal fields, through mill towns, through the slums of the great cities. Why?

With undreamed of riches in the power of the atom, in the force of the tides, in the sunlight, in the very air we breathe, why should so large a section of mankind live in misery? Why should not we—you and I and our neighbors—be able to draw upon Infinite Supply at will for any good thing we wish? Jesus told us we could:

"If a son shall ask bread of any of you that is a Father, will he give him a stone? Or if he ask a fish, will he for a fish give him a serpent?

"Or if he shall ask an egg, will he offer him a scorpion?

"If ye then, being evil, know how to give good gifts unto your children; how much more shall your heavenly Father give.. . . . to them that ask him?"—Luke 11:11-13.

Then why should we, like many a poor, starving miner back in '49, be walking over millions in riches, yet be unable to lay our hands upon even a trace of them?

Perhaps the story of Charles Page, as given in the July *American Magazine,* may be of help in pointing the solution. Page is now a millionaire oil operator in Oklahoma, but a few years ago he had little or nothing, and his wife was so sick he feared he was going to lose her as well. The surgeons at the Hospital had given up hope for her, so as all other avenues seemed closed, Page turned to God.

"Oh, Lord," he prayed, "don't take her away from me. I just couldn't bear it."

The words rang in his ears—and they had an empty ring. As a prayer, it seemed to fall flat. Why should the Lord intervene for him, if the only reason he could offer was that he couldn't bear it? Plenty of husbands just as devoted as he had lost their wives. Why should the Lord specially favor him?

The thought came home to him with the power of a blow. What had he ever done that the Lord should go out of His way to help him? What reason had he to look for special consideration from above? None! He'd been a decent enough citizen, but no more so than the average, and kneeling there he couldn't recall a single thing he had done which would entitle him to ask favors from the Lord.

The thought appalled him. What chance had he? Must he then lose the one dearest to him in all the world, just because he had never done enough to be worthy of keeping her? No! No! That was unthinkable. It wasn't too late. He would start that very minute. What was it the Master had said? "Whatsoever ye do unto the least of these my brethren, ye do it unto me."

The next morning a poor widow was in transports of joy to find under her doorsill money enough to carry her safely through the winter.

But that evening, inquiry at the hospital elicited the information that Page's wife was no better. For a little his faith faltered. Then, as he thought back over the reason for his act, it flamed up anew. Why had he helped the widow? Not because he was interested in her welfare, not even because it was the right thing to do, but because he was trying to buy off the Lord. Thinking of it in that light, it sounded ridiculous. He got down on his knees again.

"I ain't makin' a bargain with you, God," he promised. "I'm doin' this because it's the *right thing* for me to do."

This time it seemed to him his message carried. He felt strangely cheered and relieved. His prayer had gone through.

Now comes the remarkable part of this incident. His wife, much to the astonishment of the surgeons, took a turn for the better, and within a comparatively short time was well!

From that day to this, Charles Page has never failed in his Covenant with God. Times there were when everything looked black. Times when it meant a real struggle to find the Lord's share. But his faith never faltered. He knew if he did his part, he could depend upon God for His.

For a long time he gave a tenth of all his earnings. Then

he increased it to a fourth. Later to a half, and finally all
except what he needed for personal and family expenses.
He has given away literally millions.

"But don't get the idea," he warns, "that I'm telling
you how to get rich. It's the *giving,* not the *getting,* that's
important. Personally, I believe that it's only playing fair
to tithe, or give a part of your income to God. But it must
be a gift, not an investment. Do you get the difference?
If you tithe in the right spirit, you will get your reward
just as sure as a gun's iron; but the reward may not come
in the form of money. Often it's something far better than
money.. . . ."

The longer I live, the more I read and study, in books
and among people, the more firmly convinced I become
that Charles Page and his kind have found the only sure
method of contacting with Infinite Supply. In the words
of the hymn, you must "make channels for the streams of
love, that they may broadly flow."

You have heard of the wells in the great Sahara Desert.
Keep them free from sand, and they flow forever. Dam up
the crevices through which the water comes and they dry
overnight.

Just as surely as you let the sands of selfishness and greed
dam up your wells of supply, your flow of riches will stop,
too. Oh, yes, there is the occasional miser who accum-
mulates a fortune, just as there is the occasional this, that
or the other who breaks all the rules and gets away with it

for a while. But we are not looking for hundred-to-one shots. We are looking for a sure thing.

And the one sure thing I have been able to find about the Law of Supply is that we get as we give—generously or parsimoniously—it all depends upon ourselves. From the poor widow who shared her last bit of oil and meal with the Prophet, and thereafter found no end to her cruse of oil or measure of meal, down to Charles Page, the record has been the same.

The size of the gift does not matter. The widow's mite may bring far greater returns than the rich man's millions. It is the spirit in which you give that counts.

You who are starting upon life's highway, you who have traveled far and are worn and weary—make this Covenant with God:

I will give to every worthy cause, whatever may seem right and good in Your sight. Not as a bargain with You. Not to put in a nickel and pull out a dollar. But as a token of real thankfulness for all You have done for me, as a proof of my serene confidence in Your continuing supply. I will act as Your channel, carrying the good things of life from their Infinite Source to those who need them. I will not stint myself or others. I will drink deeply of the waters of the well, yet give just as generously to others, knowing there is no limit to the Supply—that the more good outlets I find, the greater will be the inflow.

A Covenant such as that is not a bargain with God—it is an evidence of your serene faith in Him. A Covenant such as that is like the Ark of the Israelites—an assurance of the Father's continuous protection and supply.

"Is any among you afflicted? let him pray. Is any merry? let him sing psalms.

"Is any sick among you? let him call for the elders of the church; and let them pray over him, anointing him with oil in the name of the Lord:

"And the prayer of faith shall save the sick, and the Lord shall raise him up; and if he have committed sins, they shall be forgiven him."

—JAMES 5:13-15.

XXII

THE SOWERS

"A Sower went out to sow his seed.

"And as he sowed, some fell by the wayside and were trodden down; some fell upon rock; and withered away; and some fell among thorns; and the thorns sprang up and choked it.

"And other fell on good ground, and sprang up and bare fruit an hundred fold."

—LUKE 8:5–8.

A manufacturer makes a good coat. He puts as low a price upon it as he can and still make a living profit. He satisfies himself that he is giving the utmost of value for the money. Then he goes out to sow the seeds of sales.

To merchants in his own town he shows the coat. He

tells them of the fine cloth he has put into it, the careful workmanship, the graceful style lines.

To merchants in other towns, he sends salesmen, with samples of the coat.

To people dwelling in rural communities, he writes letters, encloses pieces of the cloth, sends pictures of the coat, describes it in detail.

For those whose names he can not get, he puts advertisements in their papers, in their magazines, in catalogs, picturing the coat, showing its beauty, its grace, its low price.

He sows the seeds of sales. Some fall by the wayside, some fall on stony ground, some among thorns—but if his soil be well chosen, the most fall on good ground and yield fruit that springs up and increases.

We are all sowers, and the seeds we sow in good ground are seeds of success, of riches and happiness. Every word we speak, everything we do, is a seed.

When you want a better position, how do you go about it? You tell your friends what you can do. You ask them if they know of an opening for a capable man like yourself. You answer "Want Ads." You advertise your abilities. You write to likely prospects, telling them how you could serve them. Above all, you hold in your own mind the thought of what wonderful things you could do in the right job, what new avenues of service you could open, what numbers of people you could benefit. Sowing seed—and if it be sown on good ground, if it be kept watered with faith and prayer, it will presently spring up and blossom forth in new opportunities for you.

Do you want business? You sow the knowledge of your products, of their special qualities, of the things they will do, among those they will serve best, and to the extent that you pick good ground, to that extent will your crop be good.

Two things you must watch:

1st—Be careful of where you sow. There is the seed which falls by the wayside, and the fowls of the air come and devour it. There is the seed which falls on stony ground, but when the sun comes up, it withers away because it has no root. There is the seed that falls among thorns, and the thorns grow up with it and choke it. And then there is the seed that falls on good ground.

For many years I have sold books by mail. Millions of dollars worth of them. And I have found that quite as important as the letter I write or the circular I print is the list of people to whom I send them. The best letter in the world will not bring results from people who do not read books. But even a poor letter will bring a fair response from a good list.

So it is with all things. Pick your soil, and even the most amateurish planting will bring you fair results.

2nd—Be careful of your seed. Good soil will always bring forth what you plant—be it wheat or thistles. So plant only what you wish to reap.

And remember that every thought, every word, every act, is a seed—of good or ill. If you have seen suffering, know that it is the effect of wrong thought, of evil seeds. Seeds of right thought, good actions, can never bring forth crops of sorrow. Seeds of wrong thought, wicked action, can never produce happiness or content. The Law is just, unchangeable. It cannot give evil for good, or good for evil.

As Allen puts it in *As a Man Thinketh:*

"Law, not confusion, is the dominating principle in the universe; justice, not injustice, is the soul and substance of life; and righteousness, not corruption, is the moulding and moving force in the spiritual government of the world. This being so, man has but to right himself to find that the universe is right; and during the process of putting himself right, he will find that as he alters his thoughts towards things and other people, things and other people will alter towards him."

So look now to your seed. What are you sowing?

If it be seeds of timidity, inferiority, self-consciousness, fear, repression—change them now, this minute. Burn those tares of unhappiness and misery. Sow instead the seeds of riches and happiness and success. It is just as easy. It requires merely a change of base—a change in your thoughts, a change in your attitude towards the things that happen to you.

Let obstacles, let trials, let difficulties beset you; let friends or enemies stand in your way; see the angel in them—greet the Divinity in them. By digging one cellar at a time, John MacDonald built the great New York subway. By taking one step at a time, you can overcome the world.

So refuse to recognize, refuse to accept difficulties. Tell them they don't belong to you. Baptize them stepping-stones to success. Sow the seeds of success in your every thought, in your every act—and some fine morning you will wake to find those seeds of success blossoming all over the very obstacles that appeared most insurmountable. "As a man soweth, that shall he also reap."—Galatians 6:7.

Till your ground. Sow your seed. Then have no worry as to the results. If you do your part with serene faith, depend upon it, the Father will do His. You can look to Him for the increase.

"I have planted, Apollos watered; but God gave the increase."

—I CORINTHIANS 3:6.

XXIII

THE SECRET OF MATTER

"For He looketh to the ends of the earth, and seeth under the whole heaven."

—JOB 28:24.

Tell me not in mournful numbers," goes the first line of a poem we used to recite in my school days, and ends with—"and things are not what they seem."

Truly, they are not. Not in these days of black rays and violet rays which give up the innermost secrets that Nature has concealed from man for so many thousands of years.

With the aid of the "invisible light" or "black light" of the ultra-violet ray, Dr. Herman demonstrated to the Illuminating Engineering Society in Washington that many things were very far from being what they seem. Under the powerful ray of this lamp, things otherwise not distinguishable to the human eye stood out as bodly as in black-face type. Counterfeit money took on an entirely different color.

Otherwise invisible erasures were instantly seen. Even ink manufactured by the same company, but of slightly different age, changed its color entirely under the "black" rays. False teeth stood out like lumps of chocolate. False hair was easily distinguishable. Invisible ink became legible. It was even possible to read the printing on the opposite side of a newspaper.

To quote the *New York Sun*:

"In a world that always has loved a good paradox, what more delightful one could be imagined than that of seeing things by invisible light? It has long been known that such light existed and that objects could be photographed in its rays, but it is only recently that investigators have discovered a way to make it reveal its presence directly to our eyes.

"During an electrical convention in Colorado Springs the other night the garden of a hotel, flooded with beams from powerful searchlights which to human sight seemed absolutely dark, was turned into a ghostly picture in which strange and unnatural colors glowed upon shrubbery, fountains and costumes of men and women amid an enveloping atmosphere of gloom.

"The invisible light employed in experiments such as this is the ultra violet. If the human eye be compared to a radio receiving set, the ultra-violet rays may be likened to short-wave transmission which the ordinary set is incapable of picking up. If our eyes were constructed differently we might see ultra-violet; as it is, this light is blackness to our limited vision.

"In noctovision, the invention of the Scot Baird, dark rays of a different kind are used—the long-wave indra red at the opposite end of the spectrum. Baird's apparatus does not disclose objects in a dark room to the observer's eye, but transmits an image to a screen which may be many miles away."

For thousands of years, philosophers have been telling us that there are around us such entities as "things in themselves"—things we could not see or smell or touch. Now we can believe them.

For the first time, actual pictures of the *air* are being made—by the Schlieren process, perfected in Germany. The study of air pockets, which have cost so many aviators their lives, is thus made possible. Air currents, air "holes," all bow to this new method of research.

In certain German towns, the police have been furnished with ingenious devices which enable them to sound alarms unheard by any but each other. These devices are whistles which blow—not sounds, but ultra-sounds. Just as the ultra-violet ray produces light rays of such high frequency that they do not register upon the human retina, so the ultrasound waves from these whistles produces sound waves of such high frequency that the unaided ear cannot detect them. Yet the Police Post with proper "detectors" can get them at once.

As Charles Lordman says in *Le Matin:*

"Our senses are tiny receptacles of very small dimensions, not adapted to hold all the vibratory riches of the surrounding universe. An interesting tale, a la Wells, could be written—or several of them—about imaginary men provided with sense organs whose limits of action were different from ours.

"If our ears were sensitive to ultrasounds and not to sounds, we should hear—if I may use the word—the ultra-whistles of the German policemen. If they were sensitive to 'infra-sounds'—that is to mechanical waves slower than the lowest audible sounds, we should perceive at a distance the swaying of trees in the wind, the oscillations of barometric pressure and the slow movements of the earth beneath our feet.

"If our eyes were sensitive to the infrared rays, we should see and discern at a distance, even in the dark, other men and animals, and we could even distinguish many objects which emit only the heat-rays of the spectrum.

"If our retinas were directly sensitive to the Hertzian waves, life would become insupportable; for because of the formidable mixture of waves that unceasingly traverse the atmosphere, we should live in a chaos of sensation. We should have to blind ourselves to get any peace, or shut ourselves up in metal closets—metal being opaque to electric radiation. We should see a revival of the medieval knights in their steel shells!

"But if we could perceive the X-rays, and those alone, then indeed would the aspect of the universe become fantastic. In full daylight we should no longer see the sun; we should not suspect its existence from direct evidence. And in the darkened sky, we should see only certain of the stars and nebulae—those that send us the mysterious celestial X-rays of which we have recently been hearing.

"*All is appearance.* The universe is to us only what we are to it."

In short, when we say that we "see" something, we merely mean that waves of light of a certain frequency and length are beating against our optic nerves and our retina is able to detect them. Millions of rays of different frequency and different lengths pass by unnoticed. Just as, when a musical note is pitched too high or too low, our ear drums are not attuned to the sound waves and we fail to hear them, so the light waves have pitch (which we call color) and when the pitch is too rapid or too short, our optic nerve is unable to catch them.

So at last we are coming to agree with St. Paul that "Eye hath not seen nor ear heard, neither have entered into the heart of man, the things which God hath prepared for them that love Him."—1 Corinthians 2:9. Once the scientist said, in the same spirit as Job—"With God all things are possible," but these are things "too wonderful for me, which I knew not." Now it would be a hardy soul who would say that anything is impossible for God's image—Man.

"Say not ye," said Jesus (John 4:35), "There are yet four months, and then cometh the harvest? Behold, I say unto you, lift up your eyes and look on the fields; for they are white already to harvest."

Doubters scoffed at such a possibility then. Doubters still scoff at the idea now. Yet listen:

"Recent experiments with combinations of daylight supplemented with artificial light," says Floyd Parsons in *Advertising and Selling,* "proved beyond doubt that many plants can be grown from seed to maturity in a remarkably short time. Spring wheat has been brought to maturity in 35 days by using this method. A crop of clover was grown from seed to flower in 38 days.

"The possibilities for future experiments in this field are tremendous."

He then goes on to point out some of the numberless opportunities in Nature all about us, which we have scarcely begun to use, and ends with—

"It all goes to show how slow we are to understand and utilize even the most common of Nature's bounties."

Dr. H. J. Muller of the University of Texas has shown through experiments with flies that it is possible to speed up the reproduction process, producing evolutionary changes or "mutations" 150 times faster by the use of X-rays. He expects later to put that discovery to practical use with plants and larger animals.

In past ages, in the immaturity of his mental development, man dealt only with things he could see or feel or hear or taste. His five senses were the only guides he trusted. If he could not detect a thing through them, *it was not*. True—he believed in a vague sort of way that there was a God—but He was high up in the heavens out of reach of mortal sense.

Today, in his more mature mental development, man is concerned with ideas. Ideas that cannot be seen or heard or tasted or felt. Yet ideas that are just as real as any object detectible by the senses—in many cases, more real. Like Plato, we have come to believe that ideas are the perfect immaterial pattern of which all material things are but imperfect copies.

This is the age of ideas. Through them, man is for the first time learning the infinite powers in his hands.

"And God said, let us make man in our image, after our likeness; and let them have dominion over the fish of the sea, and over the fowl of the air, and over the cattle, and over all the earth."—Genesis 1:26.

Long before they had discovered all the known elements of matter, scientists knew exactly how many there were, what the missing ones consisted of, where they belonged. How? Through mind, through ideas.

Now science has penetrated the secret of matter in the earth and the stars, and can literally do for itself in a few days what Nature has been doing for us through ages. How? Through the product of man's ideas—the X-ray.

To quote Waldemar Kaempffert in the *New York Times*—

"It takes a million million atoms to fill the head of a pin, yet the X-rays indicate the position of every one. Atoms have ceased to be the smallest hypothetical units of matter. They have become as real as bricks—the architectural material of a new chemistry which is mimicking nature.

"Clutch a piece of iron. It seems substantial, dense, continuous, all that is implied by the word "solid." Look at the stars above. How remote from us, how remote from one another! Stellar distances must be measured by light-years—so empty is space. Yet the piece of iron that you clutch is relatively just as empty. Magnify it to the dimensions of the solar system, and its atoms would be separated millions of miles. Hundreds of comets have swept through the solar system without colliding with a planet. A comet far smaller than an atom might theoretically swim through a seemingly solid piece of iron just as readily. Science has compelled us to modify the traditional conception of "solid" matter.

"With the introduction of the X-rays into the chemical laboratory we have crossed the threshold of a new scientific era. Suppose a metal is wanted that can be rolled out into a sheet or drawn into a wire without cracking. The chemist draws a space-lattice in which each atom is tied to three others on either side. Thereupon he indicated how that metal is to be produced. Thus the metallurgist of the future will literally compose in his mind, or on paper, alloys to meet specific industrial requirements."

"If our planet were constantly covered with clouds," said Flammarion, "we should know nothing of the sun, nor the moon, nor the planets, and the world system would remain unknown, with the result that human knowledge would be condemned to an irremediable falsity. Illusion forms the unstable basis of our ideas, our sensations, our sentiments, our beliefs."

Illusion—yet we are beginning to lose some of it. The ultra-violet ray of understanding will dispel more.

"Whatsoever things are true, whatsoever things are honest, whatsoever things are just, whatsoever things are pure, whatsoever things are lovely, whatsoever things are of good report; if there be any virtue, and if there be any praise, think on these things."—Philippians 4:8.

Our ancestors thought the earth was a fixed object. Our children today know that it moves, but only as they learn it from books. Our ancestors thought the earth was flat. We know it to be round, but only as it is proved to us. Our senses would still tell us it is a fixed body—in spite of the fact that it is rushing through space at a dizzying speed, the plaything of fourteen different movements, making a complete revolution every 24 hours.

We would never know from our five senses that the air we breathe has weight. We cannot sense the electricity all about us. We cannot detect more than a small part of the light or sound waves, or the odors, in the air around us. In short, if we depended on our five senses, we should be as ignorant of all that is going on about us as is the savage.

And yet people can still be found to say—I see a certain thing, or I feel a certain thing, or I hear a certain thing, *so I know it to be so.* Man, man, the things your five senses tell you, are the things you can be least sure of. They don't know the hundredth part of what is going on around you—and least of all do they know the things they seem surest of.

What can your ears tell you of the music and lectures and reports that are being broadcasted all about you this very minute? What can your eyes tell you of the images that are being telegraphed past you in every direction through television, or the mirages that appear on a million light waves? What reliance can you place on your unaided sense of touch? Remember, in school boy initiations, how they "branded" you by first blindfolding you, then burning a piece of bacon rind under your nose, the while they clapped a chunk of ice against the place to be "branded"? And if you had no advance information of what was really going on, the ice hurt as much as a hot iron, for the sensation of intense heat and intense cold is just the same.

Or your sense of taste? Remember how they fed you— still blindfolded—a raw oyster, telling you all manner of dreadful things? And how readily your sense of taste accepted those suggestions?

To trust the testimony of your five senses rather than the testimony of your reason is foolish in this day and age. As far as the physical senses are concerned, today is the day of uncertainty. According to them, the moon is larger than the sun, and the earth is the center of the solar system.

Our new conception of the universe is based entirely on mind. According to the Einstein theory, we are not only somewhere in space, but somewhen. It is not *events* which are happening now, but our perception of them. If it takes years for light to travel from the planets to us, what we see through our telescopes is not what is happening there now, but what happened years ago. It is as though we had years ago been marooned on a remote island and a passing steamer dropped a 10-year-old newspaper giving us our first knowledge of the war. To us, with nothing by which to reckon time, that war would be now. To the world, it is past and gone.

More and more we live in a world of mind's making. Just as, in many industries, the profits now lie in the things that formerly were thrown away, so the future of the race lies in the fields that heretofore have been not only unexplored but undreamed of. "For the invisible things of Him from the creation of the world are clearly seen, being understood by the things that are made."—Romans 1:20.

Quoting Floyd Parsons again—

"Although the most abundant of all nature's elements, air still offers the inquisitive scientist unmeasured opportunities for investigative work. Oxygen is found in the air in a perfectly free state and yet we have not perfected a way to utilize this most common element on a large scale in concentrated form. Eventually cheap oxygen at a dollar a ton will revolutionize all of the metal industries as well as gas manufacture. Laboratory practices in chemistry and medicine will likewise be materially improved.

"For years science has discussed the possibility of the development of a safe explosive; one that would reduce the hazards of industry, be unworkable in the hands of assassins and yet would be abundant and low in cost. Liquid oxygen would seem to be the substance sought."

Dr. J. F. Norris, President of the American Chemical Society sees the power in the atom changing our whole life. He sees the synthesis of food without the slow process of passing through the vegetable kingdom. He sees our knowledge of matter so broadened that what we know today is but the foreground of the great picture that is to come.

"Their line is gone out through all the earth, and their words to the end of the world. In them hath He set a tabernacle for the sun. His going forth is from the end of the heaven, and his circuit unto the ends of it; and there is nothing hid from the heat thereof."—Psalms 19:4, 6.

Dr. Umberto Pomilio, the noted Italian chemist, visions the emancipation of mankind from the use of coal and other energy-producing materials, and atomic energy heating the world.

An English engineer, John L. Hodgson, told the British Association for the Advancement of Science that the internal fires of the earth could be made to supply fuel for the world's needs for centuries to come, and proceeded to suggest a plan for utilizing this boundless heat.

"For we know in part, and we prophesy in part.

"But when that which is perfect is come, then that which is in part shall be done away.

"When I was a child, I spake as a child, I understood as a child, I thought as a child: but when I became a man, I put away childish things.

"For now we see through a glass darkly; but then face to face: now I know in part; but then shall I know even as also I am known."—I Corinthians 13:9-12.

Dreams wilder than the wildest of Jules Verne's stories are becoming everyday realities now. Why? Because man no longer puts a limit upon himself or his powers. He knows that anything is possible to him, and thereupon proceeds to turn the seemingly impossible into everyday reality.

Remember, in *The Mysterious Island*, how Captain Nemo killed the pirates with a gun that used no bullets, but shot a mysterious ray, fatal to anything it touched? A wild dream of the imagination, we thought then. But Dr. Robert W. Wood of Johns Hopkins found that sound waves of a high frequency can be directed in a well-defined beam.

And when testing them in the water, a fish happened to swim through the path of the rays. The next moment that fish *was a dead fish!*

In chemistry, they have what they call catalytic agents. Take a little potassium chlorate, as an instance. Heat it. Nothing happens. But add just a touch of manganese dioxide—and the chlorate gives up oxygen, while the manganese remains unchanged. The manganese is a catalytic agent. It releases the constituent parts of the potassium chlorate, while itself remaining unaffected.

Mind is the great catalytic, but we are only beginning to learn how to use it. It brings out the real from under all the forms which appear to our naked senses. It shows us the substance beneath.

Do you know where we get the word substance? From sub and stare—to stand under. Substance is the *real* that stands under all its visible forms. When you look at an object, you do not see the substance—you see only what corresponds to that substance to your eyes. You get only a small and unimportant number of the light rays it refracts.

"While we look not at the things which are seen, but at the things which are not seen. For the things which are seen are temporal. But the things which are not seen are eternal."—II Corinthians 4:18.

When you look at yourself in the glass, you do not see your real self—you see only your idea of it, the idea you have been accustomed to accept because it is all your physical senses have been able to grasp. The real substance you have never seen.

The millions of protons and electrons of which it is made—each a miniature solar system—are entirely beyond the ken of our ordinary senses. The perfect image of God in which the real body is made—we can't see this with our eyes.

These are mental concepts. They must be grasped mentally. They must be controlled mentally. But once we do grasp them, once we do control them, our body becomes the servant instead of the master—it becomes the image and likeness of its Creator.

It is only this real substance that matters. And it is to help you to find this real substance that "stands under" all the imperfect outer forms, that this book is written.

"I have heard of Thee by the hearing of the ear: but now mine eye seeth thee."

—JOB 42:5.

XXIV

THE MYSTERY OF LIFE

"So God created man in his own image, in the image of God created He him; and male and female created He them.

"And God saw everything that He had made, and behold, it was very good."

—GENESIS 1:27, 31.

In the northern part of Africa, near the rim of the Great Desert, there dwelt a Sheik named Ibn Ben Said. Ibn was rich. Camels he had by the score. Flocks of sheep and herds of asses.

In his youth Ibn Ben Said had been a mighty hunter so when, upon a time, his men brought in a young lion cub whose parents they had killed, Ibn determined to tame it.

The cub was playful as any kitten, and its antics amused the Sheik through the long afternoons. Months passed, and the little cub grew from a prankish kitten into a powerful lion. But still he had the run of the tent. Still Ibn Ben Said fondled him and amused himself with him.

But it was getting more difficult to handle him. The herdsmen feared him—wanted a chain put upon him—begged the Sheik to set some powerful young fellows in charge over him. The Sheik laughed at such thoughts—was this not the cub he had trained and raised? What though it was no longer content with asses' milk and scraps from the men's supper? What though it must have juicy joints cooked especially for it? Was it not the Sheik's pet?

One day the Sheik was away, and the joint was not forthcoming. The lion cub growled and roared, finally lost patience, pounced upon a young lamb and for the first time made its own "kill."

That taste of blood was the beginning of the end. The cub ate and slept—then hungered for the taste of blood again. It would slink off, where none of these two-legged creatures could see, pounce upon a lamb—and feast its fill.

But the herdsmen had found the remains of the previous feast. And when the young lion slipped from the tent, there was the Sheik waiting for it, whip in hand. A lash, a roar—and the cub was gone forever. In its place stood the primitive terror of the desert, crouching over its kill. The taste of blood had been too much—the pet had turned and rent its master.

You see similar incidents every day. A man starts a

business. It is his pet, his hobby. It grows—and he is master of its every detail. He delights in experimenting with it, gets the utmost pleasure from the management of it.

But after a while it reaches such proportions that it demands more and more of its owner's time. Instead of a pet, it becomes the master. Until finally it grows so big and unwieldly that it crushes its owner beneath the load—and you read of another man gone the way of the nervous breakdown.

THE FALL OF MAN

As I read the Scriptural narrative, the fall of man was in similar wise.

"God created man in His own image." What is God? Mind, Spirit. He has not a body. He is not a corporeal being. If He created man in His image, then He created man as a spirit, as mind—"in the image of God created He him."

That was the true man which God created, the image of Himself, the real *substance* of man. And He gave to this *real* man dominion over all the earth.

Then in the next chapter of Genesis we read how "God formed man of the dust of the ground and breathed into his nostrils the breath of life."—Genesis 2:7.

First the mental image, then the material body.

Scientists are agreed that all matter is made up of atoms, and that the atoms in turn consist of minute particles of electrical energy called protons and electrons. So the simile of man's body being made of the dust of the ground is in no wise farfetched, since the dust of the ground and the body of man consist of the same particles of electrical energy.

These bits of energy whirl round and round, the electron revolving around the proton with mathematical precision.

But whence comes the energy, and whence comes the intelligence that regulates it? For to keep the arrangement they do, these buttons of force would have to be able to count! That requires mind. Surely no one would contend that these minute particles of energy have a mind? So the Intelligence that regulates them, that supplies their energy, must come from without—must be the Divine Mind that permeates all of life. Back we come to God—the Creator.

God gave man "dominion over every living thing that moveth upon the earth." Surely his own body was no exception. His body is made of electrons and protons whose every revolution is directed by Mind. And man's mental self is the image and likeness of God. Therefore, it is reasonable to assume that the real man was given control of everything about the bodily man.

You have seen pictures in the newspapers that had been

telegraphed from distant places. Look at them under a magnifying glass and you will see that they are made up of an immense number of dots. Use a powerful glass and the dots seem so far apart that it is hard to get the outline of the picture.

That, in effect, is what your body is like—an infinite number of dots, each dot representing a whirling mass of protons and electrons. Can't you imagine the fascination of playing with such an aggregation of energy, of making it into different forms and then bringing it back into the Divine mold, the mental *substance* that stands under all the different forms?

But like the young lion or the infant business, this body grew beyond the control of Adam. He ate of the tree of knowledge of good and evil—he came to delight so much in this material body of his, in its pleasures and sensations, that he presently lost control of it. Instead of a plaything, it became the master. Instead of a pet, it turned and devoured him. He forgot his power over it. He became so lost in bodily sensations that his Divine self—the image and likeness of God—was completely overwhelmed and forgotten in grosser, fleshly pleasures.

That was the serpent which tempted Eve. That was the apple from the tree of Knowledge of Good and Evil with which she did beguile Adam. That was the Fall of Man.

Jesus came to this earth to reveal to man anew his

sonship to the Father, to redeem him from subservience to the body. "Verily, verily, I say unto thee, except a man be born of water and of the Spirit, he cannot enter into the Kingdom of God. That which is born of the Flesh is Flesh, and that which is born of the Spirit is spirit."—John 3:5-6.

We must put off the carnal mind, as Paul tells us, and go back to the mind which has dominion over all things— the mind which is the image and likeness of God. "It is the spirit that quickeneth," says Jesus (John 3:63), "the flesh profiteth nothing. The words that I speak unto you, they are spirit and they are life."

To put it another way—His words must be spiritually discerned, but, so discerned, they are light and life to us. "To be carnally minded is death; but to be spiritually minded is life and peace."—Romans 8:6. Throughout His earthly career, Jesus adjured His hearers to seek first the Kingdom of God—and all things else would be added unto them. And He told them that this Kingdom of God or Kingdom of Heaven was within them!

If they wanted to get back to the Garden of Eden, if they even were looking for happiness, and health, and plenty, let them seek it at the source—in the Kingdom within, in the realm where God gave man dominion over all things. "Call unto me and I will answer thee, and show thee great and mighty things, which thou knowest not."— Jeremiah 33:3.

At the meeting of the British Association for the Advancement of Science last September, the veteran Sir Oliver Lodge expressed a strong disbelief in any doctrine of materialism.

"I do not think that life is a form of energy which can be transmuted," he said. "There seems to be a guiding principle ad extra—*from the outside*—which interacts with the material universe *yet is not of it*. Physical science is not comprehensive of all reality."

Heretofore, scientists have pictured the universe as being like a clock which will eventually run down. What if it did, asked Sir Oliver. What would happen? In his opinion, the same Intelligence which wound it up originally would wind it again. Obviously, that Intelligence is outside the material universe, apart from and above it.

We are all wound up, and that we ever run down is our own fault for not keeping in touch with that same Intelligence, for not using the dominion He has given us.

Every cell in our body is an entire organism in itself, a little storehouse of energy, capable of performing all the complex functions of life—eating, reproduction, excretion and motion.

"Under the microscope," says E. C. Wheeler in the *Popular Science Monthly,* "a single cell may be seen at its most important task—that of renewing and perpetuating itself. This it does, by dividing to form two complete cells where one was before. These in turn divide. And so the life force continues its process of renewal.

"That is how every living thing grows.

"The invincible power of the life force was demonstrated in a recent experiment by Dr. Chambers. His subject was a single egg cell from the sea, less than a thousandth of an inch in diameter. The cell began the process of division, creating within its own substance two opposing streams in the form of tiny whirlpools. As it did so, Dr. Chambers caught up the opposite sides of the cell with extremely fine needles and stretched them out in an attempt to arrest the whirling motion of division. But the tiny unit of life would not be denied.

"Instead of surrendering, it tore itself viciously away from the needles which held it, and so fulfilled its destiny.

"One important significance of these discoveries by Dr. Chambers is that they tend to bear out the fascinating theory that the basis of all life and all matter is electricity."

But back of all that energy is Intelligence—the Intelligence which first wound up things, which first released the energy. When you find your life energy beginning to run down, go back to that same Intelligence for rewinding.

You have seen boys with little magnets of steel, picking up pins, bits of iron and the like. After they have been used for a time, the magnetism gradually dies out of them and they no longer attract even the weight of a pin.

What do the boys do then? Throw away the useless magnets? No—they rub them against stronger magnets or re-magnetize them with an electric current and their power is completely restored.

That is what you must do with your body. Mind is the source of all power. Go to it—set your mental power-house to work reconstructing in your body the perfect image of it that is in Divine Mind.

The real you, the substance underneath all this outer layer of body or energy, is the image and likeness of God, one with Him, endowed with the same power—a God-given dominion over all things.

Use this power to do your own winding up, your own recharging. Get back the control over your body which was yours in the beginning, which Jesus came to redeem for you. Know that the image in which you were made was perfect then, is perfect now. Know that the *substance* which God made is the same now that it always was, and that it is this substance, this mold, on which you must model the perfect body which should be yours.

Know that you have that perfect mold, that real spiritual substance, underneath all the outer forms, then forget the body that you know and proceed to rebuild along the perfect lines imaged in the mind of the Father.

"He giveth power to the faint; and to them that have no might he increaseth strength.

"Even the youths shall faint and be weary, and the young men shall utterly fall:

"But they that wait upon the Lord shall renew their strength; they shall mount up with wings as eagles; they shall run, and not be weary; and they shall walk, and not faint."

—ISAIAH 40:29-31.

XXV

THE ELIXIR OF LIFE

*"For I have no pleasure in the death of him that dieth,
saith the Lord: wherefore turn yourselves and live ye."*

—EZEKIEL 18:32.

Through the wisdom granted to the world through
the first man, namely through Adam and his sons,
who received from God Himself special knowl-
edge on this subject, in order that they might prolong their
life, God most high and glorious has prepared a means for
preserving health and for combatting the ills of old age and
retarding them."

Thus, in part, reads the *Opus Majus* of Roger Bacon,
the greatest mind produced by the Middle Ages. The part
quoted refers to the so-called Elixir of Life, and was translated by Dr. Robert Bell Burke, Dean of the University of
Pennsylvania.

"There is a medicine," Bacon says, quoting Aristotle's
Book of Secrets, "called the ineffable glory and treasure

of philosophers, which completely rectifies the whole human body."

This medicine is supposed to have been discovered by Adam or by Enoch and secured through a vision, and Bacon goes on to give a number of instances in which it was successfully used to prolong life for a hundred years or more.

One of the men so benefited is said to have stood before Augustus Caesar, who marvelled to see that although more than a hundred years old, he was strong, robust and active.

But Bacon fell into the common error of his age in thinking that this "ineffable glory and treasure of philosophers" must be a material medicine, a tonic or a physic, and he thereupon proceeded to outline a formula that can be compared only with the gland-diets of today.

"If what is tempered in the fourth degree," his formula reads, "what swims in the sea, and what grows in the air, and what is cast up by the sea, and a plant of India, and what is found in the vitals of a long-lived animal, and the two snakes which are the food of the Tyrians and Ethiopians, be prepared and used in the proper way and the minera of the noble animal be present, the life of man could be greatly prolonged and the conditions of old age and senility could be retarded and mitigated."

What is tempered in the fourth degree is gold. What

swims in the sea is the pearl. What grows in the air is a flower. What is cast up by the sea is ambergris. The plant of India is aloe. And what is found in the vitals of a long-lived animal is the "bone" in the stag's heart.

Truly a noble concoction, but not much more ridiculous than the eating of monkey glands today, which forms the basis of some modern rejuvenating systems. Primitive man was no more foolish when he tore out his enemy's heart and ate it to add to his own that enemy's strength.

There is an Elixir of Life, but it is not put up in bottles. Neither will you find it in the glands of a monkey or the vitals of a stag. Bacon was right when he said that "God most high and glorious has prepared a means for preserving health and for combatting the ills of old age and retarding them." But he should have known from a study of Jesus' works that God never had recourse to drugs or medicaments to cure His children or to keep them well.

DO WE LIVE LONGER THAN OUR FOREFATHERS?

Much has been written about the increased span of life in these days of modern hygiene and preventive medicine. Since 1855, the average age increased from 39.77 years to 58.32 in 1924—a gain of 18.55 years. But this does not mean that the middle-aged man of today can expect to live 18.55 years longer than his father or grandfather. His increased expectation is only two or three years. The place where medical science has brought up the average is at the other end—in decreasing the enormous death rate among children.

But don't let that discourage you. Two or three years extra may be all you can expect from the help of medical science, but there is another Source which is not so niggardly.

Life's battle is generally thought to be fought in the morning. The youngster of twenty-one, starting in business or the profession, feels that he must make his success by the time he is forty—or his case is hopeless. And the man of forty, with nothing accumulated and seemingly little done, looks back at his life and feels that he is through—a middle-aged failure.

People have the idea that success belongs to youth, that if you can't grasp it while still in your thirties, you might as well give up trying. And most business houses seem to foster that idea. Read the want ads—"Man wanted for important executive position. Must be under forty."

As if youth were a matter of years! Most men don't hit their stride until they are forty. It takes the majority of us that long to get the background of experience and sound judgment necessary to successfully carry on a modern business. At forty, a man should be just starting on his most productive work.

Do you know at what age you are most valuable? Not twenty. Not thirty. Not forty. *But sixty years of age!* The average age of the men who head the leading business and industrial organizations of the country is sixty years!

Youth and health and enthusiasm are wonderful things. Properly directed nothing can hold them back. But they need direction. They lack experience, and the mature youth of forty with health and enthusiasm, can begin to cash in on an asset far greater than money—the sound business judgment acquired from his years of experience.

For it is not the number of years you have lived that make you old. It is how you have lived them. You will find them—men and women of sixty, seventy, eighty, with skin as smooth, faces as un-lined as a youngster of twenty. You will find men and women of thirty with skin as sallow, faces as drawn as though they were in their dotage.

Youth and age are states of mind. There is no physiological reason why you should grow old. The cells of your body can continue renewing themselves forever.

WHY DO PEOPLE DIE?

Fifteen years ago, Dr. Alexis Carrol of the Rockefeller Institute decided to ascertain how long a piece of the heart of a chicken (still in the egg, unborn) would live if left to itself except for care and feeding.

So he cut out this piece of chicken heart, put it in a glass jar and surrounded it with proper nourishment.

The cells continued to multiply themselves exactly as when in the embryonic chick—in fact, distinct pulsations of the heart could be detected under the microscope for months. Then the cells began to multiply so fast that they overran everything. Left alone, they would now be an enormous mass, for *they double in size every forty-eight hours!* But each two days they are trimmed and the excess thrown away.

In the fifteen years, thousands of generations of cells have formed, generated and passed on. Yet they keep perpetuating themselves at as lively a rate as ever. To all intents, they are immortal.

If these cells, with proper care, can live forever, why does a chicken die? Why do we grow old and die?

So far as scientists can see, there is no principle limiting life. There are numberless reasons why people die, but no physiological reason why they *must* die. If their bodies could be taken at intervals, washed free of poisons and properly nourished, they might live forever!

The reason they die is because the complete bodily machine even of a chicken is far more complex than any one set of cells. And it is this complexity which spells its doom. One set may be injured, or another may fail in its duties, bringing poisons into the blood that play havoc with the whole machine. Post mortems have repeatedly shown that even in deaths from old age it is only a few sets of cells that have atrophied or given away. The rest seemed good for an indefinite period.

In short, science has proved that our bodies are made up of potentially immortal cells. It is merely the organization of them which is faulty, letting one or two sets bring the whole to an untimely end. How then can we improve the organization?

How would we do it if the organization of cells in our body were a factory, each cell a worker, each group a gang with a definite job? We would look to the head of it first, would we not? We would ask why it was he was letting one or two groups ruin the work of all the others. We would insist upon better direction upon his part, more active management. We would urge him to get behind the lagging groups, hold before them the perfect model on which to pattern their work, give them the personal attention necessary to spur them on. And there is no reason why we cannot do the same thing with our bodies.

When Lord Clive was a young Captain in the Indian Service he at one time commanded a small force garrisoning the town of Arcot.

Suddenly the enemy came down upon him with an army twenty times the size of his own, and laid siege to the town.

The walls were old and offered little resistance to the cannon of the besiegers. Whole sections were levelled every day. But every night, as soon as darkness fell, Clive's indefatigable garrison cleared away the debris and built new and stronger walls behind.

For fifty days the enemy kept up the siege, massing their troops in heavy attacks against the breaches, only to find the new walls more impenetrable far than the old. And at last, after a score of repulses, they drew off defeated and discouraged.

Just so it is with your body. Every day the enemy tears down millions of cells, effects great breaches in your defenses. Every night, if your commander is of the right sort, your garrison cleans away all the rubbish, rebuilds the walls stronger and fresher than ever. The forces of disease can rant and rave and attack in massed formation, but so long as you keep the torn down walls cleared away, so long as your commander puts up a smiling confident front, they will have nothing to mount upon and will be driven back defeated and dispersed.

How long do you suppose Clive would have lasted had he felt like that? How hard would his garrison have fought for him, slaved for him?

Doctors are agreed that old age is simply the failure of the body to eliminate waste and worn-out tissue. Arteries become clogged, the fresh cells can no longer get through and the patient gradually weakens and dies.

And the reason? Not years, but a state of mind. A man reaches forty, or fifty, or sixty. He thinks he has passed his prime. So he lets down. Gradually he ceases to look forward—that way only death seems to lie. And spends his time instead bemoaning the glories of his "vanished" youth.

Ceasing to look forward, he ceases to be of use in the business world, ceases even to be value to those around him. He is relegated to a life of inactivity. His mind and all about him becomes torpid. Presently the life-giving cells, lacking incentive, lacking any urge to keep on, give up the struggle. People think that is when this man dies. It isn't. He has been dead a long time. He died when he lost his forward look.

CHOOSE YOUR AGE

A man is never old until he stops growing. When he no longer looks forward to bigger, better things, when he feels that he has done his best work, you might just as well call the undertaker. He is through.

But he need not be. As long as he has an active interest in life, as long as he can look forward confidently each day to bigger, greater accomplishments than on the previous day, he is young—he is growing. Look out for such an one—he will do big things.

Too old to learn? That myth was exploded long ago. You are never too *old* to learn. Too busy—yes. Too lazy—often. Too "sot"—if the truth were told.

Experiments made with groups of adults between 20

and 24, and others between 35 and 50, showed that both learned new languages (an admittedly difficult subject) more rapidly than did children.

Other tests have repeatedly shown that adults learn many subjects faster than children of 12 to 15 years, though heretofore that has been thought to be the age at which we learn most readily.

Professor Thorndyke of Columbia University recently stated that no man or woman under 50 years of age need be discouraged from trying to learn anything he wants to learn, from fear of being too old. The basis of that old saying about being too old to learn was more in lack of opportunity than lack of ability. Even in men and women of advanced age, the ability to learn decreases so slightly each year (less than 1 per cent.) as to be scarcely worth noticing.

"I certainly never heard of an old man forgetting where he had hidden his money," says Cicero. And he added that the aged remember everything that interests them. They retain their faculties as long as their interest and application continue.

There is no giving up point. When George De Saulles was appointed to the Canadian Senate at the age of 79, many of his colleagues protested that he was too old. He is still there—and on September 27 last he was 100.

Gladstone became Premier of Great Britain for the fourth time at the age of 80. Cato began the study of Greek at 80, and Plutarch started Latin at the same age. Tom Scott at 86 took up Hebrew.

At 96, Titian finished a famous painting. Michelangelo was still busy at 89. At 103, Chevruel was adding new laurels to his crown as a scientist. Right here in New York is a woman of 93, Mrs. Catherine Stewart, who started painting at 75 and is still getting more pleasure and profit out of it every day. There is a steamboat captain on Lake Champlain still plying his trade at 97. While in the *New York Sun* some months ago I read an Associated Press dispatch telling that Zaro Agliz, 150 years old, of Constantinople, was finding the work of porter too heavy for him, so the Prefect of the city had appointed him doorkeeper for the Municipal Council!

As Chauncey Depew put it, it is all in finding an interest in life. "I have always found life filled with interesting things," he says. "Every day there is something new—in spite of the fact that I am 93. Every day I take a mental inventory. 'Chauncey,' I say, 'how do you find yourself this morning? What's on the good side? What's on the bad side?' And I find, somehow, I always come out on the optimistic side."

The reason so many men's minds seem to stop where they are at 45 or 50 is not lack of ability to learn more, but lack of willingness to readjust their mental furniture. Their mental furniture is so firmly screwed down to the flooring of their mind that to bring in radically new ideas would require a ripping up of the whole mental structure, and this they are too complacent or too lazy to chance.

> "I will Restore to You the Years that the Locust Hath Eaten."
>
> —JOEL 2:25.

One of the youngest men I know was born 70 years ago. He came to New York recently to take a new position—the kind of job he had been longing for all his life, but never before had the courage to tackle. Now he is not only making good at it, but he is happier than he ever has been, with a fresh grip on his youth that should last him for years. With Viscount Cowdray, he can say that it is not the end of the journey, but the traveling that makes life worth while.

It is a law of mind, you know, that whatever a man fixes his attention upon is drawn toward him. If he fixes it upon senility and decay, he will get it. But if he fixes it upon some active accomplishment, he will get that.

When you feel yourself slipping, when the ideas no longer seem to come as readily as of old, start something new. Take on a bigger, harder job. Forget yourself and forget your years in your new work. There is no biological reason, you know, for dying at 70, or 80, or even 100. The animals live to five times their adolescent period. The least that can be expected of you is to equal the record of the animals.

The elephant comes of age at 21 and lives to be 100 or more. Turtles frequently reach 300. The swan reaches 70 years and frequently tops 100. Alligators live several hundred years.

It is not as though there were any Biblical warrant for our present short span of years. There is not. In the sixth chapter of Genesis, you will find—"And the Lord said— My spirit shall not always strive with man, for that he also is flesh. Yet his days shall be an hundred and twenty years." And the Patriarchs of old surpassed that by even more than our occasional centenarian surpasses the average run of mankind today.

James Whitcomb Riley wrote a poem about a man who had lived to three score years and ten, had the hang of it now and could do it again.

That is what you men of 40, 50, 60 and upwards must do. You have lived long enough to have the hang of it now, so start this minute to live your years over again. It can be done. "Thine age shall be clearer than the noonday. Thou shalt shine forth. Thou shalt be as the morning."—Job 11:17.

In the thirteenth edition of the Encyclopedia Britannica you will find, under "The Why and Wherefore of Death," confirmation of the fact that the cells of the body are held to be potentially immortal, nothing like death being inevitable or inherent in them. Not even senescence, or old age, is a necessary concomitant of cellular life. It is because they are mutually dependent upon each other for nutritive material that when one or two groups die, the others follow.

Our problem, then, is one of management. We must keep each group so thoroughly alive, so actively alert, that none will ever act as a brake upon the others. How shall we go about it? What is the "means for preserving health and combatting the ills of old age prepared by God"?

First, by realizing that the source of all life is God, Mind. "In Him was life, and the life was the light of men."—John 1-4. And that the surest way of renewing your life forces is to turn to Him as the flower turns to the sun, or the small boy takes his magnet to the electric current for recharging.

Second, remind yourself often of the entire newness of your body. Every cell is constantly renewing itself, casting off the old, rebuilding anew. The very oldest part of your body—no matter what your years—is only eleven months old.

Third, go back to the perfect image of God, to the real substance of which you are made, for the model on which to rebuild. Hold that model ever before your mental eyes. Let it be the first thing in your thoughts of a morning, the last at night, and your subconscious cannot help but build as you direct.

Fourth, realize that you HAVE a perfect body now. That the substance which stands under the outer form, "the image and likeness of God," cannot be other than perfect, else it would not be His image. Since the mold is perfect, it is just a matter of holding that mold before your mind's eye until you can truly absorb it, and *you* will be perfect.

It is not necessary to wait for death and another life to realize God's image. It is not even necessary to wait eleven months while your cells are being rebuilt. All of life is in the body now. "That which hath been is now; and that which is to be hath already been; and God requireth that which is past."—Ecclesiastics 3:15.

You have the perfect image of God. You have the substance. You were given dominion over all the earth and over every creeping thing upon the earth. Use your dominion. Realize that you HAVE youth, you HAVE health, you HAVE the perfect image in which you were made. Believe that ye receive them and ye shall HAVE them.

That is the way to take your body out and cleanse it of the poisons and imperfections of wrong belief. That is the way you can steep it in proper nourishment. That is the way you can keep it everlastingly young and active.

Take it out daily—wash away the worn-out tissue of belief in age and decay—nourish it with the recollection of your God-given dominion of the immortal substance beneath that outer form, "made in the image and likeness of God."

"And I saw a new heaven and a new earth. And there shall be no more death; neither sorrow nor crying; neither shall there be any more pain. For the former things are passed away. And He that sat upon the throne said—Behold, I make all things new."

—REVELATION 21:1, 3.

XXVI

PATHWAYS OF THE MIND

"That the God of our Lord Jesus Christ, the Father of glory, may give unto you the spirit of wisdom and revelation in the knowledge of Him:

"The eyes of your understanding being enlightened; that ye may know what is the hope of His calling, and what the riches of the glory of His inheritance in the saints."

EPHESIANS I:17-18.

Have you ever been in the filing department of one of the great insurance companies?

Millions of records—millions and millions of names—but all so carefully put away, all so thoroughly indexed, that you can find any record you may want from all those millions at a moment's notice.

Just such a filing department is your brain. There are six billion compartments in it, six billion cells that will accept and retain anything you may file away in them. In all that mass of information, how are you to find what you want?

How do you find it in an ordinary file? Isn't it by association? Take John Smith, as an instance. You have had certain dealings with John Smith which you wish to be able to refer to at will. How do you go about it?

First, you associate his name with the letter S. You put a folder in your file under the letter S, containing certain data about John Smith. If your file is a large one, you make further sub-divisions. You divide the S file into Sa, Sb, Sc, etc. And you put your folder under Sm. Perhaps you even have a Smith sub-division, in which case you differentiate this Smith from other Smiths by the name John.

You have made it as easy as possible to refer to the record of John Smith.

But perhaps under the heading of Real Estate, or Accidents, or Law or some other title, there is matter relating to John Smith which cannot be moved into Smith's folder. What do you then?

Put a note in Smith's folder that under Real Estate or whatever title it is, there is additional matter relating to John Smith. And in the Real Estate folder, put a note reading—"For additional information as to John Smith, see his folder."

Thus you get cross-references. Thus you get a pathway from Smith to Real Estate and vice versa. After a time, when you have made the trip often enough, you find yourself unconsciously going on to the Real Estate folder after you have finished with Smith's. And whenever you think of Smith, you also think of Real Estate.

It is the law of Suggestion.

That is all memory is—association and suggestion. You wish to recall some event. You go back along the pathway of things associated with that event until you reach the event itself. It in turn leads you on to minor details, to people you met in connection with it, to things which happened in consequence of it.

What is a habit but a pathway worn so smooth to certain compartments of the brain that they function without conscious effort on our part? Our daily habits are nothing more than paths of the mind—well worn paths which we can follow with our eyes closed. To change those habits, we must cultivate new paths. But we must do not only that—we must abandon the old entirely, let weeds grow in them until they are impassable.

When a man drinks to excess, he cannot merely cut down his drinking and become instead a moderate drinker. He cannot indulge only periodically and hope to become the master. No—he must stop entirely. He must let the briars grow so thickly in that old pathway that the sight of a drink will not set his mouth afire with thirst, his salivary glands watering with anticipation. On the contrary, he must open a different pathway. He must make the sight of a drink start in train the thought of how strong he is, what perfect control he has over his appetite, how fine a thing it is to have overcome all taste for, all desire for drink and to be able again to look the world in the eye. He must definitely lead his thought into this new path until it in turn becomes so well worn that he can follow it blindfolded.

Intemperance, immorality, sickness—many of the ills flesh seems heir to—can be traced to the pathway worn in our minds, by certain trains of events, by certain suggestions.

To the impure in heart, the saying that—"to the pure, all things are pure"—sounds ridiculous. Knowing the association of thought which certain words or events call up in his mind, he thinks the minds of others follow the same path.

Yet the same event may stir up quite different emotions in each of a dozen people. To one, it may mark a guilty person. To another, it seems the proof of innocence. All depends upon the path which the idea takes in the mind of each.

A draught of cool air blows through a window. To one, it seems a breath of fragrance from on High. To another, it suggests colds and chills and fever. The one gets from it health and strength. The other sickness. The air is the same—it is the paths their thoughts take that is different.

"It is not the things that *happen* to us which matter," says some wise old philosopher. "It is the way we *look upon* the things that happen."

When an epidemic is reported in the papers and its

symptoms painstakingly described, people hundreds of miles away who could by no stretch of the imagination have been exposed to contagion, will come down with those symptoms—will even die from them. Why? Suggestion. Reading of the epidemic with a fearful mind, they start their own minds working along those same pathways of thought, with the inevitable result that it sets to work the forces which bring about the very conditions they fear.

Merely imaginary? Of course. But that is all any disease is—yes, though it carry with it every evidence of emaciation and travail and suffering. It starts in the mind. The mental image must be there before it can evidence itself in the body. Not only that, but *whatever image is there* will evidence itself in the body, be it sickness or perfection.

"You are wrong there," people write me triumphantly, "for I had a growth or a tumor or a sickness I'd never even heard of—much less held a mental image of."

Quite, quite true. You don't realize the mental combinations which the trains of thought you suggest finally result in. No more than you realize the chemical reactions your mind figures out in the digestion of your food, and its assimilation into your blood. All you do is to put the food into your stomach. Your mind looks after the rest. But have you ever noticed how often you have put perfectly good food into your stomach, which agreed with every one else, but which you feared you "couldn't eat"—

and your mind carried out the suggestion you gave it and caused you to lose that food?

It is not necessary to think of sickness in order to start such a train of thought. Anger or hate or envy often have the same result. The great Surgeon John Hunter once remarked that his life was in the hands of any rascal who chose to anger him. Some one did—and he died!

Fear, hate, envy, lust—all of them are mental states, but all are breeders of disease. And as long as such a condition which caused disease is present, what chance have you of curing it with drugs?

There was an article on this subject in *Colorado Medicine* of July, 1924, by Albert C. McClanahan, M. D., which was so good that I quote parts of it below.

"There is nothing occult," he said, "about the physical effects of beliefs introduced into the mind by suggestion, and there is nothing imaginary about them. Few things are more familiar.

"Embarrassment dilates the capillaries of the face and causes blushing. Sudden fear contracts the facial capillaries, causing pallor; contracts the arrectores pilorum, causing the hair to rise; accelerates the heart; depresses the respiration. Grief congests the conjunctiva, stimulates the secretory activity of the lachrymal glands, and causes weeping. Surprise tinged with resentment will almost infallibly arrest an attack of hiccups. Conscious volition will move any voluntary muscle in the body.

"Now, what are embarrassment, fear, grief, surprise, resentment, attention, imagination and volition? They are mental states. If it is incomprehensible that an intangible mental state—a mere thought or emotion—can reach across the gap that separates the spiritual from the material and produce a physical effect, it is so only because we have made it so. There is no gap, so far as our experience is concerned, between the spiritual and the material.

"The effect of mental states upon bodily conditions is all a part of an orderly universe."

And he goes on to state that—"If a mere correction of judgment can cure organic disease when such disease is due to autosuggestion, what warrant is there for denying that a like remedy can effect a like result even where the organic disease is due to a physical cause? Recall again the quick congestion of the salivary glands at the mere sight of an expected feast; note once more the sudden pallor and the trembling hands of fright; observe the epidemic of irrepressible yawns evoked in any company by the first clandestine gape; observe the abounding, virile health of the young man accepted by the lady of his choice, and the dejected malnutrition of the victim of unrequited love; note once more the mantling blushes of the maiden shy and suddenly embarrassed, and be more hesitant to deny that an intangible mental state can produce a definite, visible, measurable physical effect.

"How often has the sound of water trickling from a tap

proved an effective substitute for a catheter? How many toothaches have been cured by the mere decision to visit the dentist?"

Further in his article he gives the remedies usually prescribed for scarlet fever, rheumatism and typhoid, and while he thinks these remedies have properties which may be helpful, he asks if any one longer believes that any of them has ever *cured* scarlet fever or rheumatism or typhoid?

"Yet," he writes, "the victims of scarlet fever, possibly of chronic rheumatism, certainly of typhoid fever, have got well under their administration—as sufferers from hundreds of other organic diseases have got well under the administration of thousands of other equally casual remedies. And before they got well under the administration of such remedies as these, they got well under the administration of the dried viscera of strange reptiles and other messes weirder still. And before that the beating of a tom-tom by a highly decorated medicine man was the most effective means of restoring the pathologically altered organism to a state of health.

"What cured these sufferers? Vis medicatrix naturae is the answer that comes obediently to mind. They just naturally got well. But did they? The vis medicatrix naturae, once so successfully invoked by the beating of a tom-tom, and later by the entrails of a lizard, notoriously failed to respond to these inducements after men became familiar with the magic of mercury and venesection and huge doses of nauseous herbs. These also lost their potency for persons whose faith had been intrigued by the higher potencies of the infinitesimal doses of Samuel Christian Friedrich Hahnemann. And these at last went down before a faith that blandly denied the very existence of pathology for anybody who had been delivered from the thralldom of mortal mind.

"In all of these mediums of cures the thing that cured was the suggestion that went along with the medium. Analyze your vis medicatrix naturae, and you shall find that one of its chief ingredients is the confident expectation of getting well. Destroy that expectation, and nature's power to heal will be as definitely crippled as if you had lowered the vitality of the tissues by insufficient nourishment, by extremes of temperature, by poisons, or by any other means. Fortify that expectation, magnify it, multiply it, and—if the history of therapeutics teaches anything— you will accomplish the cure of many diseases—even of many organic diseases—that would not 'just naturally get well,' and you may accomplish such cures even under the administration of drugs or gestures that have no inherent power of their own to cure any pathological condition whatever."

The effect of thought upon the health will be more fully covered in the next chapters, so let us turn here to the pathways of ideas—those riches of the mind over which so many people think they have no control.

According to the English psychologist, Graham Dallas, a new thought or idea passes through four definite phases.

1st—Preparation. You have a problem to solve. You study everything relating to it that you can. You fill your mind with all the facts pertaining to the problem.

2nd—Incubation. You let go of the problem with your conscious mind. You pass it along to your subconscious and forget it—secure in the knowledge that the subconscious is weighing every phase of it carefully. Meantime you go on about your everyday affairs, attending to those ordinary duties which the conscious mind is capable of taking care of unaided.

3rd—Illumination. Those who do not understand the processes of the mind tell you of the wonderful idea that suddenly dawns upon them, solving the problem they have been working over for hours or days or weeks. What actually happens is that their subconscious has weighed all the facts, come to its conclusion and passed that conclusion back to the conscious mind.

Spurred on by confident faith upon the part of the conscious mind, there is no question the subconscious cannot solve in this way. But so many of us make a correct solution impossible by interrupting the deliberations every few minutes with worry and fear, or by telling ourselves that we cannot solve the problem. Of course, when you tell the subconscious that, it doesn't bother about the problem further. It accepts your judgment that it cannot be solved, and goes on to something else.

4th—Verification. When the conscious mind receives the conclusion (the good idea) from the subconscious, it analyzes it in the light of all the facts it has, to see if the answer is correct. It *tests* it.

Perhaps the answer is negative, because of the fear and worry of the conscious mind. In that case, the problem must be sent back to the subconscious with the confident assurance that there is a solution, that the subconscious HAS it and can speedily find it.

Perhaps the answer is incomplete, solving only one phase of the problem. Refresh your mind again with every angle and send it back for further developing.

Don't talk about a new idea too soon. Let it ferment until it is complete, until it becomes so strong it pops out of itself—full born and perfect. Steam has little power as long as it escapes freely from the spout of a kettle. But stop up the spout, and it will presently blow off the lid!

Thoughts have little power as long as they escape through your mouth as fast as they are formed. You must dam them up for a while, set them some definite task to do, before they generate real power.

The trouble with many people is that they do not appreciate the difference between remembering and thinking. You give them a problem and they sit down, go through their brain files and look over everything connected with that problem they can find. If one of these files happens to contain a record of the solution of a similar problem, they use it. If not, they wait helplessly for some one to solve it for them. That is not thinking. That is merely passing your memory cells in kaleidoscopic review before your mental eyes.

Real thinking—connecting all these related items of information, and drawing logical conclusions from them, is something entirely different. It is like holding two pieces of electrically charged wire close to each other, and letting a spark spring between them. It is taking two memory cells, holding them before your mental eyes and connecting them with the spark of a related idea. Of course, that is an effort—probably the greatest effort there is—and many people are too mentally lazy to make such an effort.

"Many a man has made the mistake," says John Grier Hibben, President of Princeton University, "of not realizing that there are other functions of the mind besides memory. It is the creative function which is important. Happy is the man who has found the secret of life, the secret of delving deep into the well of knowledge."

What is the creative function? It is to draw conclusions from the facts filed away in your brain cell files—to connect them together and make of them something greater than the sum you now have. In other words, to take the 2 and 5 you find in your little file drawers, mix them together in such manner that you are able to deduce the unknown X, and make the total equal, instead of merely 7, 14!

Women do it every day. They call it intuition. It is merely reaching out after the unknown quantity without stopping to reason it out—*and finding it!*

Every great scientist, every inventor, every writer, every successful business man, must do it every day. *You* can do it.

Robert Louis Stevenson used to call the millions of little brain cells his "Mental Brownies," and he would set them deliberately to work comparing notes, drawing conclusions, bringing him the sparks, the ideas he sought.

W. A. League of Richmond, Virginia, wrote me that the simile of these little Brownies has been of greater help to him than anything he has found. It rid him of worry. It gave him the courage to tackle difficulties which before seemed insurmountable.

"The first thing I saw after unlocking the door of my filing department," he wrote, "was my own private office, nicely furnished with a big roomy desk. Immediately in front of my desk are two windows which afford me full view of the surroundings; on either side is a very efficient receiving apparatus, equipped with sensitive diaphrams that enable me to hear all that is said and done; just below the window is an automatic air intake which brings in fresh air at regular intervals; a little below is the speaking apparatus through which I can speak and explain the ideas as they are presented by my Brownies. There is nothing right that this organization cannot do.

"Immediately we set sail for treasure land. I am glad to report that, thanks to you, we are returning simply loaded with treasures—we have money, for example, in great stacks—enough to satisfy all those who have patiently waited; enough for charity of all kinds; and enough left to supply everything in abundance.

"The first problem I asked my Brownie to solve was a big one. The proper way to obtain financial independence. The next morning he informed me that we should push the sales of an educational service that I had been dabbling with for some time. Proper methods of approach, good sales talks, everything necessary for success were given men by the Brownies. For example: Saturday we closed a deal with $60.00 commission; Monday we earned $30.00; Tuesday $145.00.

"The customers are satisfied because they receive great benefits from their small investments; the house is satisfied because they do a big volume of business; I am satisfied and very thankful because it affords independence. We are just getting started and while we are not directly after the dollars—that is incidental—we are glad of the opportunity to serve.

"Thanks to you for presenting me with the key."

Now about *you*—have you looked over your mental storehouse lately? Have you cleared new paths to take the place of old, careless habits? Have you blocked off those that were worn into ruts?

Let's start now getting those Brownies busy on constructive work. They like it. The more you give them, the happier they will be, for it leaves them no time to be dull or listless or get into mischief.

Let's first look over the job you have. Let's try to look at it with the eyes of an outsider. Aren't there things which could be improved? Aren't there ways of doing things which would save time and money? Aren't there short cuts you could use?

Put down on paper every way you think of in which methods or product or service could be improved. Then put your paper away for a few days and forget it. Go back to it at the end of a week, and see how much you can better it, how many more short cuts you have found.

But don't take it to the boss even then. Remember, ideas are like a stream. They gain power by being damned. Dam yours for a little while until they are so big and so strong they carry everything before them. Then use their power to carry you on to advancement and success.

"Happy is the man that findeth wisdom, and the man that getteth understanding.

"For the merchandise of it is better than the

merchandise of silver, and the gain thereof than fine gold.

"She is more precious than rubies: and all the things thou canst desire are not to be compared unto her.

"Length of days is in her right hand; and in her left hand riches and honour."

—PROVERBS 4:13-16.

XXVII

THE DANGERS OF LIVING

Eat meat, and you'll have apoplexy,
Eat oysters, toxemia is thine;
Dessert, and you'll take to paresis;
Have gout if you drink too much wine.
Drink water, and get typhoid fever;
Drink milk, get tu-ber-cu-lo-sis;
Drink whisky, develop the jim jams;
Eat soup, Bright's Disease—think of this!
And vegetables weaken the system,
Cigars mean catarrh and bad breath;
While coffee brings nervous prostration,
And cigarettes bring early death.
So eat nothing, drink nothing, smoke nothing;
And if you would live, have a care,
And don't breathe at all, pray remember,
Unless you breathe sterilized air!

BY JAMES COURTNEY CHALLISS.

FROM LAUGHTER MAGAZINE.

The American people pay more than $50,000,000.00 every year for cathartics alone. Their total bill for medical and hospital treatment is estimated at $2,000,000,000.00. What are they getting for all this money?

In *The New Yorker* a short time ago was an article which so well reflects the attitude of many doctors toward this vast expenditure, that I give you parts of it here. It purports to be a couple of doctors talking things over in one of the big hospitals.

"I've been thinking a lot about this profession of ours," said the first. "You fool around, and guess right every now and then, and save somebody's life, and get to feeling all noble about it—then somebody comes in with a little bellyache, and you give him a pill or two, and the next morning you wake up to find he's dead. You get to wondering whether you really cured that first guy, or whether luck cured him, and whether the best part about the medicine you gave him was that it didn't hurt him any."

"There aren't but three medicines in the world," answered the second medico, "castor oil and quinine and morphine—well, if you consider iodine a medicine, let that in, too. Every time you give a dose of anything else, you're shooting in the dark. The better doctor you are, the less chance you take of bumping somebody off. The best you can say for most of the compounds is that they don't do much harm."

"But," said the senior, "you grant that they have a psychological effect on the patient. Anybody feels better after a dose of some terrible stuff."

"Sure," answered the other, "good for his mind if his belly can stand it. I just mean to say, in the case of an ordinary sick man, you know there isn't much you can do for him. If he is going to be cured, nature will do more for him than anything else. You give him a little medicine, hoping it will help nature out a little and trying to be sure it won't hurt him. Study medicine for six years, and you find out that *nobody knows anything about it.*"

Yet almost every magazine and newspaper is full of advertisements urging you to use more drugs, more remedies for this, that or the other imaginary ailment. As Spencer Vanderbilt put it in one issue of *Advertising and Selling*:

"It looks like a concerted policy on the part of many prominent advertisers to turn the good old easy-going American people into a race of hypochondriacs.

"It's getting so you can't look through the advertising pages of any of our better known periodicals without feeling queer all over. Every other advertisement, so it seems, asks you what's the matter with you, and before you have a chance to reply, tells you what you need to correct just that condition. Are your teeth coated with film like scum in a stagnant pool? Is your breath such that people leave the room every time you exhale? Does the food you eat give you the vital nourishment you need, or do you eat just because it's 6:30? Are you often constipated for weeks at a stretch?

"The other evening I was looking through a recent issue of a leading monthly magazine. At 9:11 when I began, I was in good health and excellent spirits; temperature and pulse normal. At 9:14, I felt the need of a little sodium bicarbonate. At 9:18, I staged a gargling act. At 9:20, I sprayed my gums with iodine, in defiance of the poison label on the little brown bottle. At 9:24, I tripped myself while trying to execute a difficult maneuver with a coil of dental floss. Meanwhile I was becoming feverish and my blood pressure had risen. At 9:45 prompt, I fell to the floor in a dead faint."

We buy more nostrums and pay more money for health protection than any nation under the sun. Yet we are far from being the healthiest nation. Our average citizen loses 10 per cent of his time through sickness, and half a million of our people die every year from diseases which doctors regard as preventable or curable.

The common cold is responsible for more illnesses resulting in more unnecessary deaths than all other ailments put together. A simple enough ailment, surely, yet the drugs of today seem no more effective in preventing or curing it than did the "snail water" of our ancestors, or the "powdered

Pharaoh" or dried entrails of a snake which were so popular a thousand years ago.

Why?

Is not the answer that the nostrums people took never did have any healing efficacy—that the good they did was merely in proportion to the physician's and the patient's faith in them?

Fear is the basis of all sickness—and fear is being ingrained in us through the schools, through newspapers and magazines, through the advertisements of every nostrum on the market.

Does a woman bring forth a perfect child? Beware! Have it X-rayed. It may be developing Ricketts. So-and-so's preparation will make it right.

Have you a perfect digestive apparatus? Too bad! It is probably twenty-four hours late in performing its work. There is not enough yeast in your food—or iron—or what-not.

Are you feeling like a two-year-old, in tip-top shape, ready to grapple with anything the world may hand you? That's all wrong! No man has any business feeling as good as that when any one of a hundred insidious ailments may be creeping upon you. Get examined! Learn all the things that are wrong with you. Join the Worry Club!

Soon we shall be as bad as the Annamites of Indo-China, who have taken hygiene so tragically that they refuse to eat strawberries, fish, oysters and various other foods for fear of possible contagion. They have worked themselves into a state of terror, worrying over ailments that seemed of no consequence until science taught them how terrible they are. They are depriving themselves of all joy in life— just to be able to keep on living.

Logan Clendening, M. D., contends that, with all our advances in medical science, the average life expectancy has been increased only one-tenth of a year in the past 75 years, and he strongly opposes the annual physical examinations which certain agencies are now urging so insistently.

"I have seen the plan in operation," says Dr. Clendening, "and I have seen practically nothing result but grief and unhappiness. The number of people who supposed themselves well and who were symptomless, and who found on examination a condition of disease which could be materially remedied—the number of people whose lives were lengthened—was so small as entirely to be minimized in the face of the dead load of meaningless sorrow entailed. What usually happens is this: Most of the patrons of such a system are men; most of them have considerable financial responsibility, and most people who have considerable financial responsibility are no longer young. Therefore a middle-aged man is the usual victim. In the great majority of cases, if such men have anything to be found wrong with them, it is a slight defect of the heart, some kidney change and a beginning of hardening of the arteries or hypertension.

"This report is handed to a man who believed he is in good health. He looks up things in an encyclopedia or medical book and decides he has received his death sentence. If he had not had the examination, he might have lived twenty-five years without a symptom."

What many doctors forget—and what few people realize—is that the medical practice of today will be in the discard tomorrow and some entirely new theory the vogue.

Professor Simpson of Edinburgh University was asked to go to the University library and mark the medical books that were no longer worth keeping. "Take every text-book that is more than ten years old," he directed the Librarian, "and put it down the cellar." And many doctors go even further. A famous surgeon—author of several authoritative works—told me that most medical or surgical works more than two years old were of no more value than waste paper.

For 1300 years the fallacious ideas of Galen were regarded as the Law and the Gospel of medical practice. The science of medicine stood still all that time because it was content to accept, and people were content to believe, what had been handed down as truth.

Then came Harvey—the doubter—and proved Galen wrong, established the circulation of the blood. After him

came Pasteur and Lister, to prove the old adage that cleanliness is next to Godliness.

For what is Godliness but God-likeness, perfection of
body and mind? And of all the essentials to this, next to a
clean mind comes a clean body.

Before the time of Pasteur and Lister, every wound was
expected to fester, to suppurate. Why? Because no effort
was made to keep it clean. These scientists discovered
the importance of cleanliness—and modern surgery is the
result.

What was the greatest discovery in the world war?
Dakin's Solution—a cleanser. It does not heal. It does not
cure. It cleanses. And allows Nature to carry on its healing
undisturbed.

Medical science has practically rid the world of plagues,
of typhus, of yellow fever, or a dozen old-time scourges of
mankind. How? Not through drugs. Through cleanliness.
Through purifying water supplies. Through sewage dis-
posal and drainage systems. Until after the Civil War, our
cities were cesspools where cholera and other diseases of
filth took enormous toll of life. The air was foul with steam-
ing abominations from the noisome liquids that filled gut-
ters and pools. What did away with the plagues of cholera
and the like? Not drugs—SANITATION!

What was the basis of Moses' Sanitary Code, which
brought the children of Israel through the wilderness

without dysentery or typhoid or any of the attendant ills an army on such a march would expect today? Cleanliness!

Keep your body and your surroundings clean and Nature will attend to the rest.

Germs? What of them? What though there are billions all around you all the time? Seldom, if ever, is disease caused by germs alone. Germs are like dogs, which fawn upon you if you fear them not and devour you if you try to flee them.

As long as your health is good, as long as your body is clean and wholesome, you need pay no attention to germs, though the air be so full of them you can almost feel them. The trouble must start from within. Rome did not fall because the barbarians under Alaric or Attila were stronger than any of the hordes which had attacked the legions before their day. Rome fell because it was rotten within. And all the germs in the world will not hurt you unless your defenses give way from within.

If you feel that you must have medicine to fight off these germs, by all means take it. But don't contribute your money towards that $2,000,000,000.00 which goes every year for drugs and medical treatment. Instead, use the medicine which God provided so abundantly—fresh air, sunshine and water. God is in them. Life is in them. So use them—absorb all you can of them.

The Metropolitan Life Insurance Company had an

advertisement entitled: "Water—$10 a glass!" which told how some specialist had ordered a rich patient abroad to a water-cure. How he drank water—lots of it—no medicine—just water. Counting doctor bills, and steamship and railroad fares and hotels, he estimated that water cost him $10 a glass. But he felt it was worth it. He came back well!

A friend who met him at the pier laughed at him when he heard the story. Asked the reason, he explained that he had had the same trouble, had even received the same prescription, but drew his water from the family faucet and got the same results!

THE WILL TO BE WELL

"There is probably no physician," said Dr. Joseph Collins in the February Harper's, "who has not seen patients whose disorders had resisted his efforts, restored to health by an appeal only to what is popularly called the mind. There is one medium in which Nature does her best work. It is fearlessness. Apprehension halts Nature. Fear fetters her.

"One of the reasons why training in Psychology would be a valuable thing for every practitioner is that it would teach him that disease cannot be standardized—that the individual must be considered first, then the disease."

When you realize that of all the beds in all the hospitals in the United States one in every two is for a mental ailment, you begin to see how important the mental attitude of the patient is. Just think—as many mental cases as all other kinds put together! And yet doctors can still be found who pin all their faith to drugs or diet, who disregard the mind as utterly as though it had no power whatever.

In experiments conducted by the New York Homeopathic Medical College and the Flower Hospital, fifty students were given capsules containing either plain sugar of milk or one of four slight poisons. Half were given poison, half sugar of milk, but no student knew which he had received.

The students then reported their reactions in sealed envelopes. Some, however, noticed such virulent symptoms that they brought them to Dr. Boyd's immediate attention. What was his amusement to find that practically every one of these was a student *who had received no poison at all!*

What caused these virulent symptoms? Certainly nothing they had eaten, nothing physical that had been given them. Then what? Wasn't it the mental suggestion that poison had been administered to them? And this mental fear was far more potent than the poison itself proved to be to those who received it.

What is it kills the victim of the witch-doctor? What is it gives power to the Voodoo priestess? Fear—the suggestion to the victim that he has been marked for evil or death.

What is it ails most mental cases in the hospital? Fear—

fear sometimes so subtle that they would have difficulty recognizing it themselves. Patients in hysteria relive highly emotional experiences of the past. Shell-shocked veterans relive the sights and sounds of the trenches.

And what is the cure? First, bringing those fears out into the open—recognizing them for what they are. Second, using the proper counter-suggestions to overcome them.

When a child thinks he sees some fear-some creature in the dark, you don't try to drive away those bogies. No—that would confirm their reality in the child's mind. Instead, you turn on the light and show him the *nothingness* of his fears. When a victim of delirium tremens sees green tigers and pink snakes about to attack him, you don't try to kill these animals. You show him their unreality. When a sick person thinks he has something the matter with him, just as imaginary as green tigers, you don't operate to remove the trouble from his body. You correct his mental picture.

Drugs, appliances—what good are they when the trouble is mental, as all trouble is? They may help to start a different train of thought, they may even provide a crutch upon which to lean for a while, but a real cure must go to the heart of the cause—the mind.

I remember one woman who wrote me:

"I have been bothered with constipation for the past ten or more years—taking medicines, etc. Thence other ailments, such as eyesight being dim and fainting spells, due to my taking medicine so strong. Then when I get used to one kind of pill, its supposed power dies only to take something stronger. I have paid so much money out to doctors, etc., that I am financially embarrassed. First they tell me to get my tonsils and adenoids out which was done, and then they extracted nine teeth, and people tell me I have such nice teeth, but at the roots acid condition appears to be eating the enamel—and lately I am afraid to look at the mirror—rather in it, because I see these defects. And another thing they tell me to do, is to wear glasses—which I have done. I don't see why I have to contend with all these things. Physicians tell me all these things have come from the bad condition of my stomach. I am only a young lady 25 years of age, and discouraged now on this account."

An aggravated case, of course, but don't you and everyone of us know a dozen almost as bad—people who have started doctoring for one trouble, have been treated for every imaginable ailment, yet whose last state is far worse than their first? Drugs lead only to more drugs. Even though they seem to correct one condition, they bring about a worse.

If you bought a new automobile and some of the parts seemed to function improperly, what would you do? Take it apart yourself? Buy a lot of patent remedies and feed them to it? Of course, there are some people foolish enough to do that, but most have the good judgment to take the car back to the maker or his agents and have the difficulty adjusted by someone who understands it. We call that "servicing" a car, and anyone who buys a car expects a certain amount of such service.

The Hand that made your body is just as ready to "service" it as any automobile maker is to "service" his product. All you have to do is to appeal to Him just as confidently as you would to the auto manufacturer. He has not put any time limit upon His "service." In fact, He has repeatedly *invited* us to bring our troubles to Him. "And it shall come to pass," He promises, "that before they call, I will answer. And while they are yet speaking, I will hear."

What many people and even some doctors forget is the ability of this body machine of ours to adapt itself to almost any circumstances. People worry about their foods and their surroundings and the pace of modern life. They don't need to. Given the necessary mental support, this body of ours can adapt itself to any condition. As Dr. Raymond Pearl of *Johns Hopkins* says:

"A fundamental characteristic which is possessed by the living organism and lacked by the non-living, inorganic machine, is adaptability . . . ability to do something to meet any situation which arises in a manner which conduces to the continued survival of the doer.

"This adaptability is not confined to food seeking,

overcoming material obstacles, finding a mate. It functions also in the internal workings of the human body, to prevent disaster—as when one kidney is removed, the other promptly increases in size to meet adequately the enlarged demand."

Few people have even a faint idea of the wonderful biological powers of every organism in their body. Most have heard that a tonsil will grow back after being removed unless every vestige of it has been cut out. But do you know that such solid substances as bones can grow again? Some years ago, Dr. Jas. R. Wood of New York removed the entire lower jaw bone of a woman, leaving only the periosteum or membrane, and putting in a framework to hold the teeth in place. Not only did the entire jaw bone grow in again, but as it grew the teeth resumed their original places in it!

"I know that, whatsoever God doeth, it shall be forever. Nothing can be put to it, not anything taken from it."—Ecclesiastes 3:14.

Dr. Ernest P. Boas, Director of the Montefiore Hospital of New York, says that the word "incurable" should be removed from the dictionary. There is no such condition. "In the present state of medical knowledge," he declares, "the pronouncement of the sentence 'incurable' on a patient implies a knowledge greater than the physician possesses."

Every one knows that ignorance killed Washington. In his day the practice was to bleed a sick person. If the patient was not relieved, they bled him again.

Washington had a sore throat. The physician opened a vein and bled him. Next day, throat no better. Doctor bled him again. Throat worse. After the third bleeding, Washington protested. "But," says Dr. William Mather Lewis, President of George Washington University, "the bleeding was continued right up to his death."

Today we know that the loss of blood and consequent vitality hastened the death of Washington, as it did that of thousands of others. For doctors did not then recognize Nature as the supreme Doctor. But how do we know that the popular treatments and remedies of today won't be just as thoroughly discredited a week or a month from now, especially when doctors themselves tell you that most medical books are worthless after two years?

"What is *unknown* about maintaining and perfecting the health of mankind is far greater than what is known," says Dr. Chas. V. Chapin, President of the American Public Health Association. "The opportunities in the scientific field are as great today as before the days of Harvey, Lister and Pasteur."

In medicine, as in all other learning, it is only your tyro who knows it all—who condemns everything that differs from his own school of thought. The greatest minds realize how little is really known, how much merely guessed at, what a vast sea of knowledge still remains undiscovered. There are plenty such men in the medical profession. Cabot of Harvard, Pearl of Johns Hopkins, Carrel and Loeb and others at the Rockefeller Foundation. You seldom hear sweeping condemnations of any new line of thought from such men as these. All they ask is to *know*—to have the chance to test and investigate and get at the kernel of truth under no matter how many layers of prejudice. They have no fear of new methods leaving them out of a job, depriving them of their livelihood. They know that service such as theirs will always be in demand.

Such men will be the first to tell you that real health never came out of a medicine bottle or pill box. And never will. Nature is the only source of life. Nature is the only curative agent. And when I speak of Nature, I mean God—the Great Mind that is over all and in all.

Don't give up your pills and your nostrums. Don't give up your patent foods and appliances. Use them—as long as you have faith in them—as long as you think they are doing you good.

But when you have come to the end of these, when you have exhausted the remedies that human ingenuity can devise, then try the power of Mind, then go back to the methods the followers of Jesus found so effective.

"The spirit of the Lord is upon me, because He hath annointed me to preach the Gospel to the poor; He hath sent me to heal the broken hearted, to preach deliverance to the captives, and recovering of sight to the blind, to set at liberty them that are bruised."

—LUKE 4:18.

XXVIII

THE OLD MAN OF THE SEA

*"I will praise Thee; for I am fearfully and wonderfully
made; marvelous are Thy works.*

*"My substance was not hid from Thee, when I was made
in secret, and curiously wrought in the lowest parts of
the earth.*

*"Thine eyes did see my substance, yet being unperfect;
and in Thy book all my members were written, which
in continuance were fashioned, when as yet there was
none of them."*

PSALMS 139:14–16.

On the fifth voyage of Sindbad the Sailor, his vessel was wrecked and he with difficulty made his way to the shores of a fertile isle.

Thankfully he got to his feet and took his way inland, hoping to find some human habitation where he might get help. In a little while he reached the bank of a small stream. Sitting there, very weak and infirm-looking, and apparently unable to cross the stream, was an old, old man.

Sindbad thought him a shipwrecked sailor like himself, so he took him upon his shoulders and carried him across the stream. Once on the other side, however, the old man refused to get down. He wrapped his skinny legs about Sindbad's chest and with his hands clutched Sindbad's throat so tightly that, do what he would, the latter could not shake him off.

For days he stayed there and Sindbad was like to perish from exhaustion, but still the old man kicked and pinched and choked him into subjection. It was only when he used the power of his *mind* to contrive a way out, that Sindbad finally got rid of his awful burden.

You have an Old Man of the Sea who, every little while, perches upon your shoulders—upon yours or those of some member of your family. Usually his hold is insecure. You succeed in shaking him off. But with some, he gets his skinny old legs around their chest, his talons upon their neck, and holds on and on until they give up and die.

That Old Man of the Sea is Sickness.

Has he ever had his clutches upon you? Has he, by chance, a strangle hold on you now? Do you want to know how to shake him off?

Drugs won't do it. Mankind has been pinning its faith

to drugs and nostrums for several thousand years, yet the Old Man of sickness is as rampant today as he ever was. As a matter of fact, examination of mummies shows that the Egyptians of thousands of years ago suffered from fewer diseases than do we. For more than a thousand years, there was no medical profession, there were no physicians among the Jews, and—call it cause or effect, as you like—the Psalmist declares: "There was not one feeble person in all their tribes."—Psalms 105:37.

Then how shall you get rid of this old devil who is at the bottom of more misery than all other causes together?

Only one person has ever been completely successful in mastering this Old Man of the Sea. That one was Jesus. So our best chance would seem to be to study His methods, to follow the directions He so carefully laid down.

To begin with, we have His assurance that it can be done. We know that He cured all manner of diseases— not by drugs or potions or dieting or exercise—but solely through the power of Mind—of the Father in Him. "It is not me," He said, "but the Father in me; He doeth the works." And He assured us again and again that the same Father is in us, and that the works which He (Jesus) did, we too can do. "He that believeth in me, the works that I do shall he do also. And greater works than these shall he do."—John 14:12.

Not only have we His definite assurance of this, but He proved it with His own disciples. They were plain working folk, most of them unable even to read or write, yet by dint of much teaching and example, He was able to send them out two and two and have them report signs and wonders second only to His own. "And the seventy returned with joy, saying, Lord, even the devils are subject unto us through Thy name."—Luke 10:17.

That power was not confined to His immediate disciples. Even those who were not direct followers were able to cure in His name, solely through their belief in Him. Remember how the disciples, in their zeal, stopped such a one and Jesus rebuked them for it? "Master," said John, "we saw one casting out devils in Thy name, and he followed not us; and we forbade him, because he followed not us. But Jesus said, Forbid him not, for there is no man which shall do a miracle in my name, that can lightly speak evil of me."—Mark 9:38-39.

For more than two centuries, the healing power of Jesus abode with the early Christians—right up to the time when Christianity was made the State religion. Then it became so buried in form and ritual, in ceremonial and pomp, that the real spirit of Jesus' teachings was lost. And physical healings became so rare as to *be* miracles.

But the power is there, the same power Jesus gave to His followers when He bade them—"Go ye into all the world and preach the Gospel to every creature. And these signs shall follow them that believe; In my name shall they cast out devils; they shall speak with new tongues; they shall take up serpents; and if they drink any deadly thing, it shall not hurt them; they shall lay hands on the sick and they shall recover."—Mark 16:15, 17, 18.

Let us then analyze *how* He did these wonderful works, how His followers were able to do the same.

To begin with, let us remember that His favorite name for Himself was the Way-shower. He came to guide, to lead. He told us that His mission was not to destroy but to save. "I have come that they might have life, and that they might have it more abundantly."—John 10:10.

Life—what is life? Isn't it the Father in us? The perfect image of God, animated by the Father?

The Father is in us now. We can't have more of Him— but we can *use* more. With most of us, the Father in us is asleep—unknown, unused. He is like the electricity all about us—static. He needs to be recognized, to be *used*, to become dynamic for us. Jesus showed us the way.

For uncounted years, the air has been full of electricity— dormant, static, except when an occasional storm lashed it into a dynamic destruction. For thousands of years, the giant power of steam lay idle, waiting for someone to harness it.

Today, steam and electricity warm and light our homes, move our trains, run huge industries. What makes the difference? The steam and electricity have not changed. They were just as powerful, just as plentiful aforetime. It is simply that someone has shown us how to *use* them.

Since Adam was first created, the life in man has been the life of the Father in him. But after his fall, man forgot his Divine Sonship, forgot the power of the Father within him. Occasionally some Prophet like Moses or Elisha would glimpse this vast power, but for the most part, mankind remained in a state of lethargy—mentally unawake.

Then came Jesus—His mission to acquaint man with himself, His Gospel that every man is the Son of God, His aim to lead all men into the Kingdom.

That mission He succeeded in as has no religious teacher before or since. But He offered so much, that mankind was reluctant to believe its good fortune. Men had been taught for so many centuries that this earth is a vale of tears, they had been told by so many powerful rulers and well-fed priests that they must expect poverty and suffering here below, butit would all be made right in some vague hereafter, that a Kingdom of Heaven here on earth seemed too good to be true.

You remember the story of the man who stood on London Bridge and offered golden sovereigns to all passers-by free. He couldn't get anyone to take them. They feared a "catch." It was too good to be true.

Barnum, after a life-time spent largely in fooling the public, wrote that he had found far more people who had lost out by believing too little than by believing too much.

So it has been with the promises of Jesus. They are so limitless, they solve every problem of life so completely, that people are reluctant to believe them true. They look for some "catch" in them. They make qualifications where Jesus made none. They can not quite grasp how such a poor, downtrodden worm as they have come to believe man to be, can have unlimited power over himself, over his surroundings—can be, in short, the son of God.

Especially do they find it hard to believe that they can rid themselves of all the ills and ailments which flesh has been heir to for so many years. They are quite willing to believe Jesus meant what He said when He told His disciples to—"Go, preach," but they think He must have referred to some vague future state when He added—"The kingdom of Heaven is at hand. Heal the sick, cleanse the lepers, raise the dead, cast out devils. Freely ye have received, freely give."

Perhaps it would help a little if we went back for a moment to what causes all sickness and disease. I know you remember the story of Jacob and his long courtship of Rebecca. But did you ever notice the shrewd understanding which Jacob had even then of the laws of cause and effect?

Jacob, you remember, was to receive Laban's daughter for his wife on condition of seven years of service. There followed another seven years before the contract was finally completed. At the end of this time Jacob desired to return to his native land, but was persuaded to remain by his father-in-law's urgency. A contract was made that for this service he should receive every spotted and ring-streaked calf, kid, or lamb that was born to the flocks or herds. Normally this would have been very poor pay, but Jacob performed a psychological trick. He went to the water courses and stripped the branches and part of the bark from the trees so that they presented a bizarre appearance to the cattle who conceived their young in this place. The Bible tells us that many ring-streaked and spotted calves and kids were born, *and that Jacob was made wealthy at the expense of his father-in-law.*

Everyone knows the shiftless habits of the mocking bird. Too lazy to rear and care for its own young, it goes to the nests of other birds which are "setting" in the interval when they are off seeking food, notes the markings on their eggs, then comes back later and *lays in their nests eggs of those same exact markings!*

One naturalist reports having found mocking bird eggs of forty different markings.

Several saints of medieval days were reported to have markings in their hands, their feet and their sides, similar to those on the risen Saviour, acquired through constant contemplation of His crucifixion.

And right now, in the village of Konnersreuth in Germany, there is a young woman on whose hands, feet and side periodically appear wounds similar to the stigmata of the crucified Christ. Various persons have testified to the truth of this, among them Dr. Wolfgang von Weisl, whose report in part reads as follows:

"In the middle of the back of each hand I perceive a thin, dark-brown scab, about the size and shape of a thumb nail. The scar is fresh and the wound itself is light red and inflamed. In reply to her visitor's questions she asserts that these symptoms can only be observed today, Saturday; tomorrow they disappear. She adds that the irregular scab can be washed off though the red stigmata remain. On her palms the same bright red scabs can also be found. At times the patient feels as if these two wounds on the back and surface of her hands touch each other. Her other stigmata I did not ask to see. Only over the wound in her heart did Theresa Neumann say she had the feeling that it was piercing deeper and working right to her heart's core."

The cause? Simply the old, well-known law that we reproduce whatever we contemplate. Whatever man looks upon with faith or fear, he will tend to reproduce in his body.

I once heard a traveler telling of a trip through Alaska. Passing through a village, one of his companions espied an Indian he knew. "Sick Man Charley!" he called. And the Indian answered immediately. Asked the reason for such a name, the traveler explained—"Oh, he was sick one time when we wanted him, so after that we called him 'Sick Man Charley.' Now they tell me he is sick most of the time."

We laugh at anyone allowing such a name to be fastened on him, but most men answer to something similar just as readily. With some it is rheumatism. Mention rheumatism, and they immediately have a premonitory twinge. "Runs in the family," they explain. "Father had it before me. Grandfather before him. Have to expect it." They ought to be named "Rheumatism." They answer to it just as surely as to their own names.

With others it is indigestion or cancer, or constipation, or colds, or one of the hundreds of ills that mankind believes itself heir to. Tell them they are no better than Sick Man Charley, and they will be highly indignant. Yet the fact remains they have "Sicknamed" themselves, and they answer to these "Sick-names" even more readily than to their proper ones.

Man thinks he can cure disease by studying it, by spreading the knowledge of it. But what has he done? *Multiplied it instead!* Just what happens? He frightens people into the very thing he is warning them against. Those diseases which he has fought with the positive weapons of sunshine and fresh air and pure water and cleanliness, visualizing these instead of the diseases, he has practically eliminated. Those which he has fought with the negative weapons of drugs (of hurting one part to help another) are just about where they were when he started.

"What boots it," asks Milton, "at one door to make defense and at another to let in the foe?" There is an old Eastern proverb to the effect that if you let a camel get his head under the flap of the tent, the next thing you know he will have his back under it, too. Let the fear of some disease get into your mind, and the first thing you know, the disease will be there, too.

Man is like the mocking bird, laying eggs marked in God's image or in the image of sickness and disease, depending upon which kind he has looked upon with desire and faith—or fear.

He sees a disease in another. He has been taught that this disease is contagious. And the fear of the disease impresses it so vividly upon his consciousness that he lays the egg of it in his own body.

The ancient Greeks understood this, and surrounded themselves with statuary depicting the most perfect figures of men and women that their artists could make. What was the result? Their children grew into men and women who for beauty and symmetry were the envy of the world.

In Genesis (1:26, 27, 31) we read: "And God said, Let us make man in Our image, after our likeness.. . .. . .So God created man in His own image, in the image of God created He him.. . .. . .And God saw everything that He had made, and, behold, it was very good."

If God were a sculptor, working in marble, what sort of image of man would He carve? Don't you suppose it would be the most perfect form of man ever conceived—more perfect than any ever made by Greek or Italian sculptors?

If God were a potter, modeling images in clay, what form of man would He model? Don't you suppose it would be the most beautiful ever molded by hands?

When "God formed man of the dust of the ground, and breathed into his nostrils the breath of life," don't you suppose He formed that image in as perfect a mold as Mind could conceive—more perfect than any statue ever formed by the hand of man?

We start then with this—that man as originally conceived by God was perfect. Each organ has a perfect Divine pattern. Each cell a definite end and purpose. As in creating the plants—"The Lord God made the earth and the heavens, and every plant of the field before it was in the earth, and every herb of the field before it grew."—Genesis 2:4-5.

No machine ever made by human hands is as efficient as this human body which God made. As an organization of distinct cells, each an essential part of the whole, each under a central head, nothing to equal it has ever been conceived. It is so flawless in its functioning under almost every variety of conditions, that no fundamental change in it has been found necessary since first it was formed into the likeness of man. It is the most perfect example of organized control in the world.

And not merely of organized control, but of reproduction. The millions of cells of which it is made have the faculty of renewing themselves indefinitely. As far as its inherent qualities are concerned, it can live forever.

Then why do people die? Why are they sick? Why do they grow old, atrophy and decay?

Why do your problems sometimes work out wrongly in mathematics? Because you depart from the rule, because you do something wrongly. It doesn't matter how good your intent may be, how much you want to work out your problem in the right way. If you don't follow the proper methods, if you depart from the principles of mathematics, your answer is going to be wrong. And the only way you will ever get it right is to erase the result these wrong methods gave you—start afresh—and work it out along right principles.

2 plus 2 equals 4. If through ignorance or thoughtlessness you put down 2 plus 2 equals 3 or 5 or any number other than 4, your result is going to be wrong and the farther you carry your figuring, the worse it will be. Erase this, go back to your original problem, start right, and you speedily arrive at the correct answer.

So it is with man. Man was first an image in God's mind. That image was perfect then, is perfect now.

Having created the image in Mind, God then breathed into it the breath of life. Therefore man is the sum of God's image and God's life energy—call it electricity, call it what you will.

If 2 plus 2 must always equal 4, must not God's perfect image and God's life energy always equal perfection? If the result seems to us imperfect, does it not seem likely that the fault lies somewhere in our conception of it, and that the thing for us to do is to erase this incorrect result and start afresh at our problem until we arrive at the perfect answer?

That is all right for mathematics, perhaps you will say, but my body is something I can see and feel and touch. I didn't make it. It is just the way I found it. And yet it has this and that and the other thing wrong with it.

True—you didn't make your real body—but are you so sure you did not make the one you are complaining of? Have you ever glanced in a mirror whose surface was marred, and thought the spots on the mirror were spots on your face? Have you ever looked into a concave or convex glass and seen the distorted images they reflect?

Your conscious mind is such a mirror and the images it reflects are no more to be relied upon than those you see in an imperfect glass. There are mists in it that come between you and the real substance of you—the perfect image which God conceived. There are wrong thoughts which have fastened themselves upon your conscious images like barnacles upon a ship. There are bad dreams of weakness and disease. There are nightmares of accidents and crippling and imperfections. All very real to your conscious mind—just as the dreams and nightmares of sleep seem real and vivid to you then.

Jesus cured the sick and the lame and the halt and the blind. How? By driving out these imperfect images, these devils of wrong thought, that stood between men and God's perfect image of them. He realized their unreality. He never inquired into the symptoms. He never prescribed physic or exercise. He treated all forms of sickness in the same way— by driving away the demon of wrong thought, by removing the mist that lay between the sick man and God's perfect image of him. "He sent His word and healed them, and delivered them from their destructions."—Psalms 107:20.

Remember, when Jesus healed the mother of Peter, how he first rebuked the fever that possessed her—and it left her? Remember how often, in curing all manner of ills, it is said that "He drove the devils out of them"? "When the evening was come, they brought unto Him many that were possessed with devils; and He cast out the spirits with His word, and healed all that were sick."—Matthew 8:16.

What were these devils? What but wrong thoughts which had fastened themselves upon the minds of these poor people and come between them and the perfect substance of themselves which was the only image God knew. The perfect image of them was always there, but it took the "invisible light" of Jesus' understanding to make its substance visible to their eyes.

There is but one right idea of your body. That is the perfect image in which God conceived it, His life energy flowing ever-abundantly and ever-renewingly through it. That is the real substance of you, under all the seeming imperfections, the substance which the "invisible light" of understanding alone can make manifest.

You remember the story of the sculptor who asked for a certain block of marble. Other pieces were offered him, but they would not do. Asked why he must have this particular block, he explained—"Because I see an angel in it." And when the block was delivered to him, he carved from it the most beautiful angel imaginable.

There is just such an angel in you, too. Hold on to the image of him. Chip off the disfiguring barnacles of imperfect thoughts, of devils of disease, of weakness, of ugliness. Use the "invisible light" of understanding to bring out the real substance under all this seeming, to show to yourself and all men the perfect image of you which is the only one your Father ever conceived, the only one He knows.

The others—the imperfect, diseased images you have heretofore known? Whenever they try to show themselves, remember that "they are of their father the devil and the lusts of their father they will do. He was a murderer from the beginning, and abode not in the truth, *because there is no truth in him.* When he speaketh a lie, he speaketh of his own; for he is a liar and the father of it."—John 8:44.

So deny them. Disclaim them. Tell them they are not yours—you don't want them—have no place for them. Remember that you are the Son of God, and as His son, you have legions of angels (right thoughts) at your command to drive away any devils (wrong thoughts) that may assail you. So call upon them for help. Command the devils to get out of you—command them in the name of Jesus Christ. "And these signs shall follow them that believe. In my name shall they cast out devils."—Mark 16:16.

But don't be content with casting out the bad. Get fast hold of the good, of the perfect image of you that is in the Father's mind. And so fill your mind with it that there will be no room for the devils of wrong thought. You can't pour water, you know, into a vessel already full. If you fail to fill his place with the angels of right thought, the devil may come back as in Jesus' parable:

"When the unclean spirit is gone out of a man, he walketh through dry places, seeking rest; and finding none, he saith, I will return unto my house whence I came out.

"And when he cometh, he findeth it swept and garnished.

"Then goeth he, and taketh to him seven other spirits more wicked than himself; and they enter in, and dwell there: and the last state of that man is worse than the first."—Luke 11:24-26.

It all comes back to this: There is but one creator—God—Good. Everything that He created is like Himself—Good.

But between His perfect image and our everyday conscious selves there frequently arises the mist of wrong thoughts, like the mists that obscure the mountain-top in the morning. The mountain-top is there, though unseen beneath the mist, just as the perfect substance of our bodies is there, though obscured by the mists of imperfection and disease.

The sun comes up and drives the mists from the mountains. And the sunlight of Truth, of Understanding, just as surely drives the mists from between us and the perfect images of us which the Father holds.

We dream in sleep and our thought forms seem to mold our bodies and our surroundings into all manner of grotesque shapes. We dream in waking, and our thought forms seem to mold the body into pitiful wrecks of accident and disease.

We wake from the sleeping dream and find our bodies perfect as when we fell asleep. We must wake ourselves from the waking dreams as well, and get back to the perfect images in which the Father made us.

Nothing is established, remember—nothing is permanent, but the one perfect God-idea. Erase any others from your thought as fast as they form. Get back to the 2 plus 2 must equal 4. There is but one right idea of each cell and organism. That is the God-idea. The God-idea of it, plus the Life-energy of the Father in you, MUST EQUAL HIS PERFECT IMAGE.

"But now, O Lord, thou art our Father. We are the clay, and thou our Potter. And we all are the work of Thy hand."

—ISAIAH 64:8.

HOPELESS TOWER

*"All things were made by Him, and without Him was
not anything made that was made. In Him was life; and
the life was the light of man."*

—JOHN 1:3-4.

He was quite the most beautiful Prince that ever
was born. Or so the story says. He was round
and fat, straight-limbed and long, and his father
and mother were exceedingly proud of him.

But on his way to the christening, his nurse tripped over
her gown and let him fall—just at the foot of the marble
staircase—and after that his legs seemed to have no strength
in them. They called it spinal trouble.

Father and mother died, and the people wanted no lame
child for King, so his uncle took the throne and the Prince
was sent to Hopeless Tower.

For a long time he lay there, very miserable and hopeless. Until one day a little old lady came to visit him. How

she got there he couldn't guess, for his room was at the top of a high tower and no one was ever allowed in it except his nurse. He couldn't even be sure of her name, for she said that different people called her so many different things. Some said she was "Stuff-and-Nonsense"; some the things that dreams are made of; but her friends called her Faith.

Faith gave to the little lame Prince a traveling cloak, which lifted him out of his bed of sickness, which freed him from Hopeless Tower and which finally brought him to the throne of his fathers.

A pretty story, perhaps you will say, but if our thoughts are the cause of all our sickness, how could a fall have hurt the infant Prince? The Prince was too young to reason, just as are many of the babies who are crippled and sickly today. Why do conditions they can't think out affect them?

If you have read the chapter on *Pathways of the Mind,* you know that trains of thought follow accustomed pathways unless we consciously send them by some other route. And that the brain is like a radio set, receiving impressions (thought waves) from those all about us. Most of us are too taken up with our conscious thoughts to pay attention to outside suggestions, but very young children, having no conscious thoughts to distract them, are particularly susceptible to the suggestions of others.

Let a child fall, or be exposed to contagion, or lie in a draught, and its parents or those around immediately image all manner of terrible consequences. These suggestions coming to the child's mind from all around him are just as potent as his own thoughts will be when he grows older, with the result that he falls victim to the very diseases his parents fear most. It is another case of "The hand that smites thee is thine own."

But the power works the other way, too. If we can change our thought and visualize only good for our children, we can bring good into their lives as surely as into our own. "I swear to you," says Walt Whitman, "that the universe shall be whole to him who is whole. It shall remain jagged and broken to him who is jagged and broken."

Man thinks—and his thoughts form the mold in which his substance appears to be. If the thought be a true one, the substance forms in the perfect image that God made. If it be a diseased one, it takes the shape in our eyes of a barnacle upon the perfect image of man.

What Jesus proved to us, however, was that this "barnacle," this seeming imperfection, is not real. It is the "devil" of wrong thought, of an imperfect mold. "Satan hath bound this woman," He said of one who was brought to Him for healing. And with His word unloosed her bonds.

Jesus came into a world which was more than half dead—dead in disease, dead in poverty and misery. Like the man in California in 1847, who sold his ranch to Colonel Sutter for a few dollars and went off in search of gold, when all the while there was gold to the value of thirty-eight millions right beneath the ground where he stood, Jesus saw men standing by the very fountain of life and not knowing that it existed!

Even after He had showed them this Fountain of Life, even after He had demonstrated its marvelous powers, men could not believe. A few did, of course. But most thought His message too good to be taken literally. Most thought the power in that fountain—if any—died with Him.

"I am come that they might have life," He said, "and that they might have it more abundantly." Who are "they"? Surely not merely the few who saw Him during His earthly career! *But all mankind!*

"God hath made man upright, but they have sought out many inventions," we are told in the Book of Books. Jesus showed us the way to regain that uprightness—showed us, indeed, that we already HAVE it, once we scrape away the barnacles of wrong thought and get down to the substance beneath. "Thou shalt be perfect with the Lord thy God."— Deuteronomy 18:13.

How shall we be perfect?

How do you get started the right way when you find yourself on a narrow road driving in the wrong direction? First, you stop your car or your horse. Then you turn around. When you find yourself headed right, you start slowly, gradually pick up speed and soon find yourself sailing serenely along on the right road.

The first thing you must do, when driving a car or when developing your body, is to stop going in the wrong direction. Drive out the devil of wrong thought. Ailments, you know, are like stray cats. If you take them in, feed them, pet them, pay attention to them, they not only make themselves at home with you but settle down and bring up a family of little ailments. You must drive them out the moment they appear. You must disclaim them, shoo them off, refuse to pay any attention to them or have anything to do with them.

If the devil wants to have a pain, let him. If he insists upon being doubled up with rheumatism, or stomach trouble or cancer, that is his affair. Let him do it. But insist that he *go off to do it*—not nest anywhere around your premises. Like the young husband whose wife awakened him in the night with the startling news that a burglar was in the pantry at her pies, your only concern need be that he "won't die in the house."

What method shall you use to get rid of this devil? Disclaim him—tell him he is not yours and that you refuse to take him in—then order him away, order him off in the name of Jesus Christ who drove him out aforetime. Order him out and claim God's perfect image for the organ he assailed.

You are God's child. Would any parent knowingly make his child imperfect? Would any sculptor intentionally turn out an imperfect image? "Doth a fountain send forth at the same place sweet water and bitter? Can the fig tree, my brethren, bear olive berries? Either a vine, figs?

So can no fountain both yield salt water and fresh."—
James 3:11-12. Yet God is the only Creator. So everything
real about you must have been made by Him. And having been made by Him, your body must be perfect. It is
only *your conception* of it which is at fault. So stop going in
the wrong direction by disclaiming, denying, any wrong
or imperfect conception of yourself. "Woe unto him that
striveth with His maker! Let the potsherd strive with the
potsherds of the earth. Shall the clay say to Him that fash-
ioneth it—What makest Thou? Or Thy work, He hath no
hands?"—Isaiah 45:9.

Second, it is necessary to turn around and get headed in
the right direction. "Ye are the temple of the living God,"
says Paul (II Corinthians 6:16). "As God hath said, I will
dwell in them and walk in them; and I will be their God
and they shall be my people."

Where God is, only good can be. If He is in you, everything in and about you must be good, must be perfect.
That knowledge is the spiritual rebirth which Jesus told
His disciples all must go through before they could enter
the Kingdom of Heaven.

2 plus 2 must equal 4. For God to be in anything must
mean that it is perfect. For us to believe—as many do—that
2 plus 2 can equal 5 or 6 or any number other than 4 in no
way disturbs the mathematical principle that 2 plus 2 equals
4. That principle can wait serenely for us to discover our
error. Our acceptance or rejection of it influences it in no

way. The only one to suffer when we misconstrue the principle is ourselves. The truth goes on just the same.

And the only one to suffer when we misconstrue the Principle of Life is ourselves. The Truth goes on just the same. When we find our mistake, erase it and start afresh, the principle is just as ready to work for us as ever.

When sickness or accident seems to lay hold upon you, disclaim it. Erase it from your mind and start at your problem over again. 2 plus 2—God's perfect image plus God's life energy—if the result is not perfect, the fault is not with the principle but with your way of applying it.

Jesus showed us the principle. He tried to get us to use it in our lives. Like the Professor of Mathematics, He worked out the examples before us, He left us explicit directions how to apply the principles to our daily problems. But—again like the Professor—He has to leave it to us to *apply* these principles. He can't work all our problems for us, else we would never progress. He showed us the way—it is up to us to apply His principles.

"The whole of creation groaneth and travaileth in pain together until now. For they wait for the manifestation of the sons of God."—Romans 8:22 19.

Realize that the perfect image of you which was in the Father's mind when He conceived you never perishes, never changes. The marble may be broken. The block may be smashed. But the perfect image lives on—unmarred, unhurt.

And if you will go back to the Father for that perfect image, you can get a new block of marble, start afresh and hew from it as perfect an image of yourself as that which is in Divine Mind.

Some people study for years before they are cured or obtain the desire of their hearts. Others get their answer at once. Why? The difference in results measures the length of time it takes each one to get the CONVICTION that Truth is true. When a man gets that consciousness, he HAS his desire.

So let go of the idea that you must wait days or weeks or months to get health or success or anything else you may want. God knows no time but NOW. You will never know any other time but the eternal present. You can't live or do anything in the future. The only time you do anything is now. "Believe that you RECEIVE"—not next week or next month—but NOW! And as you believe, it will be unto you.

Third, you must keep going in the right direction. When danger threatens, the knowledge that you are God's child and that He has given His angels charge over you, to lead you and to keep you, will drive away all fear.

When sickness or contagion is around, remember that you are made in the perfect image of the Father, His life-energy animating you; remember that in His Mind there is but one right idea for each cell and organism in your body; and He is the only Creator; therefore that one right idea is the only one you can have, regardless of any mist that may temporarily come between you and it.

When conditions seem discordant, remember that where the Father is, only good can be. And the Father is everywhere. Therefore, claim the good. Seek it out. Recognize only it. Refuse to heed or to regard as real or permanent any other condition. Hold to the good, the true, and the mists will presently clear away and show you that there never was and never is anything but good.

That is the Kingdom of Heaven—the power to see the good and the true, to hold on to them and them alone until all about you has become like them. "The Kingdom of Heaven is like a grain of mustard seed, which when it is sown in the earth, is less than all the seeds that be in the earth. But when it is sown, it groweth up and becometh greater than all herbs and shooteth out great branches; so that the fowls of the air may lodge under the shadow of it."—Mark 4:31-32.

There may seem no bigger good to lay hold of in the circumstances about you than the tiny mustard seed. Hold on to that tiny bit; refuse to see anything else, and it will grow until it fills your whole life.

"The Kingdom of Heaven is like unto leaven, which a woman took and hid in three measures of meal, till the whole was leavened."—Matthew 13:33.

A tiny bit of yeast is very small compared to three measures of meal, yet given the chance, it quickly permeates and raises the whole. Just so with the good about you. Give it the chance, and it will quickly permeate all your circumstances. It asks merely that you recognize only it, that you refuse to accept any less. It asks to be *used* in order that it may leaven everything about you.

But no man ever discovered the Kingdom through mists of anger, or jealousy, or lust, or hate. It takes the clear glass of a tranquil mind.

Why was it that, in so many cases, before healing the sick who were brought to Him, Jesus told them—"Thy sins are forgiven thee"? Wasn't it because their sickness was the direct result of anger, or lust, or jealousy, or gluttony—of seeing and laying hold of these instead of good—and Jesus, like a merciful Judge, was remitting the penalty and giving them the chance once more to find the Kingdom?

Through pride or anger or some other sin, they brought the devil of wrong thought into their lives and he proceeded to evidence his presence in their bodies. One great surgeon has said that he has been able to trace every case of cancer that has come to him to some bitterness held in the mind of the patient, some grudge, some unforgiven injury. Serene faith is the first essential to the Kingdom of Heaven—in body or in circumstances—and no man can have tranquil and serene faith who hates his neighbor, who is devoured by anger, or envy, or lust, or covetousness.

"As ye would that men should do to you, do ye also to

them likewise."—Luke 6:31. Love is the greatest requisite for entry into the Kingdom of Heaven, the Kingdom of Wholeness, the Kingdom of Harmony and Happiness. Love is the password and Faith is the key. The two together will unlock any door in this world or the next.

Why is it that women like Florence Nightingale, men like Gorgas and many another of his kind, can care for all manner of diseased people and never catch any of their ailments, whereas others who merely look upon or read about them die of their diseases? Because their hearts are filled with thoughts of unselfish service, of love for their fellow man—and "perfect love casteth out fear."

You cannot pour water into a vessel already full. When your heart is full of love and compassion for your fellows; when your mind is filled with the perfect image of the Father; you need have no fear for the devil of imperfection. Neither consciously nor subconsciously can he reach you. An established conviction is immune to outside suggestion, as has often been shown in hypnosis. A really virtuous man or woman cannot be led astray even when under the influence of a hypnotist. Like Rome, people fall not because of assaults from without, but from weakness within.

But sin is much more than the breaking of some moral law. It is not thus that "the just man falleth seven times a day." Sin is every wrong conception of some perfect idea of the Father's. That is why to enter the Kingdom of

Heaven we must be converted (turned about) and become as little children. We must forget our preconceived ideas of things and circumstances, and accept the perfect ideas of them that are in the Father's mind as readily as a little child will do. Only thus can we enter the Kingdom of Wholeness and Harmony.

THE RENEWING OF THE SPIRIT

Remember, in Rider Haggard's "She," how Ayesha not only renewed her youth and beauty, but so filled every fiber of her being with vibrant life and energy that she lived for a score of lifetimes, growing ever more beautiful with the years, until no man could look upon her without falling desperately in love and wanting her for his own?

Ayesha renewed her youth and beauty and vibrant magnetism by bathing in the Fountain of Fire deep in the bowels of the earth—a magnetic, electric flame which was said to be the source of all earth-bound energy.

You can renew yours without any such arduous journey as she was forced to undertake. More, you can renew it every day, so that each day you will rise stronger and richer and more nearly in the perfect mold of the Father than the day before. How? Through the Divine fire of the Holy Spirit.

Ayesha's Fountain of Life was an earthly fire, an electric flame which flowed through and through—but instead of consuming, renewed and strengthened every fibre of her body.

The renewing of the Holy Spirit is a Divine Fire which flows through the mind, consuming every sickly or imperfect image, and leaves only the perfect mold in which the Father imaged us.

Ayesha's fire could be used but once. Thereafter it destroyed. The Divine Fire can be used a million times. And each time it brings us ever nearer the Perfect Image of the Father, so that, as the Psalmist promised, our youth is renewed like the eagle's.

What is this Divine Fire? It is the Holy Ghost, the tongue of flame which strengthened and revivified the Apostles, the Spirit of Understanding which will revivify and renew you.

"And when the day of Pentecost was fully come, they were all with one accord in one place. And suddenly there came a sound from heaven as of a rushing mighty wind, and it filled all the house where they were sitting. And there appeared unto them cloven tongues as of fire, and it sat upon each of them. And they were all filled with the Holy Ghost."—Acts 2:1, 4.

How can you bring the Holy Ghost upon you? Through understanding faith. It is not enough to believe. That will work wonders. But to bring the Holy Ghost into your affairs takes more than belief—takes understanding.

The Holy Ghost is the Consciousness of Good. The

Holy Ghost is the CONVICTION that you HAVE God's Perfect Image—and this CONVICTION it is that consumes every vestige of wrong thought, drives out every devil of sickness or imperfection.

To bring the Holy Ghost into your being is to bring the knowledge of perfection, of harmony, of Truth.

How shall you do it? By realizing *first,* that since the Father is the Source of all life, he must of necessity be the Source of all health as well. For health is the steady inflow of Creative Life coming freely from the Father, just as electric power is the steady flow of current from the generator. Health is wholeness, harmony, perfection of functioning of every organ, strength, vitality. Health is the joy of life.

Second, whatever the Father has given you is yours eternally. He is not an "Indian giver." He doesn't give you health and then take it away from you for offending Him. The health and perfection and harmony He has given you are yours for always. He never takes them away. You may lose sight of them at times, it is true. Sin or fear may send up such a mist about you that you can no longer see God or any of His gifts. They are there just the same—apparently distorted by the mists through which you are looking, just as your image is distorted in a faulty mirror—but none the less perfect for all that. Get rid of the mist, and its mirages of imperfection vanish with it.

Third, every day is a day of creation. The faculty of every cell in your body is to create two cells, and these in turn to create more. Your body is constantly being remade. It is today what your thinking was yesterday. It is formed now in the mold you were using months ago.

In an experiment in regeneration for histology, Carl Hoffman of Lawrence College took six worms and cut them in two. Within two days the upper parts developed tails, the lower parts heads!

On the front part of each dissected worm, he split the head between the eyes. Each side filled out and each part developed another eye!

You have often heard that if a lobster or a spider loses a leg, it promptly grows a new one to replace it. Why can't man do the same? Because man puts the power in the *organ* rather in Mind where it belongs.

Yet every now and again you read of one who has brought the Holy Spirit into his consciousness, refused to accept the evidence of his senses, and thereupon had them reverse themselves.

In the English weekly, *Active Service,* Major O. S. Fisher of the British Air Forces told of a heavy fall which, according to expert medical testimony, broke his collar bone. But he refused to believe in any break in God's image, kept on using his arm, felt no pain and the bone quickly knit.

Edward A. Kimball, in his *Teachings and Addresses,* tells of having cut off the end of a finger when clipping the garden hedge. He wrapped it with a rag, then put the problem of growing back that end of finger up to the Father, feeling that it was His image and His image could not be imperfect. In a few weeks that finger was back in its perfect shape.

Thousands of cases are on record of men and women cured of all manner of disease through the prayer, the faith and understanding of themselves or others. And what these men and women have done, *you* can do. There is no such thing as an incurable disease. There is no such thing as a necessarily fatal accident. Men have been cured after being given up by a dozen doctors. Men have come back after being pronounced dead for hours. Men have lived with bullets in their brains, cuts in their hearts, holes in their lungs, broken necks, smashed backs, all manner and degree of accidents. Men have withstood 33,000 volts of electricity and lived to tell the tale. Men have fallen from great heights. And what men have done once, men can do again.

The great thing—the one essential thing—is to realize that in Divine Mind all is good, all is harmonious, all is perfect. In It is no accident, no sickness, no imperfection. Therefore these must be unreal—the distorted images of our own thoughts, pictures in the mists that have come between us and the realities in Divine Mind.

To be rid of the imperfection, we need only to dispel the mist. Medicine won't do that. Diet or exercise won't do it. What then? Only the "Invisible Light" which shines through the mist and shows the reality beyond.

Where can we find that light? In the understanding presence of the Holy Spirit. And the best way to bring that Holy Spirit into your consciousness is through constant affirmations that you HAVE the perfect image or body which the Father conceived of you—that you LIVE IN the harmonious surroundings which are the only ones He sees.

"This is a faithful saying, and these things I will that thou affirm constantly, that they which have believed in God might be careful to maintain good works. These things are good and profitable unto men."—Titus 3:8.

Emile Coué met with astounding success in treating all manner of disease. How? Through affirmations.

Originally, Coué was a hypnotist. In his little drug store, he found occasional patients whom he could hypnotize. He hypnotized them—put their conscious minds to sleep—and addressed himself directly to their subconscious.

To the subconscious, he said there was nothing wrong with whatever organ the patient had thought diseased, and the subconscious believed him. When the patient came out from under the hypnotic influence, he was well. It remained then only to convince his conscious mind of this, so he would not send through new suggestions of disease, and the patient was cured!

How do you account for it? By the fact that the disease or imperfection is not in your body—but in your subconscious mind. Change the subconscious belief—and the physical manifestations change with it. The substance underneath—the perfect image of the Father—is perfect all the time. It is only your vision of it that changes. Doctors recognize this when they give their patients harmless sugar pills, knowing that these will dispel their fears, and that when the imperfect images conjured up by fear are gone, the supposed trouble will have gone with them.

But Coué found many patients whom he could not hypnotize. How treat them? By inducing a sort of self-hypnosis of themselves. It is a well-known fact that constant repetition carries conviction—even to the subconscious mind. So Coué had his patients continually repeat to themselves the affirmation that their trouble was passing, that they were getting better and better. And this unreasoning affirmation did a vast amount of good.

If this simple and child-like method could help all manner of diseases, how much more surely the right kind of affirmations, *backed by true understanding!*

When sickness assails you, when stomach or eyes or nerves or throat tells you it is ill, don't answer, like Sick Man Charley—"That's me!" Instead, disclaim it! Tell that devil of wrong thought—be he named Cold or Rheumatism or Indigestion or What-not—that he has stopped at the wrong door. You haven't sent for him—don't want him—won't let him in. Command him in Jesus' name to get out! Then bless the organ assailed, baptize it Perfect Throat, Perfect Stomach, Perfect Lungs, in the name of the Father, the Son and the Holy Ghost. Repeat to yourself—

"There is no reality in any imperfect image of my mind. The only real substance is the Perfect Model of me which Divine Mind imaged. And in Divine Mind there is but one mold for each cell and organism, each organ and function. That mold is perfect. Therefore, since Divine Mind is the only Creator, that is the only image of any cell or organism which I can have."

Picture God, in your mind's eye, as a Sculptor. See him, like Pygmalion, modelling a perfect image of you in marble—then breathing into that image the soul of you, part of Himself, part of His Mind. You are His son.

If He were an earthly King and you His son, you would feel that you had power over everything in His Kingdom, would you not? You would consider yourself at perfect liberty to order His servants to do anything that was not wrong, would you not?

You have just as much power to order things in His kingdom as you would were you the son of an earthly king. You can feel at perfect liberty to order His angels to fetch and carry for you, to serve you in any right way. As the Son of God, you can not only order the devil of wrong thought out of you, but you can bid God's angels come and occupy the place the devil held. When you throw out the devil of imperfect vision, for instance, you can command the Angel of Perfect Sight to occupy the place in your mind vacated by the devil, and thus insure against his return. When Rheumatism or Weak Lungs or Lameness or Cold enters your sanctum, you can call upon the Angel who is the opposite of these to help you throw them out, remove all vestiges of their presence and occupy the place they coveted.

You are the Son of God. You have power to do any of these things. But you must use that power. Every use strengthens it—every surrender to sickness weakens it.

"And I shall put my Spirit in you, and ye shall live, and I shall place you in your own land."—Ezekiel 37:14.

But if God is our Father, why does He send us sickness, accidents, imperfections—or if not send them, permit them? No earthly father would ever inflict such sorrow upon his children. Yet God, we are told, loves us inconceivably more than any earthly father loves his children. Why, then, does He afflict us?

The answer is that He does not. He neither afflicts us nor allows infliction to come upon us. He does not see these sicknesses and sorrows we complain of. "For God is of purer eyes than to behold evil."—Habukkuk 1:13.

And why doesn't He see them? Because they are not real. They are no more than figments of the imagination.

If you were suffering from delirium tremens, and saw green dragons and pink elephants about to attack you, no one would expect God to step in and save you from these imaginary beasts, would he?

If your mind were temporarily deranged, and you thought you were covered with feathers like a bird, no one would expect God to remove feathers from your body, would he?

If you look in a mirror and see what appears to be a pimple on the side of your nose, but it later develops that it was merely a flaw in the glass, you will not complain because God failed to take cognizance of and remove the pimple, will you?

And when, through fear or suggestion, you allow your subconscious mind to give you a distorted image of some part of your body, you can't expect God to take cognizance of it, can you, even though it causes you intense anguish? For both the anguish and the image are just as unreal as the green dragon or the feathers or the imaginary pimple.

There is but one right idea of each cell and organism in your body. That is the idea conceived in Divine Mind, imaged in you, the Divine life-energy flowing ever-renewingly through it. That is the only real image of each cell and organism you can know. That is the only actual substance you can have.

"We all, with open face beholding as in a glass the glory of the Lord, are changed into the same image from glory to glory, even as by the Spirit of the Lord." —II CORINTHIANS 3:18.

"For which cause we faint not; but though our outward man perish, yet the inward man is renewed day by day.

"While we look not at the things which are seen, but at the things which are not seen: for the things which are seen *are* temporal; but the things which are not seen *are* eternal."

—II CORINTHIANS 4:16, 18.

XXX

THE GOOD SAMARITAN

"And Jesus answering said, A certain man went down from Jerusalem to Jericho, and fell among thieves, which stripped him of his raiment, and wounded him, and departed, leaving him half dead.

"And by chance there came down a certain priest that way; and when he saw him, he passed by on the other side.

"And likewise a Levite, when he was at the place, came and looked on him, and passed by on the other side.

"But a certain Samaritan, as he journeyed, came where he was: and when he saw him, he had compassion on him,

"And went to him, and bound up his wounds, pouring in oil, and wine, and set him on his own beast, and brought him to an inn, and took care of him."

—LUKE 10:30-34.

In the congregation of a small Church in Philadelphia was a little group of men and women who met each week at the house of one of their number to discuss their personal problems and to try to find a solution to them through united prayer.

Their thought was to prove the efficacy of the words of the Master "that if two of you shall agree on earth as touching anything that they shall ask, it shall be done for them of my Father which is in heaven."—Matthew 18:19.

Each evening was devoted to the problem of the member whose need seemed most pressing. And in addition, all present agreed to pray for the right solution to his problem at noon each day for the balance of that week.

The first one chosen was a bookbinder who owed quite a large sum of money, and could see no way of meeting his obligations. It was decided that the company should pray for aid in the payment of his debts.

The meeting was on Tuesday night, the first noon prayer on Wednesday. After lunch that day, the binder dropped into the office of a publishing house, as was his long-established custom. There he "happened" to meet a man from Washington, D. C., who was bemoaning the fact that he had missed his train to New York, where he had intended to place a large order for blank books for the Government, and the next train would throw him too late for another appointment. The binder told him that he made blank books, and within the hour closed a contract that not only paid all his debts, but proved the start of a very profitable business.

The next on the list was a jeweler who was about to call a meeting of his creditors, preliminary to bankruptcy proceedings. Within two weeks, a manufacturer whom the jeweler had never before heard of had taken over his whole business, paid off the debts and formed a partnership with him that resulted in a prosperous trade.

Every member of that prayer circle became prosperous. One young man, a clerk in a big bank, was offered the position of Assistant Cashier in another bank, and within a few years became its President! And the experience of this little group was to a great extent duplicated by other members of the same Church. For long seasons there was not a single sick person in the thousand and more homes represented by the membership of the Church. Epidemics swept over the city, but, to quote Dr. Haehnlen, "The Angel of Death passed over the congregation, taking none."

And yet we can all recall catastrophes wherein Churches and those in them were wiped out. The Church in Paris where so many worshippers were killed by the German long-range cannon. Churches shaken down by earthquakes. Churches destroyed by cyclones. And all who had taken refuge in them perishing. Wherein lies the difference between these and that little Philadelphia congregation?

Perhaps the answer is in understanding this—what were each of these groups putting their faith in? A building? A plot of ground deemed so holy that it would be regarded as sanctuary by all the forces of nature? Or in the Father Himself?

There is no more of God in a Church, you know, than in any other place. To regard it as sanctuary is to go back to the fetishes of the witch doctor. God is just as much in your home, your office or store or factory, as in the finest Church built. It is not the Church that counts—it is what people use it for. "For where two or three are gathered together in My name, there am I in the midst of them."

What made the prayers of that little circle so resultful? What brought them success and health and all good things of life? Two or three (or more) gathered together in Jesus' name (with Him in the midst of them), all concentrated on the one thought—the good of one of their number. Can you wonder that their prayers were efficacious?

"And this is the confidence that we have in Him. that if we ask anything according to His will, He heareth us. And if we know that He hear us, whatsoever we ask, we know that we HAVE the petition we desired of Him." —I John 5:14-15.

Many men think they must be ministers or evangelists or especially called by God before they can help others. On the contrary, Jesus specifically passed over the Priest and the Levite and picked a rank outsider, a Samaritan, to succour the wounded traveler. Not only that, but in choosing His apostles, He passed over the learned Scribes, the proud Pharisees, the Priests and the Levites, and picked common, ordinary men—taxgatherers and fishermen.

Emerson says in one of his essays that a chemist will tell to a carpenter the secret he would not for a king's ransom tell to another chemist. It would seem that the world has been made up of carpenters, for Jesus has been telling us these 1900 years how we can win any good thing we may ask—health or happiness, riches or success. Yet how many have availed themselves of that secret?

When Peter and John went up to the temple to pray, and the lame man asked them for alms, do you remember what Peter said?

"Silver and gold have I none; but such as I have, give I thee; in the name of Jesus Christ, rise up and walk."— Acts 3:6.

The people wondered, and ran to them, thinking another great Prophet had risen. But Peter answered them:

"Ye men of Israel, why marvel ye at this? Or why look ye so earnestly on us, *as though by our own power* or holiness we had made this man to walk?"—Acts 3:12.

And he explained to them that it was their faith in *the power of Jesus' name* which had done the miracle.

You have no power to heal anyone. Neither had Peter or John or any of the Apostles. The power to heal lies not in you, but in the truth that *every man is already whole!* Your power—like that of the Apostles—lies in your ability to help the patient rid himself of the devils of wrong thought which now assail him, of the distorted images which he sees of that which is perfect in Divine Mind.

"Then He called His twelve disciples together, and gave them power and authority *over all devils,* and to cure diseases."—Luke 9:1.

First drive out the devil of wrong thought, then the disease is cured. For when the distorted image is gone, only the perfect model which the Father made, remains.

The trouble with most sick people is that they have for so long thought sickness, their pains and discomfort are so real to them, they are so sure of their inability to do anything themselves for the affected organs, that like the lame man, they need some one to take them by the hand and lift them up.

With many, the mere presence of a doctor is so confidence-inspiring that it brings them back to health. Others feel they must have drugs to "cure" them. But all are looking for something or someone outside themselves on which to lean for help.

The part of the Good Samaritan is to extend that helping hand to lift these poor souls out of the slough of despond to set them back on the road where they can help themselves. *You* can be such a Samaritan.

How is it done? In the same way that the turning on of a 100 k. w. electric light drives away the shadows which the fitful glow of a candle had but enhanced.

Your understanding—clear, forceful, penetrating—can drive through the mists and shadows which surround a sick friend, and bring forth the true idea of him which he is too lost in the mists to see. Just two things are required:

1—A clear understanding of the unreality of evil, whether that evil be called lameness or headache or eye strain or indigestion or fever or what-not.

2—The consciousness of the perfection of God's image of the organ your patient thinks diseased, and the CONVICTION that he HAS this perfect image—that the REAL organ, the SUBSTANCE under the outer seeming, IS perfect.

You don't have to work any miracle. You don't have to cure the sick. When you can fill your consciousness with the sincere and understanding CONVICTION that he HAS God's perfect image of each cell and organism and that his disease is merely a distorted image of his subconscious mind, your conviction will dispel those shadows in his mind just as surely as the 100 k. w. light will chase them from a room—and *he will be well!*

You never heard of Jesus feeling any man's pulse, or asking how long he had been sick, or what were the symptoms. He leaned on no power but that of Truth—the Truth that God is the only Creator, and that everything He created is good—therefore anything unlike Him must be un-real. And on the basis of that Truth, he cured all manner of diseases. Never once did He fail. His apostles failed at times. Why? "Because of their unbelief." The sick man was more positive of his ailment than they were of his wholeness. You must "let this mind be in you which was also in Christ Jesus."—Philippians 2:5.

"I besought Thy disciples to cast the devil out of my son," said one poor father. "And they could not." So Jesus rebuked the unclean spirit, and healed the child. Asked then by His disciples why they had not been able to cast it out, He told them—"Because of your unbelief!" Your CON-VICTION of the perfect God-substance in your patient has to be stronger than his faith in his subconscious dream.

To dispel that dream, it is frequently helpful to rebuke the devil of wrong thought, to bid him begone in Jesus' name. "Thy word shall not come back to thee void, but shall bring that where-unto it was sent."

But don't pretend an authority you do not feel. To do that is to strengthen the conviction of disease in the patient. You are the son of God. "Ye are Gods and every one of you is a son of the Most High." If you were the son of an earthly King, you would feel at liberty to order his servants to serve you in any right way. Do you think that, being the son of God, your privileges are any less in His Kingdom than they would be as the son of an earthly king?

Then order His angels to help you. Command the devil

of wrong thought out of your patient, then order the angels of right thought to occupy the place the devil has vacated, to clean out every vestige of wrong thought, to direct the organ aright. SEE THEM DOING IT! See them, in your mind's eye, casting out the distorted images as Michael cast Satan out of Heaven. See them occupying their place, guiding, directing each cell and organism in the way it should go. See it—and BELIEVE IT!

"Stir up the gift that is within thee," counselled Paul to Timothy. Stir up the power that is in you—the power of a son of God. It is yours—but it is yours only as you USE it. The unused talent decays. The unused muscle atrophies.

But how if you have not yet succeeded in curing yourself? Should you try to help others before you have fully proved the admonition—"Physician, heal thyself"?

It is by helping others that we most surely help ourselves. Many a man, unsuccessful in fully ridding himself of some long-standing trouble, has found it disappear in trying to realize the unreality of evil in another.

It doesn't matter who or what *you* are, you know. It is not as though it were you that was doing the healing. So long as you can help another to realize that his trouble is in the distorted image of his own mind, and not in the perfect mold of the Father, that is all that is required of you. You are merely the X-ray, which penetrates through the mists which have beclouded his brain and shows him the true substance beneath. Forget yourself in the work, and the more thoroughly you forget yourself, the more surely will you act as a channel through which Good will flow from the Father to those around you.

"Strengthen ye the weak hands and confirm the feeble knees. Say to them that are of a fearful heart, Be strong, fear not, behold, your God will come. Then the eyes of the blind shall be opened, and the ears of the deaf shall be unstopped. Then shall the lame man leap as an hart and the tongue of the dumb sing."—Isaiah.

THE MODUS OPERANDI

Thirty years ago, the belief was common that the way to get rid of a cold was to wish it on someone else. With the result that when a man had a cold, and some friend caught it, the first man felt that he was rid of it—and *generally was!*

I once heard of a man who, whenever he had a headache, would go to a roomful of people, pick some one of them, and deliberately wish his headache on him. Whether the other man caught it or not I don't know, but the first always got rid of his headache!

There are billions of people in this world thinking sickness and sorrow and pain and disease. There are billions thinking hatred and malice and fear and sin. Contagion is merely allowing their thoughts to influence yours—their belief to penetrate to your subconscious and thus image themselves upon your body. And the only way to prevent this is to be continually on your guard. "Watch and pray, that ye be not led into temptation." Watch and pray— not against the bad, but to keep your mind so filled with the good that evil can find no space to enter.

If a man came to you and told you he was bothered by a belief that 2 plus 2 equals 5, and that this belief spoiled all his problems and his business, what would you do? Try to erase the incorrect belief from his mind, would you not, and replace it with the correct one? You wouldn't try to find where he got the belief, except in so far as that might help you to rub it out at its very root. You wouldn't look at his tongue or feel his pulse. You would treat him at the seat of his trouble—in his mind, his belief.

If a man came to you and told you he was troubled with a growth of feathers all over his body, you would know such a thing to be so palpably impossible that you would not even bother to look for the feathers—you would simply try to blot the belief from the man's mind. When you had done that, you would know he was cured.

When a man tells you he is troubled with a growth of boils, or pimples, or smallpox, you must treat his belief in these in the same way you would treat a belief in feathers— by blotting the belief from his mind. When you can do that, they will be gone from his body as well.

For the only place those boils or pimples really exist is in his mind. His subconscious has objectified them for all to see, but if you can, by the X-ray of your understanding, see *through* them to the perfect reality beneath, your perfect vision communicates itself to his subconscious and erases his distorted image.

Have no fear as to whether you are good enough or holy enough to help another. You don't bother to clean each speck of dirt off the wires that bring your light and current. You know it will not dim the light, or make the current less powerful. The wire is merely the channel through which the electricity comes. And that is all you need to be to help another—a channel through which the Truth of Being may pass to him. "Let this Mind be in you which was also in Christ Jesus." It is Divine Mind which does the healing—not you. All you need to do is to make the connection with the power-house of Divine Mind by dissipating the mists of evil, seeing through them to the real substance beneath and thus making the contact with that underlying reality.

It doesn't matter whether you have been studying a day, a week or a lifetime. Try your power! You will never develop it until you do.

Suppose a baby were to say—"My legs are so weak and puny, it's no use my starting to kick yet. I'll wait until they grow big and strong." What would happen to that baby's legs? They would stay weak, would they not? They would never grow strong until he used them.

A doctor studies for four or six years because he has to learn all about all manner of disease. You don't. The less you know about disease, the better off you are. All you need to know is the perfect image of the Father. A doctor studies disease because he expects to see disease manifest. You study perfection because that is all you must ever see.

For that reason, when you want to help another, the first one you must cure is yourself. Not, mind you, of any ailment or imperfection you think *you* have—but of the ailment the *patient* seems to have. When you can convince *yourself* that his ailment is unreal, that he HAS the perfect image of his Maker, your belief will speedily communicate itself to him.

So the first thing to do is to disabuse your mind of the thought that you have to *do* anything. Relax. And bid your patient relax. You can command the devil of wrong thought to come out of him—yes. Command it as the Son of God—and in Jesus' name. You can pray the Holy Ghost to enter into him and burn every distorted or imperfect image from his mind. You can command the Angel of Perfection to enter into him, and occupy the place the devil has vacated. Then sit and realize the perfect image in which your patient is made. Realize that—and watch it becoming manifest in him.

Our bodies are just like rubber balls, you know. Squeeze them (hold the wrong thoughts of them), and they show up in distorted shapes. Let go of them and they promptly resume the perfect image in which they were made.

Dr. W. A. Hammond, former Surgeon-General of the U. S., said that the body would live indefinitely if it were not that the eliminating processes become defective. And what most disturbs these eliminative processes is fear, anger, worry, tenseness, strain. Let go! Relax! What is it spoils singers? *Trying* to sing. What is it spoils pianists? *Trying* to play. What is it spoils golfers? Tenseness. The first thing the music teacher or the vocal instructor or the golf "pro" teaches is to relax, to *let* your muscles work in their natural way.

Don't worry about elimination. Know that the Truth is the law of elimination to anything unlike itself. Then realize the Truth, fill yourself with it, and everything unlike it must go.

But what of those poor souls who believe this to be a vale of tears, who think God sends each of us a certain amount of sickness and we ought to "bless the hand that smites us"?

There is a saying that "Experience is a dear teacher, but fools will learn from no other," and it applies to suffering as well. Suffering is a sure way into trouble, but it is not the way out. More often it is simply the door to more suffering. You never get rid of anything, you know, by calling it yours. The supreme need of humanity is not suffering, but enlightenment. All suffering is caused by someone's wrong thinking about something which is essentially right in Divine Mind.

In his *Teaching* and *Addresses*, Edw. A. Kimball tells of a patient whom he found dying. "He was in the extremity of belief, eyes closed and sunken, face pallid. He could not utter a sound; he could not even open his eyes. Something had to be done for that man right away. I said to him, 'I want you to repeat what I say, and if you cannot utter the words aloud, make your lips go so that I shall know you are thinking it. Now you say, 'There is one infinite Life.'—now make your lips go. He made them go. 'And that Life is eternal Life,—and that Life is my Life'; and I kept saying that over and over again. After awhile he began to make a little noise. Then the words would come faintly. Then he began to open his eyes, and finally he got so he could speak plainly enough to ask me to let up on him. 'No,' I said, 'I will not let up on you; you say it,' and I went after him again. I kept after him until he could say it as plainly as I could.

"His body resumed its natural condition; his eyes were wide open, and that work healed that man, and all he had to do was to manifest the evidence of convalescence. That healed him; in other words, that was Life's idea.

"Very likely, if I had told him, *God is Life,* he would not have lived; because there would not have been any marked relationship between God and him. What I said was, 'There is one Life, and that Life is eternal Life,' and that broke the sense of a dying life. 'And that Life is my Life,' was bringing that Life down into his own experience as an idea, and that conscious idea broke the mesmerism of death."

Kimball did not stop to ask what was wrong with the man. He did not treat fever or sore throat or heart trouble.

He declared the Truth. He thought the Truth. He held on to the Truth—and made his patient hold on to it—until it broke through the outer seeming and manifested itself as life and health.

Every good treatment goes forth with all the power of Truth. And every treatment that has this Truth in it has power. It cannot be wasted or lost. "The words that I speak unto you," said Jesus, "they are spirit and they are life." And in the Proverbs (18:21) you read—"Death and life are in the power of the tongue."

PRINCES IN THE KINGDOM

When James and John went to Jesus and asked Him what places He had in mind for them in His Kingdom, He told them: "Whosoever will be great among you, shall be your minister; and whosoever of you will be the chiefest, shall be servant of all."

After the resurrection, when Peter was protesting his love for Him, what task did Jesus set him to prove it: "Feed my lambs!"

And if *you* would be a Prince in this Kingdom which Jesus came to lead us into, what must *you* do? Serve—serve your neighbor—help him in whatever way it is given you to help. "For inasmuch as ye do it unto the least of these my brethren, ye do it unto me."

You are the Son of God. "Ye are the sons of the living God."—Hosea 1:10.

If God were an earthly King, what would that make you? A Prince, of course. But to be treated as a Prince, you have to act like one. You couldn't go around, shabbily dressed and in poverty and want, and expect anyone to regard you as a Prince. Not even yourself. You would have to act the part, to feel and speak and do as the son of a king should.

You are the Son of God. But to become a Prince in His Kingdom, you must USE your sonship. "Yea, a man may say, Thou hast faith, and I have works. Show me thy faith without thy works, and I will show thee my faith by my works."—James 2:18.

Picture yourself at the throne of God. Can't you see yourself at the Father's feet, His angels grouped around, ready to do your bidding as His own?

And since the keynote of His Kingdom is Service, what should your bidding be? What but to help you bring some poor, wounded traveler, who has been beset by the robbers of sickness or want, into the Kingdom? To help you bind his hurts, pour into them the oil of understanding, leave for him the pennies of Truth to start him afresh on life's way.

What is the Oil of Understanding? Isn't it a knowledge of that which stands under the outer seeming—an ability to peer beneath the surface and bring forth the substance beneath?

When you say a man understands chemistry, you mean that he can take some supposedly simple substance like coal, and resolve it into all its native elements of carbon and ash and sulphur and phosphorus and gas. When you say a man understands the Truth, you mean that he can dig beneath the distorted images of disease and bring forth the perfect mold which is beneath.

Can you think of anything more worthy to make you a Prince of the Kingdom than acting the part of the Good Samaritan to those who are wounded on life's highway? Can you think of anything that will provide you with better equipment when you finally undertake your journey into the Great Beyond?

You don't need to obtrude yourself upon strangers. You don't need to force your views upon your friends. Without their knowledge, without argument or discussion on their part, you can help them. When next you hear that a friend has met with an accident, when some one tells you of another who is sick, instead of fastening his troubles upon him by inquiring into all the symptoms and causes, give five minutes of your time and thought to driving away from him those devils of wrong thought, realizing for him the innate perfection which is his. Picture yourself then as a Prince in God's Kingdom, and as a Prince, send to your friend the Angel of the Perfect Organ which he thinks diseased, to drive away and replace the devil of wrong thought of that organ which he is entertaining.

It may not always work a cure, for your conviction of perfection may not be as strong as his conviction of imperfection, but it will at least help him.

Of course, it is better to have his active cooperation if that can be secured. But even without it, you can help.

"Stir up the gift that is within you!" Use it to help others—only then can you develop and strengthen it, so that when you need it for some loved one, it will be strong for good. "My people are destroyed for lack of knowledge."—Hosea 4:6.

Don't wait for others to lead—form a little group in your Church, or among your friends, or in your own family—a group of Good Samaritans. Meet together once a week. Pick that one of your number who most needs help and unite your prayers for him.

It matters not what the problem may be—sickness or accident or money or promotion—they are equally susceptible of the right solution through united prayer. Remember—

"Again I say unto you, That if two of you shall agree on earth as touching anything that they shall ask, it shall be done for them of my Father which is in heaven.

"For where two or three are gathered together in my name, there am I in the midst of them."—Matthew 18:19-20.

Make it your rule that each member must try to help some poor traveler into the Kingdom each day. Have some definite reminder for your daily deed. If you are a man, do like the Boy Scouts—wear your tie with the ends outside your vest or shirt until you have done your good deed—tuck them in to mark the good deed done. If a woman, turn the settings of your rings in toward the palm of your hand as a reminder, turn them out when you have done your part. Then "count that day lost whose low descending sun views from thy hand no worthy action done."

"Then shall the righteous shine forth as the sun in the Kingdom of their Father. Who hath ears to hear, let him hear.

"The Kingdom of Heaven is like unto treasure hid in a field; the which when a man hath found, he hideth, and for joy thereof goeth and selleth all that he hath, and buyeth that field.

"Again, the Kingdom of Heaven is like unto a merchant man, seeking goodly pearls:

"Who, when he had found one pearl of great price, went and sold all that he had, and bought it."

—MATTHEW 13:43-46.

L'ENVOI

"And He said, So is the Kingdom of God, as if a man should cast seed into the ground;

"And should sleep, and rise night and day, and the seed should spring and grow up, he knoweth not how.

"For the earth bringeth forth fruit of herself; first the blade, then the ear, after that the full corn in the ear."

—MARK 4:26-28.

For thousands of years, we have been taught that nothing good can come to us without struggle.

For countless generations, we have been told that this earth is at best a vale of tears, with very little of good in it, and to get any of that good, we must fight for it like hungry dogs over a bone—take it away from others if we want to enjoy it ourselves.

In short, the general belief is that there is not enough good to go around. To make sure of ours, we must build a wall around everything we have, hold on to it with all our might, yet keep ourselves ready to jump out and grab more as opportunity offers.

The others? Well, it is too bad about them, but somebody has to suffer, and, anyway, it will all be made right for them in the next world.

That is the doctrine which Priest and King preached for thousands of years before Christ. That is the doctrine which robber baron and the "hard-boiled" among industrialists have sought to perpetuate ever since. But that is not the doctrine Jesus taught.

As I understand the promises of the Bible, God is our Father. And like any other loving Father, He gives us all of good. It is ours—and there is more than enough for all of us. "What man is there of you, whom if his son ask bread, will he give him a stone?

"Or if he ask a fish, will he give him a serpent?

"If ye then, being evil, know how to give good gifts unto your children, how much more shall your Father which is in heaven give good things to them that ask him?"—Matthew 7:9-11. The reason we do not manifest more is that the walls of fear and pauperism we have erected around ourselves are just as potent to keep further supply *out* as to keep what we have *in*.

What we must do is tear down these walls and *let* the good which is all around reach us.

God is the Creator of the whole universe. He knows where all the gold and silver and diamonds and other precious things are. He put them there.

We are His children. If He were an earthly father, what would we expect of Him? To share His riches, to enjoy His great possessions. Every good earthly father shares with his children. Is God any less loving, any less generous than the best of His creatures?

"The Spirit itself beareth witness with our spirit that we are the children of God;

"And if children, then heirs heirs of God, and joint heirs with Christ."—Romans 8:16-17.

God has all wealth. We are His children. Therefore *we* have all wealth. Why then do we not manifest it?

Why? "Because of our unbelief." We cut ourselves off

from God by doubting our sonship. We know He has all things, yet we think He gives them grudgingly, and takes away even more readily than He gives. We build around ourselves high walls of doubt and fear and unbelief, and then rail at Him because His bounty does not flow over these walls to us.

"Consider the ravens; for they neither sow nor reap; which neither have storehouse nor barn; and God feedeth them. How much more are ye better than the fowls?"—Luke 12:24.

All of good is yours. In its substance—in the invisible realm which you cannot reach without understanding—you HAVE it. *Claim it*—hold on to it—and like the little leaven in the three measures of meal, it will soon leaven your whole loaf.

As things are now, you may seem to be surrounded with want and disease and all manner of evil things. Refuse to accept them as yours. Disclaim them. Never take them in, but send them to seek homes with those who are looking for such.

Pick from among them only the good—no matter how infinitely small that good may seem to be. Then plant it and nourish it and be thankful for it. Soon, like the tiny mustard seed, it will grow into a tree in whose shade you can find shelter and rest all your days.

In Eugene O'Neill's new play—*"Lazarus Laughed,"* one of the guests tells how Jesus raised Lazarus from the dead after he had lain for four days in the tomb, tells how frightened all were, how they gazed awe-struck after the departing Master.

"And Lazarus, looking after Him, began to laugh softly *like a man in love with God!* Such a laugh I had never heard. It made my ears drunk! It was like wine. And though I was half-dead with fright, I found myself laughing too!"

Why did Lazarus laugh? He had been for four days on the other side of the Great Divide, and he *knew* there was nothing to be afraid of over there—nothing fearsome in death! He had seen God—*and he knew Him for a God of Love!* Why shouldn't he laugh, at all the fears, at the pretense, at the excuses we contrive, just to keep out of the way of God! Lazarus *knew*—and knowing, he laughed, he exulted in the consciousness of Love's allness.

At the head of a band of followers, Lazarus laughs himself through all earthly obstacles. To the Christians, he is almost another Messiah. To the Greeks, the Fire-born son of Zeus. But to the Romans, he is the enemy of empire. For in removing the fear of death, he takes from them the sword with which they hold all their subject peoples in leash. "What do I fear," asks Caligula, "if there is no death?"

"Love," says Lazarus, "Love is man's hope—love for his life on earth, a noble love above suspicion and distrust. Hitherto, man has always suspected life, and in revenge life has been faithless to him.

"Most men's lives are long dyings. They evade their

fear of death by becoming so sick of life, that by the time death comes they are too lifeless to fear it.

"Oh, if men would interpret that first cry of man fresh from the womb, as the laughter of one who even then says to his heart—'It is my pride as God to become Man. Then let it be my pride as Man to recreate the God in me!'"

There is nothing to fear in death. More, there is nothing to fear in life. So let us laugh at the silly pretensions of disease. Let us laugh at such ghostly spectres as poverty or want in such a world of plenty as we know this to be. Let us laugh at the idea of evil having power over us when our Father is Love—and Love is all about us like the air we breathe.

"If God so clothe the grass, which is today in the field, and tomorrow is cast into the oven, how much more will He clothe you, O ye of little faith?

"And seek not ye what ye shall eat, or what ye shall drink, neither be ye of doubtful mind.

"For all these things do the nations of the world seek after. And your Father knoweth that ye have need of these things.

"But rather seek ye the Kingdom of God; and all these things shall be added unto you."

—LUKE 12:28:31.

ABOUT THE AUTHOR

Born in St. Louis, Missouri, in 1885, Robert Collier trained to become a priest early in his life, before settling on a career in business, achieving success in the fields of advertising, publishing, and engineering. After recovering from a chronic illness with the help of mental healing, Collier began studying New Thought, metaphysical, and success principles. He distilled these theories into widely popular and influential works that included *The Secret of the Ages* and *Riches Within Your Reach!* Collier died in 1950.

DON'T MISS THESE PROSPERITY FAVORITES
FROM TARCHER/PENGUIN

Think and Grow Rich by Napoleon Hill
The landmark classic—now revised and updated
for the twenty-first century.
ISBN 978-1-58542-433-7

Think and Grow Rich, Deluxe Edition
by Napoleon Hill
A keepsake volume of Napoleon Hill's original
masterpiece, featuring leather casing, gold stamp-
ing, a red-ribbon place marker, gilded edges, and
marbled endpapers. Suited to a lifetime of use.
ISBN 978-1-58542-659-1

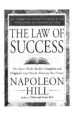

The Law of Success by Napoleon Hill
Napoleon Hill's first pioneering work, featuring
the fullest exploration of his formula to achievement, now redesigned in a single volume.
ISBN 978-1-58542-433-7

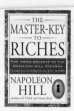

The Master-Key to Riches by Napoleon Hill
The actual handbook that Napoleon Hill gave to teachers of his ideas—a master class from the greatest motivational writer of all time. Revised and updated.   ISBN 978-1-58542-709-3

The Magic Ladder to Success by Napoleon Hill
Napoleon Hill's distillation of a lifetime of ideas in a compact, powerful primer. Revised and updated.   ISBN 978-1-58542-710-9

Your Magic Power to Be Rich! by Napoleon Hill
A three-in-one resource, featuring revised and updated editions of the classics *Think and Grow Rich; The Master-Key to Riches;* and *The Magic Ladder to Success.*   ISBN 978-1-58542-555-6

The Think and Grow Rich Workbook
The do-it-yourself workbook for activating Napoleon Hill's winning principles in your life.
ISBN 978-1-58542-711-6

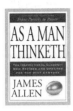

As a Man Thinketh by James Allen
Revised and updated for the twenty-first century,
this is one of the world's most widely loved
inspirational works—as a special bonus it includes
an updated edition of the author's first book, *From
Poverty to Power.*   ISBN 978-1-58542-638-6

The Secret of the Ages by Robert Collier
The classic on how to attain the life you want—
through the incredible visualizing faculties of
your mind.   ISBN 978-1-58542-629-4

The Master Key System by Charles F. Haanel
The legendary guide on how to enact the
"Law of Attraction" in your life.
ISBN 978-1-58542-627-0

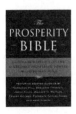

The Prosperity Bible
This beautiful boxed volume features complete
classics by Napoleon Hill, Benjamin Franklin,
James Allen, Florence Scovel Shinn, Ernest
Holmes, and many others.   ISBN 978-1-58542-614-0

A Message to Garcia by Elbert Hubbard
History's greatest motivational lesson, now
collected with Elbert Hubbard's most treasured
inspirational writings in a signature volume.
ISBN 978-1-58542-691-1

The Science of Getting Rich by Wallace D. Wattles
The time-tested program for a life of prosperity—
features the rare bonus work "How to Get What
You Want."   ISBN 978-1-58542-601-0

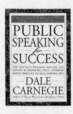

Public Speaking for Success by Dale Carnegie
The definitive, complete edition of Dale
Carnegie's public-speaking bible—now revised
and updated.   ISBN 978-1-58542-492-4

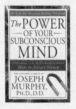

The Power of Your Subconscious Mind by Joseph
Murphy, Ph.D., D.D.
The complete, original edition of the million-
selling self-help guide that reveals your invisible
power to attain any goal.   ISBN 978-1-58542-768-0